1983

VIRGINIA WOOLF'S *The* YEARS

VIRGINIA WOOLF'S

The YEARS

The Evolution of a Novel

Grace Radin

THE UNIVERSITY OF TENNESSEE PRESS
KNOXVILLE

Frontispiece: From VIRGINIA WOOLF: A BIOGRAPHY,
copyright © 1972 by Quentin Bell.
Reproduced by permission of Harcourt Brace Jovanovich, Inc.,
the Author's Literary Estate, and The Hogarth Press.

*Clothbound editions of University of Tennessee Press
books are printed on paper designed for an effective
life of at least 300 years, and binding materials
are chosen for strength and durability.*

LIBRARY OF CONGRESS CATALOGING IN PUBLICATION DATA

Radin, Grace, 1934-
  Virginia Woolf's The years.

  Bibliography: p.
  Includes index.
  1. Woolf, Virginia Stephen, 1882-1941. The years.
I. Title.
PR6045.072Y3437   823'.912   80-22590
ISBN 0-87049-307-8

for George

ACKNOWLEDGMENTS

My thanks

to Ruth Z. Temple, who first encouraged me to explore the Woolf manuscripts;

to Lola L. Szladitz and her staff at the Berg Collection, for their unfailing patience and courtesy;

to David V. Erdman, friend and mentor to all those who love Virginia Woolf;

to Louise DeSalvo, companion in research and friend in need;

to Carol Orr, my thoughtful and conscientious editor;

and most of all, to my family.

I would also like to thank the following:

Quentin Bell, for permission to quote from unpublished documents in Virginia Woolf's Literary Estate.

The Henry W. and Albert A. Berg Collection of English and American Literature of The New York Public Library, Astor, Lenox, and Tilden Foundations, for permission to quote from Virginia Woolf's manuscripts of *The Years* and *Professions for Women*.

The Hogarth Press Ltd. for permission to quote from *The Years* and *A Writer's Diary*.

Excerpts from THE YEARS and A WRITER'S DIARY by Virginia Woolf are reprinted by permission of Harcourt Brace Jovanovich, Inc., copyright 1937 by Harcourt Brace Jovanovich, Inc.; copyright 1953, 1954, 1965 by Leonard Woolf.

CONTENTS

ABBREVIATIONS AND PROCEDURES

TY	*The Years*	The novel as published
TP	*The Pargiters*	The original holograph draft
AWD	*A Writer's Diary*	Leonard Woolf's selected edition of Virginia Woolf's journals
DVW	*The Diary of Virginia Woolf*	Ann Olivier Bell's more complete edition of Virginia Woolf's journals (Roman numerals after initials indicate volume numbers)
LVW	*The Letters of Virginia Woolf*	The published letters of Virginia Woolf edited by Nigel Nicolson and Joanne Trautman (Roman numerals after initials indicate volume numbers)
PWH	"Professions for Women"	The holograph of the speech
PWT	"Professions for Women"	The typescript of the speech
BA	*Beginning Again*	Volume III of Leonard Woolf's memoirs—1911 to 1918
DAW	*Downhill All the Way*	Volume IV of Leonard's Woolf's memoirs—1919 to 1939
G	Galley proofs	The March 1936 galleys of *The Years*
P	Page proofs	The 15 December 1936 page proofs of *The Years*

When quoting from Virginia Woolf's manuscripts I have preserved her idiosyncratic spelling and punctuation.

Words that have a line through them in her draft are enclosed by parentheses: (word).

Words that I have inserted to clarify meaning are enclosed by brackets: [word].

Ellipses within quotations indicate that I have left out words in the original text unless I have indicated that the ellipsis is the author's.

Most readers of this study will not be fortunate enough to have access to Woolf's unpublished MS. Many may be able to read the edition of the "1880" section published as *The Pargiters* by Mitchell A. Leaska. His edition also includes a transcript of the holograph and typescript of the speech "Professions for Women." I have included page references to Professor Leaska's edition for all the quotations in my study that refer to the portions of the MS he has transcribed. Page references to the Leaska edition are in italics and follow the volume and page references to the holograph, e.g.: *TP*, I, *23*, *10*.

Readers will note some discrepancies between Professor Leaska's text and mine. Both of us worked directly from a body of manuscripts which contains many crossed-out words, words written in margins and on facing pages, and passages repeated with slight variations. Each of us made subjective decisions as to what to include and what to leave out. For the most part, I have included only the canceled words that seem significant to the meaning of the passage.

I use the term "chapter" to indicate the large divisions of the novel that have dates as titles, such as "1880." Woolf herself refers to these divisions at different times as "parts," "sections," or "chapters." I refer to the episodes within chapters as "scenes" when they involve changes in place or time. Here again I differ from Professor Leaska, who terms the "1880" chapter a "Novel-Essay" and subdivides it into individual "essays" and "chapters." Chapters I and II of my study discuss the material included in his edition.

I call the descriptive passages that open chapters "preludes" and those placed within a chapter to separate scenes "interludes." (Woolf referred to similar descriptive introductions to chapters in *The Waves* as "interludes.")

At the head of each of my chapters I have included a brief synopsis of the scenes from *The Years* that will be referred to in that chapter.

This should help the reader keep straight the many characters and incidents in *The Years* while making his or her way through my discussion of the earlier versions.

THE PARGITERS:
Dramatis Personae (Major Figures)*

Abel Pargiter
Rose, his wife
  their children:
          Morris
            Celia, his wife
              their children:
                      George (North)
                      Peggy
          Eleanor
          Edward
            his friends:
                  Gibbs (later Milly's husband)
                  Tony Ashton (Ashley)
          Delia
            Patrick, her husband
          Milly
          Bobby (Martin)
          Rose
      the Pargiters' maid: Crosby
      Abel Pargiter's mistress: Mira

*(Names changed in *The Years* are indicated by parentheses.)

Digby Pargiter, Abel's brother
Eugénie, his wife
  their children:
                  Maggie or Magdalena
                    Renny, her husband
                  Elvira (Sara or Sally)
                    their friend: Nicholas Pomjalovsky or
                              Brown (in both versions)

Mr. Malone
Mrs. Malone, Rose Pargiter's sister
  their daughter:
                  Kitty
                    her teacher: Lucy Craddock
                    her friend:
                            Nelly Hughes or Brook
                            (Robson)
                              her parents: Mr. and Mrs.
                                Hughes or Brook (Robson)
                              her brother: Jo

INTRODUCTION

This is the story of *The Years*, of how it was written, and of how its nature changed as it was revised. For Virginia Woolf, this novel, the last to be published before her death, was very special. It was to be her *summa*, the work which would contain "millions of ideas but no preaching—history, politics, feminism, art, literature—in short a summing up of all I know, feel, laugh at, despise, like, admire, hate and so on" (*AWD*, 25 March 1933, p. 198).

Readers of the novel as we know it might find this ambitious declaration puzzling, for though all sorts of ideas are suggested in its pages, their expression is often indirect or incomplete. Apparently, during the long period of revision and compression that preceded its publication, Woolf's original intentions lost their force.

It is impossible to isolate any one factor as decisive in bringing about the novel's transformation, but a note that sounds frequently in Woolf's diary expresses her fear of becoming shrill and one-sided, of allowing her ideas to destroy her art. Seen from this vantage point the story of the evolution of *The Years* becomes the story of a struggle to embody ideas in imaginative fiction, to write a work that expresses the deepest beliefs of its author without losing its balance and integrity.

Eventually, as the extreme difficulties of this task became apparent, Woolf deleted many of the ideas she had expressed directly in her original draft and incorporated them in the pamphlet *Three Guineas*, which she published in 1938 as a complement to *The Years*. It was her hope that readers would see the connection between the two works and would regard them, as she did, as "one book" (*AWD*, 3 June 1938, p. 295). But for a time the connection was lost, and it is only in recent years, as readers turn to these seminal works and their drafts to learn more about Woolf's social theories, that they are being read as she wished.

Soon after the publication of *The Years*, Virginia Woolf was to write: "I myself know why it's a failure, and that its failure is deliberate" (*AWD*, 7 March 1937, p. 277). This seems a strange remark for an author to make, though it is at least partly attributable to her anxiety as she waited for the first reviews to appear. It does reveal Virginia Woolf's fear that the original impetus for the work had been lost and that what she had meant to say would not be understood.

The Years was not a failure in the eyes of the public when it was published in 1937, for it became a best-seller both in England and the United States. As time went by its reputation faded, and it came to be ranked below the level of her most highly regarded novels.[1] Today a new generation of readers is turning to *The Years*, finding in its pages a more serious social and political comment than can be discerned through the graceful prose of her more lyrical novels. And *The Years* rewards careful reading, for though its tone is quiet, its fabric is rich with meaning, and some of Woolf's most memorable writing can be found in its pages.

As I have read my way through the manuscripts, proofs, and fragments of typescript that remain as evidence of the process Woolf went through as she shaped the final form of *The Years*, I have been led to wonder whether another unwritten novel lies hidden in these scratched-out passages and cancelled galley proofs. If she had stopped revising sooner, or if her work had gone on for another year, what book would we be reading today as the last novel published in her lifetime?

---

[1]Although the early reviews were mainly favorable, many of the later critical studies echo E. M. Forster's view that "in *The Years* as in *Night and Day*, she deserts poetry, and again she fails . . ." (*Virginia Woolf*, 17). Until recently, the strongest dissenting note was sounded by Hafley, who called *The Years* "possibly the best, and certainly one of the most interesting of Virginia Woolf's novels" (132).

These are questions that can never be answered, any more than we can truly understand what motivated her at crucial points to turn the novel in the direction she did, though the details of her biography and revealing comments in her journals and letters provide many fascinating clues. All we really have to go on are the facts, as they can be found in the documents, and in the memoirs of Leonard Woolf, who lived with her through nearly five years of struggle with *The Years*.

The documents that have survived provide a picture of the way Woolf worked, but it must be noted that though these materials are extensive, they are in no way complete. The major source we have seems impressive, for it consists of eight bound notebooks that appear to be a handwritten first draft of the novel.[2] Yet Leonard Woolf's memoirs tell us that when Virginia Woolf was creating a novel, months of mental activity preceded the actual writing of a draft, so that characters and scenes had come alive in her mind long before they appeared in any text. In his memoirs, Leonard Woolf recalled that he

. . . had never known any writer who thought, ruminated so continuously and consciously over what she was writing, turning her problems over in her mind persistently while sitting in a chair in front of the winter fire or going for her daily walk along the bank of the Sussex Ouse. She was able to reel across the last ten pages of *The Waves* stumbling after her own voice and the voices that flew ahead only because of the intense, conscious thought she had given the book for weeks and months before the words were actually put on paper.[3]

In the case of *The Years*, the long period of planning that took place

---

[2]This manuscript, and all other documents mentioned here, except for eight pages of typescript in the library of the University of Sussex, England, are preserved in the Henry W. and Albert A. Berg Collection of English and American Literature of The New York Public Library, Astor, Lenox and Tilden Foundations (referred to hereafter as Berg). Quentin Bell, Virginia Woolf's official biographer, has informed me in a personal letter that he does not know of any documents relating to the writing of *The Years* other than those in these two libraries.

[3]*BA*, 33.

before the writing of the holograph is attested to by evidence in the draft and in her journals.[4]

As we examine the six years' history leading from Woolf's first inkling of the idea for *The Years* in 1931 (which came to her as she prepared a speech to be given before a feminist organization) to the publication of *The Years* in 1937, it becomes clear that some of the materials that documented the evolution of the novel have been lost. The holograph itself contains many variant versions of scenes, and after it was completed in 1934 further revision continued, probably in typescript.[5] The only documents that may have survived from this period are eight sheets of undated typescript preserved in the Library of the University of Sussex.[6] Aside from these fragments, we have no idea of what the alternate versions were like, except for what we can glean from Woolf's journal entries.

It was not until March 1936 that the first galleys were set in type, and it is our good fortune that a nearly complete set of galley proofs pulled at that time is still in existence, preserved along with the holograph in the Berg Collection of English and American Literature of the New York Public Library. The Berg Collection also possesses page proofs of the "1917" chapter, which were pulled in December 1936, just before the novel was published; these last are quite close to the chapter in the Hogarth Press first edition, except for a few minor changes in wording.

[4]The way in which Woolf developed the character of Elvira-Sara in her mind months before Elvira appeared in the holograph will be examined in ch. III below, pp. 40–42.

[5]There is also a strong possibility that a typescript was made up at the same time as the holograph. Leonard Woolf, describing his wife's writing habits, said that "She wrote only in the morning from 10 to 1 and usually she typed out in the afternoon what she had written by hand in the morning . . ." (*BA*, 232). Woolf herself called the revised version she typed after completing the holograph her "first wild retyping" (*AWD*, 17 July 1935, p. 252).

[6]With the permission of Quentin Bell and through the courtesy of John Burt of the Library of the University of Sussex, England, I have been supplied with copies of the extant typescript pages. They correspond approximately to part of the holograph version of the "1910" chapter of *The Years*. Since the typescript is undated, it is impossible to know just when it was written, but the content of the pages is close enough to the holograph to suggest that they were written either concurrently or soon after the holograph was completed.

This collection of documents, though incomplete, is substantial enough to provide a great deal of insight into how Woolf worked. The holograph, which is many times the length of *The Years*, is replete with details that have been expunged from the final text. What, we may ask, is its relationship to the novel that finally emerged? Some clues may be found in Woolf's journal entries. It happens that just when Woolf was beginning to face up to the arduous task of revising her long, discursive first draft she was reading Turgenev in preparation for writing an essay on his work.[7] She was struck by his idea of form: "T.[urgenev]'s idea that the writer states the essential and lets the reader do the rest. . . . T. reduces the possibilities. The difficulty about criticism is that it is so superficial. The writer has gone so much deeper. T. kèpt a diary for Bozarov: [*sic*] wrote everything from his point of view. We have only 250 short pages. Our criticism is only a birds eye view of the pinnacle of an iceberg. The rest under water" (*AWD*, 16 Aug. 1933, p. 210).

Like Turgenev, Woolf was beginning to see her manuscript as the base of an iceberg that could be submerged beneath the surface of the finished novel, giving it substance and depth. In his case the technique was consciously arrived at, for he deliberately wrote Bazarov's diary for his own benefit. Woolf's approach was more spontaneous; she seemed to use her first draft as a way of writing out her thoughts, talking to herself as she went along about the problems of craft she was encountering.

This way of working was not new to her. Woolf's recently published letters reveal that as early as 1909, when she was writing an earlier version of her first novel, *The Voyage Out*, she gave a copy of her draft to her brother-in-law Clive Bell. When he criticized one passage, she sent him an explanation: "Those bare passages of biography were not meant to remain in the text. They are notes to solidify my own conception of the peoples characters. I thought it a good plan to write them down; but having served their purpose they

[7]The essay Woolf wrote on Turgenev at that time can be read as a commentary on what she was trying to do in *The Years*, since many of the qualities she finds in Turgenev's works can also be ascribed to *The Years*. "The Novels of Turgenev," *Collected Essays*, I, 247–53.

will go."[8] Thus we can see that to understand Woolf's method we must regard the unpublished draft more as a source book than as a first version of a novel that could be ready for publication after a little polishing and revision. At least in the two novels that nearly span her writing career, Woolf achieved her elusive, impressionistic style by paring down a more detailed original manuscript.

But, at least in *The Years*, Woolf did more than cut. As she chipped away at her manuscript, hoping to reveal its underlying form, she realized that her scenes lacked continuity, that using a set of characters from the same family moving forward through time was not enough to unify her work. Doubtless it was this realization that led Woolf to develop what I call the reverberative structure of *The Years*: the series of echoes and re-echoes of words, phrases, and incidents which link one scene to another. The pattern of repetitions in *The Years* has been noted by others and has formed the basis for Allen McLaurin's excellent analysis of its structure in his *Virginia Woolf, The Echoes Enchained*, but what my examination of the documents reveals is that almost all of the repetitions were not present in the original draft. They seem to be a device she discovered as she revised, for as I compared the holograph to the proofs and the published novel I was able to watch Woolf at work inserting these key phrases and their variations into the text.

Another discovery made in the course of my research is that the passages describing the weather and setting the scene that begin each chapter and that separate scenes within chapters were not added to the novel until the final months before publication. Though it is difficult to imagine *The Years* without these richly suggestive preludes and interludes, their late appearance in the text suggests that they were nearly an afterthought.

For many years studies of Woolf have emphasized the aesthetic and psychological values of her works and have placed her, for better or worse, among the novelists of "sensibility." Scant attention has been paid to her social theories, perhaps because they cluster around feminism, a point of view that has only recently been restored to serious consideration. For this reason *The Years* and its documents

[8]*LVW*, I, 382.

are at the heart of the current reappraisal of Woolf, since it is in these uncut documents that her social and political theories are developed most fully.

The first to undertake a careful examination of *The Years* MS was Charles G. Hoffman. Beginning in 1968, he published a series of articles describing what he found in the unpublished drafts of *Orlando*, *Mrs. Dalloway*, and *The Years*. In his article on the MS of *The Years*, published in 1969, he pointed out the discrepancy between Woolf's intention to write "a sequel to *A Room of One's Own*—about the sexual life of women . . ." and the content of the novel that was the result of that impulse (*AWD*, 20 Jan. 1931, pp. 165–66). Hoffman was also the first to comment on the striking difference between the "Novel-Essay" format of the first section of the holograph and the more conventional structure of the published novel. My analysis of the evolution of *The Years* is indebted to Hoffman for his pioneering efforts.

Recent revival of interest in *The Years* has led to the publication of Mitchell Leaska's edition of the "1880" section of the holograph of *The Years*, which he has titled *The Pargiters*. With the able assistance of Lola L. Szladitz, curator of the Berg Collection, and David V. Erdman and his editorial staff at The New York Public Library, Leaska has transcribed most of the contents of the first two volumes of the holograph. His edition also includes a transcription of the typescript and holograph notes for the speech Woolf gave before the London National Society for Women's Service, which became the impetus for the novel.

The main focus of my own study is the manuscript notebooks, since these pages contain a wealth of details that has been excised from the published novel. Beginning with an analysis of the speech that sparked Woolf's initial impulse to write a feminist essay, I have followed her through the chapters of her draft, using diary comments and other biographical materials wherever they provide insight into the circumstances surrounding her work.[9] My first six chapters deal with the holograph notebooks, and in all but Chapter

[9]At present, Virginia Woolf's complete journals are being published, but at this writing only the entries dated before 22 Dec. 1924 are in print.

V, which describes the two episodes that are not included in the published novel, I have used the corresponding chapters of *The Years* as a basi͘ for comparison. Chapter VII carries the history of the writing of the novel forward from the end of the holograph to the date of publication; its focus is the set of galley proofs pulled in March 1936, which provide most of the documentation for the last stages of revision. In Chapter VIII, I undertake a detailed comparison of the galley proofs and published version of the "1917" chapter of the novel.

My method has been quite selective. I have chosen to follow certain trends, such as the deletion of sexual and ideological material and the changes in the depiction of one character, Elvira (Sara in *The Years*). I have paid less attention to stylistic variations than to changes that significantly alter form and meaning. Now that many of Woolf's unpublished documents are being given increased attention, I look forward to the day when comparative studies of the MSS of all her novels will produce insights into her creative processes that go far beyond what can be learned from a study such as mine, which centers on the evolution of a single work.

I

Germination

.

The story of the writing of *The Years* begins with an idea conceived in a bathtub on a January morning in 1931, an idea for a feminist essay to be based on a talk Virginia Woolf was to give the next night to a group of women in the professions. The spark of inspiration came, as Woolf's beginnings often did, just as she was struggling with the conclusion of a novel, in this case, *The Waves*. Endings were always difficult for her, and her mind seemed to seek release from the effort by charging off in a new direction.

Her new idea was so exciting that she found it very difficult to shake off its obsession and return to the writing of *The Waves*. *The Waves*, Woolf's most experimental work, was a series of dramatic monologues without plot, action, or narrative transitions for which she had plumbed interior experience to its depths. Now she found herself drawn swiftly back to the outside world, to facts and arguments, politics, and the concerns of daily life.

Virginia Woolf was forty-nine years old when she addressed the London and National Society for Women's Service on that January night.[1] Since 1925 she had published *Mrs. Dalloway*, *To the Lighthouse*, and *The Common Reader*; she had come into her own as a serious novelist and critic. The popularity of her fantasy, *Orlando*, had given her access to a wider reading public, and she had become a symbolic figure to women who shared her aspirations and regarded her as a spokeswoman for those of her sex who wished to enter fully into the artistic and intellectual life of their time. In 1928, when she gave two lectures on women and literature to the students of the women's colleges of Cambridge, her sister Vanessa remembered that there was an atmosphere of "triumph—a kind of ovation."

[1]The society was a direct descendant of the first women's suffrage committee. Its object was the bettering of the economic position of women by increasing their opportunities for employment. Phillippa Strachey, Lytton's sister, was secretary until 1951. For a brief, lively history of the society, see Rachel Strachey's pamphlet *Women's Suffrage and Women's Service*.

1

A Room of One's Own, the essay based on the two college lectures, dealt mainly with women as writers, though many of the questions she explored pertained to all women. Now, three years later, when Woolf found herself addressing the London and National Society for Women's Service, she was able to generalize from her experience as a writer to speculate on the obstacles women would encounter as they began to move into all the professions.

As we trace the history of *The Years*, we will come to see how her speech, and the incipient essay it inspired, was transformed first into a "Novel-Essay" and then into a more conventional work of fiction, and how some of the ideas developed for the original essay found their way into *Three Guineas*, the pamphlet on women and war that was published as an offshoot of *The Years*.[2] And we will see how the first hints of the themes she would deal with in her novel, the methods of revision she would use, and the special problems she would face, can be discerned in the holograph and typescript of the speech she gave on that January evening in 1931.

Some of the impetus for Virginia's speech that night came from her fellow speaker, Dame Ethel Smyth, a seventy-one-year-old composer and one-time militant suffragette. Ethel was a new friend who had attached herself passionately to Virginia. All through the preceding autumn the two had spent afternoons together, going over Ethel's memoirs of her early struggles to become a composer and to further the women's cause.[3] Virginia was both fascinated and repelled by Dame Ethel's indomitable egotism, but the story of her friend's

[2]The diary entry describing Woolf's thoughts in her bath (*AWD*, 20 Jan. 1931, pp. 165–66) has two notes attached to it. Where Woolf says that she has "conceived an entire new book," an editor, presumably Leonard Woolf, has added a note suggesting that the new book planned here was "Eventually *Three Guineas*." Virginia Woolf herself, however, had already appended another note: "(This is *Here and Now*, I think. May '34)" which also appears in the published edition. *Here and Now* was one of the many provisional titles for *The Years*, and Woolf connects her original idea with the novel, not the later pamphlet. Since *Three Guineas* was based on the research for the essay that became the "Essay-Novel," Leonard Woolf is not incorrect in his notation; it is possible, however, that Leonard did not know of the close connection between *The Years* and *Three Guineas*, since there is no evidence that he read *The Years* in its earlier form before the essays had been deleted.

[3]During this period Ethel Smyth was preparing material for her collection of autobiographical essays, *Female Pipings in Eden*.

unswerving effort to achieve recognition and equality in a man's world made a deep impression. In an early section of the typescript of her speech, Woolf paid tribute to her: "(She is of the race of pioneers, she is one of the ice-breakers, the gun-runners, the window-smashers, the armoured tanks who climbed the rough, drew the enemies fire, and left behind her a pathway for those who came after her, not yet smooth and metalled road—but still a pathway)" (PWT, 1, *xxvii*). Because this part of her tribute to Ethel has been canceled in the extant typescript, it is doubtful that these words were spoken that night; nevertheless, it is unusual to find Woolf, who abhorred violence, giving even fleeting approval to such militant tactics. In this instance her sympathies outweighed her reservations: "I never know," the deleted passage continues, "whether to be angry that such heroism was needed, or glad that such heroism was shown" (PWT, 1, *xxvii*).

Her own work, Woolf went on to tell her audience that night, had not demanded such extraordinary valor. Paper and pen and a stamp to mail one's essay to an editor were all a young woman required to launch her on a career in journalism, and these were more readily available than artist's models and studios, or an orchestra to perform a composer's works.

Yet she saw now, as she looked back, that she had fought her own psychological battle, a struggle she had shared, she suspected, with many another daughter of the middle class. It was a battle with a phantom she called "The Angel in the House," after the heroine of Coventry Patmore's famous paean to Victorian womanhood.[4] This is the "Angel" her typescript describes:

> (She was the woman that men wished women to be . . .) she soothed, conciliated, sacrificed herself took the hash if there was only chicken enough for one and in short was so constituted that she never had a wish or a mind of her own but preferred to sympathise with the wishes and needs of others. Above all—I hope I need not say it—she was pure. There were a great many things one could not say without bringing a blush to her cheek. (PWT, 3–4, *xxix–xxx*)

The "Angel" had tried to dictate what Virginia might write about

---

[4]*The Angel in the House*, in *The Poems of Coventry Patmore*, 61–205.

and how she should approach her material, especially when she wrote for a paper owned and edited by men and reviewed books written by men. "Be sympathetic," the "Angel" warned her, "be tender; flatter; use all the arts and wiles which I heaven help me have used 'til I am sick of the whole thing . . ." (PWT, 5, *xxxi*). Such pressures, Woolf suspected, had destroyed the creativity of many a talented woman of the past. "Writer after writer, painter after painter and musician I daresay too she has strangled and killed. One is always meeting their corpses laid out in biography" (PWT, 6, *xxxii*).

In addition to the typescript, there remains a brief holograph draft of the speech, which probably preceded the typescript.[5] Although the typescript version may be closer to the actual words Woolf spoke that night, comparison with the handwritten draft affords an insight into the process of distillation and modification that was part of the writing method we will find Woolf using again and again when she revised *The Years*. In the typescript, the young aspiring journalist whom Woolf conjures up as an example for her audience is reviewing a novel by someone like Arnold Bennett, but in the holograph version of the speech, the subject of the review is a memoir of the last war written by a participant: "If I were reviewing books now, I would say this was a stupid and violent and hateful and idiotic and trifling and ignoble and mean display. I would say I am bored to death by war books. I detest the masculine point of view. I am bored by his heroics, virtue and honour" (PWH, 121, *164*). The holograph version is a spontaneous outburst, an expression of anger, irritation, and disdain for the "masculine point of view." As was her wont, when Woolf rewrote she softened her remarks and placed them in a broader context, believing that this would make them more palatable and persuasive.[6] Here, as we will find in *The Years*, the handwritten drafts

[5]The holograph draft of the speech is incomplete. It is entitled "Speech" and is dated "21st Jan. 1931"; it is located in Virginia Woolf's working textbooks. Berg, "Articles, essays, fiction and reviews," vol. 4, 1930–31, pp. 117–33. The typescript, which appears to be complete, is undated, but it is likely that Woolf followed her usual practice of jotting down her ideas in longhand and then revising as she typed. Since the speech was given on 21 Jan. 1931, the two versions probably were written at nearly the same time.

[6]The value of writing freely and polishing later was something Woolf had learned from keeping her diary. In 1924 she had written, "What I was going to say

seem to function for her as a way of venting her own anger and frustration, freeing her to write her final version more reasonably, with a wide readership in mind.[7]

Here in this early speech, Woolf also touched on one of the major themes that she would explore in *The Years* and *Three Guineas*: the connection between "the masculine point of view" and the causes of domestic tyranny and savage warfare. This "masculine" attitude was not, in her view, natural to all males. It was an abstraction called "masculinity," defined by social expectations and instilled through education, that had acted throughout history to constrict and deform what was best in human nature. Only by changing the upbringing of both sexes, she believed, could the direction of civilization be changed.

These passages also suggest one of the questions that would occupy Woolf's thoughts throughout her exploration of the ways in which the lives of men and women might be changed. How was one to distinguish between the "heroism" of an Ethel Smyth and the "heroics" of those who led men into senseless battle? How were women to prevent themselves from adopting the "masculine point of view" as they struggled to achieve an equal place in society? Would they be able to change social institutions by infusing them with more humane values, or would their efforts be just one more source of conflict and polarization? The life and character of Rose Pargiter, the militant suffrage fighter in *The Years*, who later proudly wears her medal for

---

was that I think writing must be formal. The art must be respected. This struck me reading some of my notes here, for if one lets the mind run loose it becomes egotistic; personal, which I detest. At the same time the irregular fire must be there; and perhaps to loose it one must begin by being chaotic, but not appear in public like that" (*AWD*, 18 Nov. 1924, p. 69).

[7]Woolf frequently expressed her belief that the expression of anger and resentment weakened and distorted a work of art. In an essay entitled "Women and Fiction," written in 1929, she notes that this element was seldom absent from the work of women writers, who, like Negroes and working-class men, had a personal grievance against society. At that time she was optimistic enough to think that women's new freedom would help them to write more objectively. Nevertheless, the documents show that Woolf herself had never expunged anger and bitterness from her soul, and that it was only through careful editing that she moderated the tone of her writing. *Collected Essays*, II, 141–48.

war service on behalf of the very government she had spent her life attacking, dramatizes this dilemma.[8]

The holograph of Woolf's speech touches on one of the difficulties she faced as a writer, a difficulty that was to surface again and again in the years to come. She feared that even if she were able to conquer her personal "Angel" and allow herself to write about her deepest feelings and experiences, the men who read and judged her work would not tolerate the degree of frankness in a woman's writing that they were willing to accept from men.

> Take Mr. Joyce or Proust, one of the achievements of their books is their honesty, their openness, their determination to say every-thing. For women, the prudery of men is a terrible bugbear. . . . Now men are shocked if a women said what she felt (as Joyce does). Yet literature which is always pulling down the blinds is not literature. All that we have ought to be expressed—mind and body—a process of incredible difficulty and danger.   (PWH, 121-22, *164*)

In the typescript Woolf broadens her view and includes male writers like D. H. Lawrence in her concerns. He too had suffered as an artist because he had defied convention. The opposition his writing had aroused had, in her opinion, injured his imagination and distorted his personality. She feared the same fate for herself if she took up the role of an iconoclast: "The moment I become heroic the moment I dash my imagination against an obstacle; it shrivels up and hardens. I become a preacher, not a writer. . . . I become hard and

[8]Jane Marcus suggests that Woolf expressed her fear of Ethel Smyth's violent nature in the character of Rose, "whose image of herself as 'Pargiter of Pargiter's Horse' is similar to Dame Ethel's self-image as the daughter of a general in the Royal Artillery. A good friend of Emmeline Pankhurst, Dame Ethel was the composer of 'The March of the Women,' battle song of the suffragettes. Im-prisoned, she conducted the march from her jail cell with a toothbrush. Like Rose Pargiter she became a patriot during the war, supporting the very government she had fought, not refusing its honors as Woolf and Margaret Llewelyn-Davies did. The odd scene in the novel in which Rose buys violets for Sara, then knocks her against a wall (calling her a 'damned liar' as Sara later remembers), suggests the combination of affection and violence which characterized the friendship of the composer and the novelist." Marcus, "*The Years* as Greek Drama, Domestic Novel, and *Götterdammerung*," 297–98. In a letter to Ethel, Woolf comments on a quarrel they had in the street: "In another moment you would have felled me to the ground with your fist" (*LVW*, V, 70).

shrill and positive. . . . in short I cease to be a writer . . . (PWT, 13–14, *xxxix*).

This was the impasse that Woolf was to arrive at repeatedly in the long, arduous course of writing *The Years*. How was she to write about what she wanted most to express, how reach down and bring up the truth as she saw it, without preaching or insisting, without distorting her art? A note of regret sounded in her voice as she told her audience in 1931 that the time was not ripe for what she had to say. "We will wait another fifty years. But it seems to me a pity. . . . I will wait until men become so civilized that they are not shocked when a woman speaks the truth about her body" (PWT, 14, *xxxix–xxxx*).

Her experiences as a writer were different from what her listeners would encounter as they entered other professions, and she told them that she looked forward to gaining new insight into women's nature as a result of their growing freedom to explore all their potentialities. Yet women would surely go through many changes as they undertook new roles. Woolf believed that there were profound differences between men and women that would make women's progress in a man's world more difficult. Nevertheless, these differences should not be erased.

For Virginia Woolf, the distinctive qualities that made a woman what she was came from the divergence between her upbringing and experience and those of a man.

> Her experience is not the same. Her values both in art and in life are her own. . . . And you are bound to find when you come to practice your innumerable professions that your differences of outlook will bring you to loggerheads with some respected chiefs of your profession . . . that you will have to make your profession adapt itself to your needs, your sense of values, your moral sense your sense of what is due to humanity and reason.
> (PWT, 8–10, *xxxiii–xxxvi*)

Woolf thought that the way women were brought up and the role they played in the family had developed in them a sensitivity to others and an awareness of the rich fabric of physical and emotional life that was denied to most men, who had been forced into narrow specialties at an early age in order to achieve advancement in their careers. It was her hope that the professions would be humanized by the entrance of women, so that new possibilities would open up for both sexes.

Yet the future held dangers for women. In competing with men at work they would meet with a great deal of opposition and derision and would feel pressured to become as ego-bound and careerist as the men. It would take strength and courage to retain their individuality, and, she warned "it is of the highest importance that you should not add to your burdens a very heavy and unnecessary burden, the burden of bitterness" (PWT, 17, *xxxxi*).

Despite these obstacles, Woolf saw the future as an opportunity for a new growth of understanding and a new kind of dialogue between the sexes. The note on which she ended her brief talk was optimistic and visionary:

> You have earned the room; you have paid the rent for it . . . that is perhaps enough at the moment. But then, as Dame Ethel asks, what will be the next step? There will be one. And I predict that the next step will be a step upon the stair. You will hear . . . somebody coming. You will open the door. And then—this is at least my guess—there will take place between you and someone else the most interesting exciting and important conversation that has ever been heard.   (PWT, 21–22, *xxxxiv*)

In *A Room of One's Own*, Virginia Woolf had described her vision of a young couple who meet and share a cab. Woolf, who had been pondering the relationship between the sexes in her essay, felt a peculiar sense of gratification at the sight. She conjectured that when she saw the couple get into the cab "the mind felt as if, after being divided, it had come together again in a natural fusion." This realization led her to another question. She asked herself "whether there are two sexes in the mind corresponding to the two sexes in the body, and whether they also require to be united in order to get complete satisfaction and happiness?"[9] At this point she began to develop her concept of androgyny, a theory which suggests that each human being has the potential for both male and female qualities of mind. If these were fully developed, she suggested, the androgynous being would be able to move freely from one side of his or her nature to the other and would not be constrained from developing any talent or interest out of fear of being branded unmanly or unfeminine.

[9]*A Room of One's Own*, 167–71.

In "Professions for Women," Woolf predicts that when women moved out of their conventional roles as wives and mothers and explored their full potentialities they would become more androgynous. This last passage expresses the hope that men would be changed by these new women, so that they too would have the chance to develop fully and communicate freely. It is then that the "exciting conversation" Woolf predicted will take place, between men and women who have learned how to speak to one another as human beings.

When Woolf began to plan the feminist essay she had thought of in her bath, she tentatively entitled it "The Open Door," or "A Tap on the Door," which suggests that she planned to focus her essay on that hoped-for moment when such a conversation would be possible (*AWD*, 23 Jan. 1931, p. 166; *AWD*, 20 Jan. 1932, p. 178). And it is to that vision of a fruitful new relationship between the sexes that she will return at the very end of *The Years*, when Eleanor Pargiter sees a young couple, who may well be the same pair that entered the cab in *A Room of One's Own*, emerging from a taxicab at the doorstep of the house in which they will begin their life together (*TY*, 434).

The speech on "Professions for Women" had given Woolf an idea for an essay, and she was so excited by it that she could not resist starting on a draft right away. But she was too much of a professional not to put it aside regretfully after a few days and return to her task of completing *The Waves*.

Though its conclusion and revision went rather quickly, *The Waves* was not ready for publication until the following August. By that time the impetus for the feminist essay seems to have lost some of its force. Though Woolf took some notes for "The Knock on the Door" in July 1931, it appears that she did not persist in this endeavor.[10]

---

[10]Our only evidence of these early notes for the essay is at the beginning of notebook 1 of the holograph of *The Years* (Berg). The first page bears the title "Notes for The Knock on the Door?" and is dated 20 July, 1931, which is just about the time Woolf finished her final typescript of *The Waves* (*AWD*, 17 July 1931, p. 172). This first effort was abortive, apparently, for after the title a number of pages have been cut out of the notebook. The next page left intact bears the date "11 October 1932," followed by the first working title of *The Years: The Pargiters A Novel-Essay Based upon a paper read to the London/National Society for Women's Service*; this page begins the holograph of the novel.

Instead, she began work on *Flush*, a little fantasy about Elizabeth
Barrett's spaniel that had been conceived as a diversion during the last
difficult stages of *The Waves*. And by the end of 1931 she became
immersed in a new project, the revision of a series of articles to be
included in a second *Common Reader*. These, along with her pamphlet,
A Letter to a Young Poet, and a few stories, were all the literary
assignments she would undertake during the first nine months of
1932.[11] Yet all during this period her mind kept turning back to "A
Knock on the Door" and collecting data for its arguments. In
February 1931, we find her talking with her physician about "the
period and professional women," following up her theories about
women's special nature and proessional life (*AWD*, 4 Feb. 1931, p.
167).[12] In September of that year she came across a passage in
Montaigne that suggests that women have voracious sexual appetites;
his remark set her to wondering why that instinct seems to have
atrophied in so many women of her generation, and she began making
up a chapter of "A Tap on the Door" on the spot.[13] Early in 1932 her
thoughts were set running on her essay once again, "owing largely to
reading *Wells on Women*—how she must be ancillary and decorative in
the world of the future, because she has been tried, in 10 years, and
has not proved anything" (*AWD*, 11 Feb. 1932, p. 179).[14]

Finally, on 13 July 1932, Woolf announced that she had been
"sleeping over a promising novel" (*AWD*, 13 July 1932, p. 182). She

[11]My source for this description of Woolf's literary activities during the early
part of 1932 is Quentin Bell's biography. *Virginia Woolf*, II, 182–95.

[12]Woolf herself was plagued by an unusual degree of discomfort during
menstruation. In letters to her sister she frequently mentions being unable to
travel, entertain, or work because of menstrual headaches or discomforts. In a letter
to Clive Bell she writes, "Possibly I see on looking at a calendar, the usual
indisposition of my sex may make me unable to come on Monday" (*LVW*, II, 360).
During the time she was working on *The Years*, she suffered from dizziness and
fainting spells that were partially attributed to menopause (Bell, II, 197). She
feared that she would be "baulked by time of life, etc.," "from completing *The Years*
successfully (*AWD*, 14 March 1937, p. 278).

[13]Virginia Woolf, unpublished diary (Berg), 3 Sept. 1931, n.p.

[14]An earlier comment that suggests she was already thinking of a novel with
some resemblance to *The Years* is recorded in her diary in Nov. 1931: "in the City
today I was thinking of another book—about shopkeepers, and publicans, with
low-life scenes" and I ratified this sketch by Morgan's [E. M. Forster's] judgment"
(*AWD*, 16 Nov. 1931, p. 176).

had been prompted to begin spinning fictional lives by reading Elizabeth Mary Wright's biography of Joseph Wright. Wright, a maker of dialect dictionaries, had been a workhouse boy whose mother had worked as a charwoman to put him through school. Woolf felt a special bond with this man, whose respect for his mother had led him to devote himself to the education of working women. It appears that Woolf had begun to feel that the feminist questions she had been mulling over might best be expressed in a novel rather than an essay—a novel that would be based on the real lives of people like Joseph Wright whom she had encountered in the memoirs and biographies she loved to read. And when we turn to the eight handwritten notebooks that comprise the first complete draft of the novel, we will find the lives of Joseph Wright and others like him reflected in its pages.

In the course of a year and a half, Woolf had moved away from her idea for a feminist essay to plans for a novel that would somehow incorporate the themes she had been exploring and the stories of people like the Wrights. What was needed now was a form that could include both, and, logically enough, that form would be the "Essay-Novel."

II

1880

.

I prefer, if I wish to tell the truth, to write fiction.

(TP, I, 13, 9)

SYNOPSIS

1880 Colonel Abel Pargiter, a retired British army officer, is at his London club. Feeling restless and "out of it," he leaves and goes to visit his mistress, Mira. Meanwhile, at the Pargiter home on Abercorn Terrace, the Colonel's daughters, Milly and Delia, are waiting for the teapot to boil. As tea is served the younger children, Martin and Rose, come in, followed by the Colonel, who has quarreled with Mira. Eleanor, the oldest daughter, returns from her weekly visit to the poor in Ladbroke Grove. Upstairs, their mother is slowly dying. After tea, little Rose wants to go to the store to buy a rubber duck. Since her brother Martin will not go with her, she disobeys orders and slips out alone. Returning home she encounters a man who frightens her by exposing himself. At home Delia goes upstairs to sit with her mother, and Morris returns from his day at the Law Courts. During dinner Mrs. Pargiter's condition worsens and the family thinks she is finally dying, but it is a false alarm. Eleanor hears little Rose crying out in bed and goes to her. Rose has had a nightmare about the man she saw but is unable to tell her sister what happened. Later that night, Mrs. Pargiter dies.

The scene shifts to Oxford, where Edward, the second son, is cramming for his exams. He is visited by two friends, Gibbs and Ashley, who are rivals for his affection. Edward thinks he is in love with his cousin, Kitty Malone, the daughter of the Master of his college. Kitty is introduced as a restless young woman who is bored with her social obligations. She admires Miss Craddock, her history tutor, but finds it hard to study seriously. Kitty visits a fellow student, Nelly Robson, whose father, a professor, is a self-made man. The chapter ends with Mrs. Pargiter's funeral.

.

We have seen how the idea for a feminist essay had remained in the back of Woolf's mind all through 1931 and most of 1932, until something in Joseph Wright's biography set her to thinking of a novel instead. By October 1932 the two threads came together; the essay and novel merged, creating a new form, the "Essay-Novel." Having hit upon a form that met her needs, Woolf began to write at once, working with such excitement that it was November before she stopped for breath and explained what she was about:[1]

> And I have entirely remodelled my "Essay." It's to be an Essay-Novel, called *The Pargiters*—and it's to take in everything, sex, education, life, etc: and come, with the most powerful and agile leaps, like a chamois, across precipices from 1880 to here and now. That's the notion anyhow, and I have been in such a haze and dream and intoxication, declaiming phrases, seeing scenes, as I walk up Southampton Row that I can hardly say I have been alive at all, since 10th October. (*AWD*, 2 Nov. 1932, p. 189)

Woolf began writing her "Novel-Essay" in the bound notebook in which she had started the essay on professions for women she had originally planned. The notes for the essay have been cut out of the book, and the new title, *The Pargiters A Novel Essay Based upon a paper read to the London/National Society for Women's Service*, announces both the form her novel will take and the source from which her inspiration came.

For the opening of her novel, Woolf recreates the occasion that had inspired it. She pretends that she is speaking before the women's group once more, and in that role she tells her audience that she has overcome her usual reluctance to speak in public because "any request made by young women who are earning, or trying to earn their livings in the professions is of such importance that to refuse it would be an act of ingratitude and selfishness" (*TP*, I, 5, 5). After further

[1]In his study of the genesis of Woolf's novels (based mainly on *A Writer's Diary*, since the unpublished documents were not available to him), Jean Guiguet posited the theory that the discovery of an appropriate form for each work served as the "active, fertilising element" that freed her to write. Guiguet, *Virginia Woolf and Her Works*, 230. The idea for the "Essay-Novel" form was the impetus that started Woolf working on *The Years* after a long period of germination; unfortunately, in this case the form proved unworkable, so that after completing the first section, Woolf found herself struggling to substitute a more viable structure.

introductory remarks, Woolf reveals her true purpose. She explains to her imaginary audience of young women that as a writer she is an "outsider" by profession, who can show them aspects of their own situation that are not always visible to insiders. It is her belief, she explains, that in order to understand themselves they must understand those who came before them: "We cannot understand the present if we isolate it from the past. If we want to understand what it is that you are doing now (I must ask you to) forget that we are in this room, this night; (in the year 1931). . . . We must forget that we are, for the moment ourselves. We must become (our grandmothers)" (*TP*, I, 12, 8).

She proposes to lead them back into the past by reading them scenes from a novel-in-progress that follows a family called Pargiter from 1800 to the year 1932. (Actually, the scene she inserts at this point is set in 1880 and is very much like the second scene in *The Years*, which opens with Delia and Milly preparing tea.) In this way Woolf hoped to show the emancipated, ambitious young women she had conjured up as her audience what it was like to grow up in a Victorian household. "You look upon us," she tells them, "with pity and contempt" (*TP*, I, 34, 28). Evidently she felt that this new generation was unable to understand the subtle pressures that kept healthy middle-class women confined in curtained drawing rooms, preoccupied with making tea and getting married.

Virginia Woolf's own lifetime spanned the transition from the Victorian era to that of the new "emancipated woman." Her sense of responsibility as a writer, which had been brought home to her when she stood on the dais before the women's group in 1931, may have led her to adopt an approach that was almost didactic. As one reads this introductory essay, it seems that Woolf saw herself speaking for her generation and sex, with an obligation to state as clearly as she could what she believed to be the truth about the important issues of her time. Thus it is not surprising that this opening speech becomes more than a conventional framing device. After the tea-table scene ends, a second essay appears in which Woolf explores the economic and social implications of the lives the Pargiter sisters led. This, then, is the pattern of the "Essay-Novel," a pattern which will persist throughout the first two notebooks of the holograph. After each scene of the novel,

Woolf inserts an interpretive essay in which she analyzes the events she has just portrayed and relates them to their historical background, using facts and quotations gleaned from biographies and other documents.[2]

This form, the "Essay-Novel," was a new departure for Woolf; by alternating her fictional scenes with explanatory essays she was abandoning her authorial detachment, placing herself in a radical stance between her novel and its readers, in order to serve as her own interpreter.[3] Heretofore Woolf's temperament and aesthetic inclinations had led her to express herself in novels that were suggestive and impressionistic, yet now we find her creating a strange, hybrid form[4] which combines story-telling with analysis that is explicitly ideological and didactic.

In the introductory essay to *The Pargiters*, Woolf makes a statement that suggests the rationale behind her invention of this new form: "I prefer, (if I wish to tell the truth) to write fiction. . . . This novel the Pargiters, moreover is not a novel of vision but a novel of fact. It is based on scores—I might boldly say thousands—of old memoirs & there is scarcely a statement in it that cannot be (traced to some biography) verified if anyone should wish to so misuse their time" (*TP*, I, 13, 9). In order to "tell the truth," Woolf has invented a special kind of fiction, a fiction buttressed by facts. And, as becomes clear some pages later, the truth she wishes to tell is a special kind of truth: "truth of fact, as distinct from truth of vision" (*TP*, I, 41, 33). For Woolf, then, truth is not an absolute—it can

---

[2]Many of the facts and quotations in the essay part of *The Pargiters* eventually found their way into the body and footnotes of *Three Guineas*. A set of holograph reading notes still exist which show the research through which Woolf found her facts. (Listed in Berg as: *Three Guineas*, holograph reading notes, undated and unsigned.) Since the notes are undated and many of the same sources are cited in both *The Pargiters* and *Three Guineas*, it is impossible to know which work the notes were originally intended for.

[3]Charles Hoffman notes that "Nowhere else, not even in the working notes for *Mrs. Dalloway* (which of all the novels except for *The Years* has the most commentary by the author while the writing was in progress), does Virginia Woolf analyze and comment on the characters to the extent that she does in these first two notebooks of *The Years*." Hoffman, "Virginia Woolf's Manuscript Revisions of *The Years*," 81.

[4]Guiguet has pointed out that Woolf also conceived of *The Waves* as a hybrid form, a "play-poem." Guiguet, 281; *AWD*, 18 June 1927, p. 108.

vary depending on its source. It is easy here to become lost in semantics, for Woolf seldom defines her terms, and it is obvious that "truth" and "fact" and "vision" are part of a cluster of concepts that we must define for ourselves. But since these are words that appear frequently in her writing, examining how she uses them in other contexts may provide some clues to their meaning here.

In "Phases of Fiction," her 1929 essay surveying novelists of the past, she named a group of writers, Defoe and Swift among them, as "The Truth Tellers." These are the writers, she says, who gratify our sense of belief, in whose work "emphasis is laid upon the very facts that most reassure us of stability in real life, upon money, furniture, food, until we seem wedged among solid objects in a solid universe."[5] It is likely that in *The Pargiters* Woolf was attempting to create just such a solid sense of reality, based on the facts she had gleaned from biographies. But, unlike Woolf, Swift and Defoe did not need to shore up their work through research—their source was life itself, as they experienced it.

Woolf, it seems, did not share their confidence in their own perceptions. This may have stemmed, in part, from the limitations of her own experience, as a woman and a semi-invalid, but as she had stated elsewhere, her whole generation suffered from a similar lack of confidence. Defoe's and Swift's certainty about the nature of reality was not available to the modern writer since "science and religion have between them destroyed belief. . . ." "It is as if the modern mind, wishing always to verify its emotions, had lost the power of accepting anything simply for what it is."[6]

The direction Woolf herself was planning to take at this point may come as a surprise to those who have followed her literary development. Earlier in her career she had repudiated the methods of Edwardian writers like Arnold Bennett, with their "enormous stress upon the fabric of things."[7] Now she was "infinitely delighting in facts for a change, and in possession of quantities beyond counting . . ." (*AWD*, 2 Nov. 1932, p. 189).

[5]*Collected Essays*, II, 58.
[6]"The Narrow Bridge of Art," in ibid., 219 and 223.
[7]"Mr. Bennett and Mrs. Brown," in ibid., 332.

Her turning away from "vision" seems even more significant than her new infatuation with facts, for heretofore the pursuit of "vision" had always been the great object of her literary quest. In Virginia Woolf's private language, "vision" seems to mean a way of looking not *at* but *through* the object, to its deepest level of meaning.[8] For her, facts and objects had always gained their significance in this way, so that, at her best, she achieved the effect she admired in Ibsen's writing: "A room is to him a room, a writing table a writing table, and a wastepaper basket a wastepaper basket. At the same time, the paraphernalia of reality have at certain moments to become the veil through which we see infinity."[9] As we continue our exploration of the way *The Pargiters* evolved into *The Years*, we will see that the infusion of vision into reality that Woolf found in Ibsen is what she herself would try to achieve in her novel. But at least at the outset Woolf appears to have set aside her search for that glimpse of infinity to focus on the solid facts of daily existence.[10]

When we turn back to the holograph, we can see how Woolf used these facts to illustrate and support the social and political themes she had touched upon in her speech, "Professions for Women." As she describes the lives of the young Pargiters in the first section of the novel, she emphasizes the way in which education and life-work will serve as a wedge between the sexes, so that even brothers and sisters

[8]Alice Van Buren Kelly, whose study of Virginia Woolf's novels focuses on the dialectic between fact and vision, has defined Woolf's concept of vision in a way that is useful and comprehensive: "in the world of vision, physical objects are not bounded, but instead transcend themselves to take on universal significance. Identity in the world of vision is unity, merging, a combining of things. Only madmen live there entirely—most often it is discovered in moments of mystical understanding. . . . It also reveals itself in patterns outside the individual life, in patterns of history, of a certain sort of immortality, and in the pattern of accumulated moments of vision." Kelly, *The Novels of Virginia Woolf*, 5.

[9]"The Novels of E. M. Forster," in *Collected Essays,* I, 346.

[10]Looking back on her work on *The Years*, Woolf was to feel that her attempt to convey the dailiness of life in this novel had been a failure, since this was not her métier. In *Moments of Being*, a collection of autobiographical writings published after her death, Woolf divided time into moments of "being" and "non-being"—times when one lives consciously and when one does not. She found the unconscious moments more difficult to write about: "The real novelist can somehow convey both sorts of being. I think Jane Austen can; and Trollope; perhaps Thackeray and Dickens and Tolstoy. I have never been able to do both. I tried—in *Night and Day* and in *The Years*." *Moments of Being*, 70.

who were affectionate companions as children find it impossible to share their feelings as they grow older. In her scenes from the novel, and in the accompanying essays, Woolf will examine the powerful economic, social, and psychological forces that create barriers between the sexes and impede the full development of both men and women. Although these themes can be found in *The Years* as well as in *The Pargiters*, they are more clearly stated and fully developed in the earlier version. And one important theme, the way the ideal of female chastity served to repress the sexual life of women, will be given far more attention in *The Pargiters* than it is accorded in *The Years*.

The first scene that Woolf introduces in the holograph focuses on Delia and Milly, who are sitting in the drawing room of the house on Abercorn Terrace, impatiently waiting for the water to boil for tea. (In *The Years* it is the father, Colonel Pargiter, who first appears, but here in the draft we meet the daughters first; the lives of the women are at the center.)

The portrait of Delia that emerges in this first scene is sharper and clearer than in *The Years*. She is an accomplished violinist who wants to go to Germany to study. Later her father will refuse to let her go, and she is already well aware that her plan is futile. Closed off from this possibility, Delia will escape into an adolescent dream of sharing in Parnell's cause. She will move, as young girls often do, from pursuit of achievement in her own right to submersion of her self in a romantic dream of fulfillment through a heroic man. In *The Years*, where there is no mention of her musical interests, she appears as a rather ambiguous and one-dimensional character.

In the holograph, even the sheeplike Milly loves to paint, but since her parents regard working from live models as a questionable pursuit for their daughter, she is limited to sketching landscapes and flowers.

For Milly, marriage and children are always the most important goals, but Delia is constituted differently. Later in the same scene, the two girls see a woman with a baby walk by their window. Each girl reacts to the sight in her own way, but in the essay that analyzes this scene Woolf explains that Delia perceives this difference in herself as a kind of defect.

> The sight of the baby had stirred in each quite a different
> emotion. Milly had felt a curious though unanalyzed desire to

look at the baby, to hold it; to feel its body, to press her lips to the
nape of its neck—whereas Delia had felt, also without being fully
conscious of it, a vague uneasiness, as if some emotion were
expected of her which for some vaguely discreditable reason she
did not feel; & then, instead of following the perambulator, as her
sister did, with her eyes, she turned abruptly into the room, to
exclaim a moment later "O My God," as the thought struck her
that she would never be allowed to go to Germany to study
music.   (*TP*, I, 44, 36)

Similar interpretive comments occur frequently in the essays; they
allow Woolf to integrate both explication and expansion of her text
into the structure of the novel. Without this commentary, Delia's cry
of despair in *The Years* appears to be a generalized response to the
limitations on her social life brought about by her mother's prolonged
illness. And since the girls' feelings as they observe the baby are not
described in *The Years*, the two sisters seem to share a longing to
marry.

In both the holograph and the published novel the sisters see a
young man emerging from a cab as they peer through the curtains,
and each secretly hopes he is coming to call on them. Eleanor, the
oldest sister, has joined them by this time, and in her role of surrogate
mother she warns her sisters, "Don't be caught looking" (*TY*, 19). In
The Pargiters the accompanying essay explains how remarks of this
kind can have a profound and insidious effect.

Both Delia and Milly blushed with a peculiar shame, when
Eleanor said "Don't be caught looking"—they wanted to look at
the young man; they knew it was wrong to look; they were caught
looking; they disliked being caught: they were ashamed,
indignant, confused—all in one—& the feeling, since it was
never exposed, save by a blush, or a giggle; wriggled deep down
into their minds & sometimes woke them in the middle of the
night with curious sensations, unpleasant dreams that seemed all
to come from one fact—that Abercorn Terrace was besieged on all
sides by what may be called street love. . . .   (*TP*, I, 47, 38)

Woolf's essay goes on to explain that "street love," which we might
call sexuality, posed a peculiar threat to the Pargiter girls because one
of the doctrines that governed their lives was that of chastity, which

meant that a middle-class girl would not be marriageable unless her
reputation and her virginity were intact. In a society where nice
women did not work for pay and where the only acceptable work
available to those who did not marry was in the servile role of
governesses, marriage was an overriding goal. Yet, paradoxically, the
"Angel in the House" insisted that young ladies should have no
awareness of sex nor interest in their bodies' sensations. These
healthy, restless young women, cut off from any worthwhile goal or
activity, must pretend that they are indifferent to men.

The ideal of chastity limited their lives in many ways; Woolf
explains that girls could not go out alone because their reputations
must be protected, and though some might venture into the slums to
do charity work, they had to avoid walking alone in the fashionable
part of the city where they might encounter eligible young men. Of
course, the more adventurous girls evaded these rules and managed to
slip out alone occasionally, but the price they paid was high. Of
necessity they constructed a tissue of lies that distorted their relations
with their parents, their brothers, and one another. The lying and
hypocrisy that flourished under the smooth surface of the Victorian
family is a theme Woolf will return to again and again in both *The
Pargiters* and *The Years*.[11]

In her essay Woolf defines the forces that "control the apparently
inevitable" behavior of people, both in novels and in real life (*TP*, I,
36). She uses the terms "Money and Love" as a kind of shorthand for
the complex psychological, social, and economic pressures that shape
human lives. It is her belief that when the motives of money and love
become confused and entangled with one another their power
becomes insidious, and the relations between parents and children are
forced into unnatural patterns. In a patriarchal society, the father uses
the giving and withholding of money to maintain his power over his

[11]Joseph Wright defines pargeter or parjeter as "a plasterer," and parget as "to
plaster with cement or mortar," or "to whitewash." *English Dialect Dictionary*, ed.
Joseph Wright, IV, 423; quoted in "Leaska, Virginia Woolf, the Pargeter,"
Bulletin, 173. Leaska and Marcus suggest that Woolf's family derives its name from
this source, and that the name connotes the process of plastering over or
whitewashing the truth, covering over the cracks in the family structure with lies
and hypocrisy. Leaska, "Virginia Woolf, the Pargeter," 172–210; Marcus, 280–
83.

wife and children. Natural feelings of love and concern motivate the
parents to force their children to conform, for they see it as their duty
to protect their daughters' chastity and educate their sons to become
heads of families in their turn. [12] The need to channel boys and girls
into different social roles meant that brothers and sisters must be
treated differently from an early age. The girls, who had shared a
happy intimacy with their brothers in the nursery, found that a chasm
opened between them as soon as the boys started school, leaving them
behind.

In both *The Pargiters* and *The Years*, the early stages of this
estrangement are dramatized through the experience of Rose, the
youngest Pargiter. Rose has always been a tomboy who loves to climb
trees and play ball with her brother Bobby (Martin in *The Years*). In
The Pargiters the episode in which Rose goes to the store alone is
clearly connected with the growing hostility between the girl and her
brother, and with her desire for independence. She and Bobby have
been engaged in a struggle over use of the schoolroom they share,
because Bobby has claimed it for his alone now that he has started
school. Because of their quarrel, Rose is sure that Bobby will refuse to
accompany her to the store.

> She had known it was hopeless to ask him when he was doing his
> prep, because now that he was what she called "a proper
> schoolboy" he was apt to sneer at her & treat her as if she were a
> baby, especially when she interrupted his work. So, holding the
> door open for a moment & looking around her as if to assert that
> though Bobby claimed the schoolroom for himself, she was not
> going to give up her claim without a fight for it—she was not a
> baby any longer to be kept with nurse in the nursery—she
> departed. Her mind was made up. She would go to Lamley's
> alone.   (*TP*, I, 50, 40–41)

In *The Years* we are told that the children had quarreled about

[12] Although Woolf herself was a young woman in the twentieth century, she felt
that she had experienced Victorian family life first hand: "our surroundings were at
least fifty years behind the times. Father himself was a typical Victorian: George
and Gerald [her half-brothers] were unspeakably* [*doubtful reading] conventional.
So that while we [Virginia and her sister Vanessa] fought against them as individuals
we also fought against them in their public capacity. We were living say in 1910: they
were living in 1860." *Moments of Being*, 126–27.

"Erridge and his microscope and then about shooting Miss Pym's cat next door" (*TY*, 117). The struggle for control of the schoolroom is not mentioned. It is only in *The Pargiters* that Rose's desire not to be treated like a baby and her resentment at being left at home while her brother goes to school are clearly shown as part of her desire for recognition and equal treatment. In the holograph her decision to go to the store alone stems directly from her resentment at the way she has been held back from growing up. In this context the frightening experience with the man who exposes himself to her on the way home from the store appears to her to be a punishment for daring to assert herself.

In the holograph Woolf describes Rose's feeling as the terrified child runs back to the house: "She did not mind banging the front door when she came in—she did not mind being found out in her disobedience . . ." (*TP*, I, 50, 60). It is almost as if she wants to be punished, to relieve some of the uneasiness she feels about what she had seen, an uneasiness that could not be expressed directly because she could tell no one what had happened.

Woolf tells us that Rose fears that if her father knew what she had seen he would be angry at *her*. As with Eleanor's warning to her sisters not to be "caught looking," guilt and shame are attached to natural curiosity about sexual differences and to seeing what one is not supposed to see.

In the essay that accompanies this scene, Woolf associates Rose's response to this experience with the difficulties a writer faces when dealing with sexual material, a problem she had alluded to in "Professions for Women":

> This instinct to turn away & hide the true nature of the experience either because it is too complex to explain, or because of the sense of guilt that seems to adhere to it of course prevented the novelist from dealing with the emotion in fiction—it would be impossible to find any mention of such feeling in the novels that were being written by Trollope, Mrs. Gaskell, Mrs. Oliphant, George Meredith, during the eighties; & if the novelists ignore it, this is largely because the biographies and autobiographies also ignore it & thus reduce the material which the novelist has to work upon, to a minimum. In addition, there is, as the three dots after the

sentence "He unbuttoned his clothes . . ." testify, a convention
supported by law, which forbids, whether rightly or wrongly any
plain description of the sight which Rose, in common with many
other little girls, saw. . . .   (*TP* 1, 61, *51*)

Continuing her discussion of Rose's experience, Woolf explains
that she realizes that such incidents, and others more serious, occur
every day. (Quentin Bell's biography reveals that Woolf herself
remembered being molested sexually as a child by her half-brother.
Like Rose, she told no one at the time; many years later she was able to
tell her teacher Janet Case what had happened.)[13] But she feels that
the experience itself was not as harmful to the child as the aura of
secrecy and guilt that surround it. This could have a lasting effect on
the child's development:

   . . . imagine the impression on the nerves, on the brain, on the
   whole being of the shock which the child instinctively conceals, as
   Rose did; & also is too ignorant, too childish, too frightened to
   describe or explain even to herself as again Rose was. Rose next
   day, of course began to observe Bobby more closely. She began to
   hunt about in the little bookcase in her father's study for some of
   his old books about the treatment of tropical diseases, because
   they had certain pictures.   (*TP*, I, 61–62, *51*)

The child's natural curiosity has been forced underground; it has
become a secret preoccupation that separates her from her playmate:
"After her adventure in the street Rose changed slightly but decidedly
in her feeling for Bobby. Again it is difficult to say how far this change
was the result of some fear or shock; how far she felt dislike for her
brother because of his sex; how far she felt & resented the change that
was making him . . . into a "proper schoolboy" (*TP*, I, 65, *54–55*).

As Bobby grows older, his experiences with his schoolmates and his
desire to be accepted as one of them alter his behavior toward his
sister. At twelve he already knows a great deal more about life than
even Milly and Delia do—he had once been walking with an older boy
when they were accosted by a brightly dressed woman who was, his
friend told him, a prostitute. "Prostitute" was a word he would never
dream of using in his sisters' presence; its casual introduction into the

[13]Bell, I, 42–44.

boys' conversation initiates him into a great fellowship: "the
fellowship of men together—a fellowship which, he began to feel,
yielded a great many rights and privileges and required even of
himself, at the age of twelve, certain loyalties and assertions, for
example it was essential to make it plain that the school room was his
room—especially when his school friends came to tea." (*TP*, I, 66,
54).

    Bobby is really rather fond of Rose and enjoys playing with her
when they are alone, but he finds that his new status among his friends
requires him to treat her with scorn. Rose begins to notice this.

> Bobby was always much rougher with her when his friends were
> there. He turned her out of the schoolroom once and locked the
> door behind him; whereupon she locked herself into the bathroom
> and sobbed. But, after the first spasm of weeping was over, she
> held what she called in her private language a "grand council of
> war", that is to say she determined that after this Bobby was in
> the Enemies Camp & she would do everything she could to thwart
> him and spite him . . . & as soon afterwards he was sent away to
> Rugby that quarrel was never entirely made up. (*TP*, I, 66, 55)

    Since Rose will grow up to become a militant feminist who is sent
to jail for smashing the Prime Minister's windows, it seems that this
childhood quarrel has planted seeds of bitterness that will become
generalized into hostility toward all men. The resentment and
jealousy engendered by the family and the educational system are
perpetuated.

    Yet, as Woolf is careful to point out, though Bobby's life may be
freer than that of his sisters in many ways, he too must learn a complex
system of reserves and deceptions. The need to be "one of the boys"
makes his school life so difficult, strange, and unnatural that Rose has
no just cause for resentment. "Had she known what her brother was
going through at school she would very likely have decided when she
called her grand council that instead of being members of opposite
camps they ought on the contrary to combine together in a blood
brotherhood"(*TP*, I, 67, 56).

    Both brother and sister are victims of an unnatural system which
forces them into rigid postures of opposition and destroys any
possibility of communication and sharing. When men and women

have been effectively turned against one another, Woolf suggests, the circumstances that oppress all of them go unchallenged.

In *The Years* the details of the estrangement between Rose and Bobby are treated rather sketchily, but the way in which Eleanor and Morris begin to grow apart is given a sensitive treatment in both the holograph and the novel. *The Pargiters*, unlike *The Years*, portrays their childhood relationship as well as the way they see one another at the time the novel opens. These two had always been very close, for Eleanor had been Morris' confidante when he was roughed up at school or when he felt discouraged because his brother Edward had taken all the prizes. Morris has never been a favorite with his father, so it was Eleanor who had gone to the Colonel and persuaded him to let Morris study for the law.

Now Morris' superior education is beginning to separate them. They are no longer able to talk to one another about what interests each most: "She often wished that she had been better educated. Morris was giving up talking to her about his cases. She found the law was so very difficult to follow & she kept back a good deal about the Levys. Morris called them 'the poor' too. They had been such friends when they were children—they had shared everything—she could remember bringing him back a piece of toffee in a pocket handkerchief" (*TP*, I, 31–32, 26–27).

Eleanor is a gentler person than Rose, and she seldom consciously resents the limitations of her life. Though they no longer share everything, she and Morris continue to have a special tenderness for one another, and she is able to make a life for herself out of her satisfaction in giving to others. Her self-effacement is in some ways the opposite side of Rose's militance. While Rose's resentment of women's inferior position causes her to turn against men and live a life of continual warfare, Eleanor accepts her position and learns to live within it. However, both have allowed themselves to be defined by men, and consequently both are less than complete.

In these first scenes set at Abercorn Terrace in 1880, the versions in the holograph and in *The Years* are quite similar in structure, but there is one important difference. In the first draft, Mrs. Pargiter is ill and will die, Woolf tells us, within a few months. In *The Years* her death takes place that very night. The depiction of Mrs. Pargiter's death within the chapter heightens its drama and opens the way for changes in the lives of the Pargiter children in the chapters to come. And, as Woolf presents it, the death serves as a climax and a moment of relief in that tension-filled house where illness has reigned too long. As Woolf revised the chapter, she added not only the deathbed scene but many images and phrases that intensify the mood of interminable expectation, ambivalence, and uncertainty.[14]

Even the weather contributes to the atmosphere. In the descriptive prelude added late in the revisions, we learn that it is an "uncertain spring," that everywhere people are apprehensive, opening and closing their umbrellas and searching the sky (*TY*, 3). Then, in the scene at Colonel Pargiter's club that was also inserted later, the uncertain family situation is explained. "His wife was dying; but she did not die. She was better today; would be worse tomorrow; a new nurse was coming; and so it went on" (*TY*, 5). The same feeling prevails at home, where Delia waits for the kettle to boil, thinking impatiently that "Everything seemed to take such an intolerable time" (*TY*, 10). Later, when she goes upstairs to sit with her mother, she notices that Mrs. Pargiter "did not look as if she were dying; she looked as if she might go on existing in the borderland between life and death for ever" (*TY*, 21).

The greater emphasis on Mrs. Pargiter's death in the final version of the novel gives Woolf an opportunity for further development of one of the major themes of the novel, the hypocrisy that made honest communication impossible for members of the Victorian middle class. Just as little Rose was damaged by her inability to talk about her frightening experience, so is the entire Pargiter family put under additional strain because they are unable to admit to one another that they resent the mother's prolonged illness and wish she would die.

Woolf shows us how they talk in code phrases when they want to allude to the hoped-for time when Mrs. Pargiter will be dead. Even in his thoughts Abel Pargiter cannot use the words. "One of these days—that was his euphemism for the time when his wife was dead—he would give up London, he thought, and live in the country" (*TY*, 6). And later, when Delia expresses her restlessness,

---

[14]In a letter to Vanessa, Virginia described a similar atmosphere of alternating hope and despair as Lytton Strachey lay dying. *LVW*, V, 5.

Eleanor will try to soothe her: " 'Look here, Delia,' said Eleanor, shutting her book, 'you've only got to wait. . . .' She meant but she could not say it, 'until Mama dies' " (*TY*, 19).

The Pargiters' discomfort in the presence of death is contrasted with the franker attitude of the poor. In the holograph, Eleanor recalls how old Mrs. Levy has planned her own funeral. In *The Years* less space is given to the Levys, but the physical reality of death as decay is brought closer by the insertion of the scene where we see Mrs. Pargiter through her daughter Delia's eyes: "Her face was pouched and heavy; the skin was stained with brown patches; the hair which had been red was now white, save that there were queer yellow patches in it, as if some locks had been dipped in the yolk of an egg" (*TY*, 21).

The realism of this sickroom scene is new for Woolf, whose earlier novels tended to romanticize death: the heroine of *The Voyage Out* dies in her youth of an exotic tropical disease, Mrs. Ramsay in *To the Lighthouse* disappears in a parenthesis, and Septimus Smith in *Mrs. Dalloway* throws himself out a window in an act of defiance that is almost an affirmation.

Now, in her fifties, Virginia Woolf had reached the time of life when many of her oldest friends were dying, and during the course of the writing of *The Years* she would lose several of them. Woolf's own mother had died when she was thirteen, and the deaths of friends made her relive that experience. At Roger Fry's funeral she recalled her feelings at her mother's deathbed: "Remember turning aside at mother's bed, when she had died, and Stella took us in, to laugh secretly, at the nurse crying. She's pretending, I said, aged 13, and was afraid I was not feeling enough. So now." (*AWD*, 12 Sept. 1934, p. 224). Mark Spilka argues convincingly that the seeds of Woolf's first breakdown were evident in her incongruous reaction at her mother's death-bed, and that the absence of sorrow suggests that because Woolf could not mourn for her mother she was not able to work through her grief at the loss.[15] Whatever effect the experience of Fry's death may have had upon her understanding of her own early reaction, she was able to make use of it in her novel. As she revised *The Years* she ascribed the same feelings to Delia.

After leaving Abercorn Terrace, the scene shifts to Oxford, where

[15]Spilka, 173.

Edward Pargiter is cramming for his exams. There, through Edward's thoughts and experiences, we will learn how the masculine point of view is impressed upon young males.

The Years focuses on Edward's evening at Oxford, as does *The Pargiters*, but in the holograph we are given additional insight into how Edward's personality was formed by having him recall his public school days. As he summons the courage to tackle his books, to beat out that "clever little Jew boy" from Birmingham, he seems to hear the voice of his old headmaster, speaking at his public school graduation:

> it seemed the voice of the names carved upon the old stone marble tablets—the names of the old boys who had fought in war after war for five hundred years; . . . whose bones lay unburied in India, who had saved Europe again and again & dying asked only that their names be written up in the old school. "No other influence," the doctor said, "has produced so great a growth of the sterner & more robust virtues—fortitude; self-reliance, intrepidity, devotion to the commonweal; readiness for united action and self-sacrifice."   (*TP*, I, 73, 61)

The public school boys have been bred and trained for warfare, and in the bloodless battleground of the examination room the rules are no different. Colonel Pargiter recognizes this when he sends his son some good port to help him study, because "you can't ram a bayonet through another fellow's ribs in cold blood" (*TP*, I, 79, 66). Here, at the beginning of the novel, a connection is already being made between the male ethos of competition and blood warfare. Edward is the son of a man who lost his fingers putting down a mutiny in India in order to establish the right of the white male to govern his possessions. As he sharpens his wits to get his fellowship, he is just as much his father's child as is Rose, who pretends she is "Pargiter of Pargiter's Horse" and will someday fight for women's rights by adopting the methods of her "enemy."

The education Edward is receiving does more than instill warlike virtues. Like his brothers, Edward is developing an attitude toward the opposite sex compounded of desire, sentimentality, and ignorance. As Edward studies his Greek, fortified with a few sips of wine, he feels a stirring of the senses, stimulated by the intensity of his concentration. He tries to resist this incipient arousal and looks to the picture of his headmaster on his desk for support against "bestiality." Through an effort of will, his thoughts become purified and his unfocused sexual impulses are replaced by an idealized image of his cousin Kitty, for whom he proceeds to write a poem. But the poem is a rather stilted imitation of the Greek verse he has been studying, since if the truth be known he barely knows his cousin, and his infatuation is based on a few polite encounters over tea and a vision of her in a white gown.

Save for a reference to Colonel Abel's gift of port, *The Years* does not develop the comparison between the examination room and the battlefield, nor does it dwell on Edward's struggles with his sexual impulses. There is, however, a detailed account in both versions of a conversation between Edward and his two friends. Since Edward has no opportunity to get to know young women of his own class, his intimate daily life is spent among the young men who are his fellow students. One of these, Hugh Gibbs, is a clumsy, athletic fellow who spends his time hunting foxes or farmers' daughters, depending on the season. Both are acceptable pursuits for upper-class young men, since casual liaisons with "common" girls are part of the system that protects the chastity of young ladies.

Edward's other friend, Tony, is a more ambiguous figure. *The Years* suggests, and *The Pargiters* makes clear, that Tony's interest in Edward goes beyond casual friendship, that his jealousy has the intensity of a lover's. The complex interaction between the three young men is in reality much more important to Edward than his romantic fantasy about Kitty.

> They had discussed every subject—hunting, philosophy, Greek, sex, in common. They had eaten together and worked together.
> . . . If he had written a poem to Tony or Gibbs it would have been quite different from his poem to Persephone [the poem about Kitty]. And without too much license, one is justified in thinking that a poem to a person whom the writer knows little, whom he idealises, whom he sentimentalizes, is always a bad poem. (*TP*, I, 95, 82)

Woolf believed that good literature that deals with both sexes cannot be written in an atmosphere in which men and women are not able to know one another—all that can be produced is sentimental nonsense like Coventry Patmore's poem, which survives to delude another generation into taking a false view of life.

Women are as hampered as men by the separation of the sexes, since the experiences that mold their brothers when they are at public school and university are unknown to the girls. The camaraderie in Edward's study is as inaccessible to Kitty Malone as it would have been to Hardy's *Jude*, though she lives in the Master's Lodge and can see Edward's light from her bedroom window.

As the focus of both the holograph and the novel shifts from one young person to another, it becomes clear that common influences create the circumstances that direct their lives. When we enter the life of Kitty Malone, we find that the special problems of her Abercorn Terrace cousins are not solely responsible for their feeling of stultification. Kitty's mother is not slowly dying; her father is a respected college Master, not a retired army man, and she lives surrounded by the great libraries and brilliant scholars of the university.[16] But what Kitty really wants is to live on a farm in Yorkshire and work the land, a desire that is so unattainable that it is only in her dreams that she can bring herself to tell her parents about it. Instead, she serves tea to undergraduates and shows visitors the sights, while her mother wonders why she is so restless. (As in the case of Delia's music, Kitty's dream of becoming a farmer is presented in only the vaguest terms in *The Years*, so that her discontent seems rather pointless.)

Although Kitty lives at Oxford, she cannot study at the university; some classes for women have been started recently, but her parents look upon this movement toward women's colleges as inappropriate for their daughter. Kitty studies a little history with a woman tutor, but her interest in the subject has been squelched by her father, who remarks one day, with "ironical courtesy," that she shares "the inability of your sex, my dear, to grasp the importance of historical facts" (*TP*, I, 107, 93).

The question of what is involved in an historical point of view and

---

[16]In letters to Ethel Smyth and Quentin Bell, Woolf describes a visit to her cousins, the Fishers, at Oxford that contains many of the details used in her portrait of the Malones' family life. *LVW*, V, 254–56.

what are the relevant facts is a consideration that runs through many of Woolf's works. In *Orlando*, in *The Pargiters*, and in *Three Guineas* one finds a running criticism of historical method, ironic yet serious, for Woolf could never see how valid history could be written without a knowledge of the daily lives of ordinary people. History as she knew it ignored these facts and concerned itself with the public lives of those in power; the lives of the obscure, and especially the lives of all but a handful of women, constituted a still unwritten history. This is the history Woolf was attempting to write in *The Pargiters*, which treats the minutiae of ordinary life with a seriousness and penetration usually reserved for momentous affairs of state.

As Woolf follows Kitty Malone through her day, she shows us how Kitty is being guided away from developing her scholarly interest or her love of the outdoors so that she can be prepared for the proper marriage that her mother envisions for her. Kitty scarcely knows why she is dissatisfied, but a visit to her friend Nelly Brook (Robson in *The Years*) gives her a new perspective on her life.

The visit makes her feel like Alice in Wonderland—she feels huge and clumsy compared to the short, stocky Brooks. As with Alice, proportions shift and change, and conventions are called into question when Kitty learns that in some houses fried fish is served at tea, and that a young man who is studying for examinations is still expected to mend hencoops and serve himself at table. In Kitty's family, the women are always waiting: the cousins wait for the kettle to boil and her mother waits for her father to come home at night before she will go to bed. In the Brook family, young Jo is neither waited for nor waited on.

Most important, it is clear that the women in the Brook family are treated as equals. Mr. Brook asks about Kitty's studies rather than about her distinguished father, and he expects his own daughter to become a doctor. Though his mother had to work as a servant to help him get his education, he is determined that his "Nell" shall have a better life. Because of this atmosphere of mutual respect, the relations between members of this family are different from any Kitty has known.

The Years focuses its account of Kitty's visit on her impression of Mr. Brook, but in the holograph as much attention is paid to Mrs.

Brook's shrewd appraisal of her daughter's friend and to the feelings Kitty has about what their marriage is really like: "Mr. and Mrs. Brook were married in a way that none of [her] parents' friends were married so that she could feel quite free with Sam" (*TP*, II, 69, *147*). In Sam's house, she senses instinctively, even an eminent historian like Chuffy would not dare to put a damp, heavy hand on her knee, and Jo Brook would kiss her, if he felt like it, as frankly as the farmer's son in Yorkshire who kissed her when she was sixteen.

In the Brooks, Woolf has given us a picture of family life as she would like to see it.[17] Everyone works, and everyone's work is taken seriously; daughter and son are both afforded a good education, yet their aspirations do not exempt them from performing household tasks or make them ashamed that their mother was a cook.

The essay that accompanies this scene recounts the story of Joseph and Lizzie Wright, whose biography Woolf had been musing over when she first conceived the idea for her novel. Like Sam Brook, Wright owed everything to his mother, who had worked hard all her life to educate her children.[18] When Joseph became engaged, the plan for married life that he proposed was revolutionary for his time. He did not wish his wife to become a "hausfrau": "It is my greatest ambition," he wrote to Lizzie, "that you shall *live*, not merely exist; and live too in a way not many women have lived before. . . ."[19] By contrasting the lives of people like the Brooks, the Levys, and each succeeding generation of Pargiters, Woolf uses this novel to explore the question of how both men and women can "live, not merely exist."

---

[17]Hoffman suggests, "Because of her limited experience of other social classes, Kitty romanticizes the Robson family, but although her wish to be a farmer is part of her romanticizing the working classes, it also represents her desire to be free." Hoffman, "Virginia Woolf's Manuscript Revision of *The Years*," 84. Actually, despite their origins, the Robsons are not working class: the father is on the university faculty and is a self-made man. Like Kitty, Woolf seems to be romanticizing the family; Mr. Robson's determination that his daughter be a doctor could be just as oppressive as the Malones' desire that Kitty marry well.

[18]The photograph of Mr. Robson's mother, described in both *The Pargiters* and *The Years*, bears a remarkable resemblance to the portrait of Joseph Wright's mother. Elizabeth Mary Wright, *The Life of Joseph Wright*, I, opposite 20; reproduced Marcus, "The Years as Greek Drama, Domestic Novel and Götterdämmerung" *Bulletin*, 289.

[19]Elizabeth Mary Wright, I, 311.

This first long chapter of *The Pargiters*, the 1880 episode, takes up approximately two and a half volumes of the holograph MS. Each scene and essay contains a wealth of detail, and many passages have been repeated and revised even in the first draft. Woolf completed the draft of the chapter by the end of January 1933—except for the Colonel Pargiter–Mira scene, which would be added in March. It is worth noting that the holograph version of the opening scene of the novel, which introduces Colonel Pargiter and Mira, is somewhat different in tone from the scene in *The Years*. There is more sympathetic authorial comment on the meaning of the relationship; despite its tawdry aspects, Colonel Pargiter's liaison is shown to be a refuge for him from the difficulties of his life.

Before moving on to the next chapter, Woolf began immediately on revisions, and on February 2 she announced, "Today I finished —rather more completely than usual—revising the first chapter. I am leaving out the interchapters—compacting them in the text . . ." (*AWD*, 2 Feb. 1933, p. 195).[20]

By "interchapters" Woolf presumably meant the inserted essays, for they do not appear in *The Years*, nor are they to be found in the later chapters of the holograph. After Woolf discarded the essays, she attempted to work her generalizations about love, money, and the oppression of women into the dramatic sequences. As they brush their teeth or take the bus, Eleanor, Kitty, and the others reflect on the ideas that Woolf had originally expressed in her essays. Though the use of multiple points of view obscures her intentions somewhat, the amount of ideological material that she was able to inject into the rest of the draft in this way is still far greater than can be found in the published novel.

Woolf's decision to delete the essays seems inevitable, for, interesting and valuable as they are to those who wish to study *The Years*, it must have become increasingly obvious to her that they were a clumsy device that impeded the narrative flow of the novel. What their presence in the early chapters does indicate is the extent to which

---

[20]Some attempts at revision of the scenes of the first chapter, with no essays and the essay content "compacted" into the text, can be found at the end of notebook 2 and the beginning of notebook 3 of *The Pargiters*. *TP*, II, 85–124, III, 2–60. Hoffman has described these revisions in detail in his study of the MS of *The Years*, 84–87.

Woolf felt the creative and analytic functions of the brain to be essentially separate.[21] Once the essays had been deleted, she found herself immersed in a struggle to merge these separate spheres of mental activity in order to try to achieve an integrated work of art.

This struggle continued as she completed her first draft and began to revise, but it was not until 1935, when she was attempting to cut her completed draft to a manageable 150,000 words, that she faced up to the need to cut many of the long political passages from the novel. It is likely that this was the moment she conceived of the idea of rewriting them as the pamphlet we know as *Three Guineas*, which was published in 1938.[22]

Woolf's diary comments during the long period of revision that followed the completion of the first draft of the novel emphasize the difficulties of trying to give a coherent form to an overflowing mass of material. Nevertheless, there seem to be additional motives for the specific decisions she made as to what to delete.

In the first section, and in the episodes that follow, the incremental effect of the cuts and revisions creates a substantive change in the impact of the novel as a whole. It appears that somewhere along the way Woolf had come to feel that she had gone too far, that the hazards she had warned of in "Professions for Women" had become nearly insurmountable obstacles. She apparently felt that she had flouted the

[21] At times she felt that the two types of thought were actually in opposition: "how my brain is jaded with the conflict within of two types of thought, the critical, the creative . . ." (*AWD*, 26 May 1932, p. 181).

[22] With only the published diary to go by, Guiguet assumes that "The sequel to *A Room of One's Own*, planned in January, 1931, had no doubt, by the beginning of 1932, split up to produce, on the one hand, *A Tap on the Door* (later *Three Guineas*) and on the other, the book that was to be *The Years*." Guiguet, 302. But the documents that are now available show that the first extant attempt at a draft of the essay that would become *Three Guineas* is dated 14 April, 1935. (Three Guineas?) "Draft For Professions," in Articles, Essays, Fiction and Reviews (Berg), 6, 125–45. This date corresponds with Woolf's account of her meeting with E. M. Forster on the steps of the London Library, when he told Woolf that the committee had voted to continue excluding women. This event inspired her to begin writing "On Being Despised," her provisional title for *Three Guineas* (*AWD*, 9 April 1935, pp.. 243–44). According to her diary, she stopped writing it a few days later, having decided that "one can't propagate at the same time as write fiction. And as this fiction is dangerously near propaganda, I must keep my hands clear" (*AWD*, 13 April 1935, pp. 244–45).

conventions of what it was possible for her as a women and a writer to reveal and in so doing had become too insistent and one-sided. By the time the novel was published she had softened, deleted, or made vague many of her strongest attacks on English society and its treatment of women and had eliminated most of the overt statements of her own beliefs.

As has been noted, some of this deleted material found its way into *Three Guineas*, though even there the tone is curiously apologetic and the arguments often circuitous when compared with the frankness of the inserted essays in *The Pargiters*. What is particularly noteworthy is that wherever the MS dealt with "women's bodies for instance . . . their passions," these passages have been deleted both from the novel and from the essay. *Three Guineas* deals with economics and politics but not with sexuality; it attacks the tyranny of fascism but only in passing mentions the tyranny of chastity.

Yet the pattern of the original holograph, which defined the underlying forces that govern our lives as money and love, placed sexuality within its definition of love and traced its effects with the utmost seriousness. Clearly, Woolf intended to show that life as lived in the private house and the streets around it was inseparable from the quality of civilization as a whole, and that the emotional and sexual alienation of the sexes from one another had caused a schism in the society. It was Woolf's deepest belief that the only solution to political and social problems lay in an open acknowledgment of all the impulses within ourselves. Yet, sadly, the differences between her first draft and the novel and essay she published reveal that there had come a moment when her courage failed.

Between the holograph and *The Years* we can discern a shift from an explicitly political novel to a gentler study of manners and relationships through the years. In addition, it is possible to trace another evolution that occurred after this first section was completed, a shift from a novel of "fact" and biographical detail to the subjective, fragmented approach that characterizes the chapters dealing with Elvira Pargiter (Sara in *The Years*). And as Elvira emerges as a major center of attention, Kitty Malone fades into the background.

In both the original and final versions of the novel, the character of Kitty is introduced with vivid and engaging detail, raising the expectation that she will remain an important figure as the years move on. But after the first chapter Kitty is seldom present, save as the glamourous Lady Lasswade who appears briefly at a suffrage meeting and at the opera, and once again in later years when she becomes both a party hostess and a woman who loves nothing better than walking alone in the country, with a packet of sandwiches in her pocket.

The space and attention devoted to Kitty in the "1880" section suggest that Woolf may have intended her to play a larger role in the novel, possibly as a counterpoint to Eleanor, so that, as in *The Old Wives' Tale*, we might have followed the course of their parallel lives. Kitty and Eleanor are women of similar age and background, and while one marries into the aristocracy, the other becomes a benevolent spinster. Their lives could have provided an opportunity to contrast the position of women in different class and social roles. Perhaps following Kitty's history more closely seemed too reminiscent of Woolf's study of Clarissa Dalloway for this course to have appealed to her, but if *The Pargiters* had remained the realistic family chronicle it appeared to be in the "1880" chapter, continuing the story of Kitty would have been a logical development.

But it was at this point that Woolf's conception of her novel was about to change. She was beginning to see her work as an experiment in integrating fact and vision and starting to work out ways of achieving this end. These new ideas will become apparent in the novel in the "1907" chapter, when Elvira Pargiter takes center stage.[23]

[23]My early investigations of the MSS of *The Years* were the subject of an article published in the *Massachusetts Review*, Winter 1975. In his introduction to his edition of *The Pargiters*, Mitchell Leaska also examines this period in the development of the novel (vii–xxiii).

III

Elvira's Scenes

.

I've brought it down to Elvira in bed—the scene I've had
in my mind ever so many months, but I can't write it
now. It's the turn of the book.

(AWD, 6 April 1933, p. 196)

SYNOPSES

1907 *Sara Pargiter, younger daughter of Colonel Pargiter's brother
Digby, is alone in her bedroom on a hot summer evening. She is observing a
neighbor's party through her window and reading* Antigone. *Her mother
and her sister Maggie return from a party. Maggie tells Sara (or Sally)
about the party. Their mother, Eugénie Pargiter, joins them, and they all
talk for a while before retiring for the night.*

1910 *Rose Pargiter, now a middle-aged woman and an active suffragist,
goes to visit her cousins Sara and Maggie, who are living together in a flat.
After dinner Sara accompanies Rose to a political meeting. Eleanor and
Martin are at the meeting, and Kitty Malone (now Lady Lasswade) comes
in late. Later, Kitty and Eleanor leave together in Kitty's limousine. Sara
returns to her flat and gives Maggie her impressions of the meeting. Sara
senses that Maggie will soon marry and leave her on her own.*

1914 *Sara meets her cousin Martin on the steps of St. Paul's Cathedral.
Martin, a wealthy dilettante, takes her to lunch at a City chophouse. Sara
gets tipsy on a little wine, and they discuss religion. Martin tells Sara about
Rose, who is in prison because she threw a brick through an official's window
as a protest. Martin accompanies Sara to Hyde Park. They pass some public
speakers on their way to the Round Pond, where they find Maggie beside her
sleeping baby. Sara falls asleep under a tree and Martin discusses his love life
with Maggie.*

.

37

In this chapter I will examine the scenes in *The Pargiters* that center on Elvira Pargiter, who becomes Sara in *The Years*. Elvira is the focus of those aspects of the novel that are visionary and poetic, in contrast with the more matter-of-fact atmosphere of the episodes centered on Eleanor. At this point Woolf began to experiment with ways of depicting a multileveled reality and hit upon the idea of alternation and contrast, with scenes focusing first on Elvira and then on Eleanor. But before turning to the "Elvira" scenes, we will try to see how Woolf arrived at her decision to develop the novel in this way.

When she had completed the first draft of the "1880" chapter, Woolf found that the flood of inspiration that had carried her through the first 60,000 words in little more than two months had begun to subside. From this point on, the progress of the novel would be erratic; sometimes it would move forward easily, but increasingly her work would be halting and slow, and plagued by self-doubt.

Woolf's practical reason for laying aside her novel at the end of the first chapter was that she had to turn her attention to finishing *Flush*, a fantasy about a spaniel she had started as a lark and now found an unwelcome burden. Yet even when *Flush* was finally dispatched to the printers and she had picked up *The Pargiters* again, she found herself restless. "No critic ever gives full weight to the desire of the mind for change. Talk of being manysided—naturally one must go the other way. . . . Looming behind *The Pargiters* I can just see the shape of pure poetry beckoning me" (*AWD*, 26 Jan. 1933, pp. 194–95). Already she was beginning to yearn for more "poetry" than her projected novel of "fact" could allow.

But Woolf could not let wayward thoughts about poetry deter her from the work she had laid out for herself. From February to the end of April she was occupied in making her revisions of the "1880" chapter and in drafting the opening scene with Colonel Pargiter and Mira and the description of Eleanor's day in 1891.[1]

The "1891" chapter serves as a bridge between the full portrait of the Pargiter clan in the "1880" chapter and the more selective, impressionistic mode of the ensuing episodes. It is only after "1891"

[1]See above, ch. II.

that the novel will begin to bifurcate, focusing alternately on the personalities of Elvira and Eleanor.

In the "1891" chapter, we meet Elvira for the first time, when another branch of the Pargiter family is introduced. Abel's brother Digby is married to Eugénie, who brings an exotic strain into the prosaic Pargiter line.[2] Eugénie, who is half-Spanish, is a sensual, imaginative woman who loves to embroider the truth with little harmless fantasies. Her daughters, Magdalena (Maggie) and Elvira, have inherited her artistic tendencies, for Maggie sees the world as a conjunction of light, shape, and color, and Elvira is a conjurer with words.

When Abel Pargiter goes to visit Eugénie on Maggie's birthday, Elvira makes her first appearance. She is introduced as a little girl of six or seven, bright and lively, but slightly disfigured because one shoulder is higher than the other. This defect makes her father and uncle uncomfortable, so that her mother tries to protect her. Elvira already shows a talent for mimicry and for making other people uneasy in her presence.

When Woolf realized that she wanted *The Pargiters* to go beyond her original conception of it as a novel of fact and history, Elvira emerges as a major character. This is probably why Woolf envisioned Elvira's first important scene as the "turn of the book." But when she attempted to write out the "1907" scene, she found she was too exhausted to begin. "Oh I'm so tired! I've written myself out over *The Pargiters*, this last lap. I've brought it down to Elvira in bed—the scene I've had in my mind ever so many months, but I can't write it now. It's the turn of the book. It needs a great shove to swing it around on its hinges" (*AWD*, 6 April 1933, p. 196).

She decided to postpone writing the scene until after her vacation in Italy. By the time she returned to England, she had formulated her new plan for *The Pargiters*:

I think this will be a terrific affair. I must be bold and

---

[2]Woolf may have named her after the Empress Eugénie, wife of Napoleon III. Ethel Smyth met the Empress after her husband's death and became her constant companion. *LVW*, V, 101n.

adventurous. I want to give the whole of the present society—
nothing less: facts as well as the vision. And to combine them
both. I mean, *The Waves* going on simultaneously with *Night and
Day*. Is this possible? At present I have assembled 50,000 words
of "real" life: now in the next 50 I must somehow comment; Lord
knows how—while keeping the march of events. The figure of
Elvira is the difficulty. She may become too dominant. She is to
be seen only in relation to other things. This should give I think a
great edge to both of the realities—this contrast. (*AWD*, 25 April
1933, p. 197)

Woolf's new scheme is ambitious; she will try to combine fact and
vision, to write a novel that is as objective as *Night and Day* and as
introspective as *The Waves*. Thus the progress of the novel is a kind of
dialectic; first she swings entirely to fact, excluding vision; then she is
tempted to poetry or vision (they are nearly synonyms here) and finally
to an idea for fusion, with both modes going on at once.

Just how to bring this about was unclear, but what Woolf
developed first was not really a synthesis but a series of alternating,
contrasting scenes. This alternation first becomes evident at the
beginning of Part II of the holograph, in the "1907" chapter, where
Elvira appears as a young woman; it is there that Woolf begins
contrasting the factual and the visionary through the personalities of
Eleanor and Elvira.

Since Woolf chose to introduce the element of vision in Elvira's first
important scene, something in Elvira's personality must have made
her an appropriate vehicle for this aspect of the novel. Yet, as we have
seen, Woolf was concerned that Elvira might become too dominant
and wished her to be seen only in relation to others (*AWD*, 25 April
1933, p. 197). Perhaps Woolf feared that Elvira might take over the
novel because she sensed that this character expressed something in
herself that could get out of control.

Elvira seems to have been a character who captured Woolf's
imagination almost as soon as she conceived of her. Although she did
not begin to write the "1907" chapter in the holograph until 3 April
1933, by that time Elvira had already been living a life of her own in
the author's mind for months. Leonard Woolf has described how his
wife would mentally inhabit the scenes of her novel long before she

wrote them out,[3] and the way Elvira developed is clearly an example of this process, for familiar references to her as an adult character appear in the journal months before her appearance in the MS as anything but a young child.

The keystone of Elvira's character will be her repudiation of society's bribes and rewards, and evidently Woolf had worked this out long before she had Elvira express these ideas in the holograph. The first of Elvira's speeches on this subject was recorded in the MS at the end of June 1933, but by the previous March Woolf was already so involved with her character that she hardly knew whether she was herself or Elvira when she turned down the offer of an honorary degree:

> It is an utterly corrupt society I have just remarked, speaking in the person of Elvira Pargiter, and I will take nothing that it can give me etc etc: Now, as Virginia Woolf, I have to write . . . to the Vice Chancellor of Manchester University and say that I refuse to be made a Doctor of Letters . . . Lord knows how I'm to put Elvira's language into polite journalese. What an odd coincidence! that real life should provide precisely the situation I was writing about. I hardly know which I am, or where: Virginia or Elvira: in the Pargiters or outside. (*AWD*, 25 March 1933, p. 195)[4]

The close identification of Elvira with Woolf's own personality becomes evident as Elvira's character unfolds in the novel. All of the young women in *The Pargiters* share some of Woolf's girlhood experiences and feelings, but Elvira alone exhibits the volatile temperament, hypersensitivity, and addiction to making up stories about people that characterized the young Virginia Stephen. Even Elvira's odd appearance reflects something in Virginia's own experience; Leonard Woolf tells us that although by any standard she was a beautiful woman, there was something strange in her appearance that often caused strangers to stare at her and laugh (*BA*, 29). In *The Pargiters* Elvira frequently refers to her dislike of being stared at or laughed at. Elvira is set apart by her deformity, so that it is

---

[3]*BA*, 33.

[4]Woolf's remark that she had been "writing about" Elvira's situation months before the scene appears in the holograph suggests that she made detailed notes on scenes before developing them in her notebook.

unlikely that she will marry and have children, and Virginia Woolf was also deprived of the natural experience of motherhood because of her precarious mental state, a psychic aberration that parallels Elvira's physical defect.

While Eleanor Pargiter typifies the stable, sensible, community-minded woman that Woolf admired but never desired to emulate,[5] Elvira's character is a portrait of an erratic, unstable, perceptive, artistic sensibility. Elvira cannot cope with the minutiae of daily life, but she perceives the deeper meaning behind the rush of daily events. Because she can participate only as a spectator, it is her function to provide a link between the life of the mind and spirit and that of the everyday world. When Elvira sits in her window listening to the birds and ironically observing the activities of her fellow humans, she becomes an authorial presence in the novel, making connections between its multiple levels.

This strange and complex creature, who seemed to come straight out of Woolf's own psyche, almost evaded being pinned down on paper. Nowhere in the manuscript are there as many scratched-out passages and illegible words as in the scenes where Elvira appears. Even Woolf's handwriting, which is relatively neat and legible when she is writing about Eleanor in what she calls her "Jane Austen" style (*AWD*, 20 July 1933, p. 209),[6] deteriorates into hen-scratchings when she tries to evoke Elvira.[7] It is as if Elvira's persona was created from a level of consciousness that is different from that which

---

[5]The depiction of Eleanor as the older sister and mother-surrogate in the "1880" episode is probably based on Stella Duckworth, Virginia's half-sister. As sources for Eleanor as she grew older, Marcus (288–89) suggests Virginia's cousin Margaret (Marny) Vaughan, whose slum settlement work influenced Leonard to become a socialist, and Margaret Llewelyn-Davies, a leader of the Co-operative Working Women's Guild. Another possible model is Margery Fry, Roger Fry's sister. The Woolfs went to Greece with Margery and her brother in 1932, and in her diary Woolf describes Margery as virginal, benevolent, and an enthusiastic traveler. Unpublished diary, 16–17 April 1932.

[6]Woolf apparently took Jane Austen as her model for objective, realistic writing. Later she came to feel that her own attempt to write in this manner had been a failure. See above, ch. II, 17n.

[7]The way her handwriting looks in the Elvira scenes fits John Lehmann's description. He said her writing looked "as if a high voltage current had been in her fingers." Lehmann, "Working with Virginia Woolf," 60–62.

produced Eleanor, a level that is far less amenable to expression through the written word.

The Years as well as *The Pargiters* reflects the difference between the two modes of perception. In *The Years* the "Eleanor" scenes are ordered and interpreted by a third-person narrator who reveals Eleanor's thoughts and shows us the world through her eyes, while the "Elvira" scenes, save for "1907," are presented solely as dramatic dialogues. We have no direct access to Elvira's thoughts in the later scenes, and the reader is forced to interpret her racing, leaping voice for himself.

Elvira's sensitive, responsive mind does not select or compose in an obvious way; a line of poetry, a street-caller's cry, or a change of light can fill her with strong emotions that must be expressed at once. Elvira's truth is the truth of feeling, of the flashes of insight that arise from the association of images that float to the surface of the mind. Childhood impressions, scraps of poetry and drama create pictures in her mind, so that what she experiences in the present is inextricably mingled with everything she has read, seen, or heard.[8]

Both *The Pargiters* and *The Years* exhibit a change in direction at the point where Elvira-Sara becomes a main character, but the two versions portray her differently. In the MS she has dimensions that are less apparent in *The Years*, in part because Elvira is a budding writer, at least in the sense that she is always taking notes, trying to comprehend her experience by putting it into words.

When we first come upon Elvira, lying in bed on that summer night in 1907, she is trying to overcome the feeling that she is insubstantial, unreal. She turns to her writing to reassure herself that she exists. First, she describes the effect of moonlight on the tree outside her window, then firmly writes down the date: "she sat up, noted everything in the room; as if it were necessary to authenticate the moment with the greatest precision" (*TP*, III, 109). When she

---

[8] Kelly's description of Sara in *The Years* suggests that for perceptive readers she retains many of the qualities that are more clearly developed in Elvira: "Sara borrows or coins for each member of the family a phrase that shows in miniature that person's way of life. But at the same time she herself diffuses her identity into every crook and cranny of the world and assembles the fragments of fact she sees in stories that transform the scattered shards to unified visions." Kelly, 211.

has completed her description, including even a little pencil sketch of the room, she adds, "this is perfectly & exactly true to the best of my belief. She felt that she had made a mark which in years to come she would still find there; that she had asserted once and for all the fact of her existence" (*TP*, III, 109).

The close identification between Virginia Woolf and her character at this point will be clear to anyone who has read Woolf's many comments on the way her writing helped to stabilize her life. The connection with this passage is especially direct because the scene that Elvira sees when she looks out her window is taken from an essay entitled "A Dance at Queen's Gate" in Virginia Woolf's 1903 journal, a little book in which she wrote a series of descriptive essays. [9] The essay in Woolf's 1903 journal recounts her experience when she was awakened on a warm evening by the sound of dance music and looked down from her window to observe the goings-on at a party being given in a house across the mews. Her description was the "mark" that she herself had made when she was just a few years older than Elvira is in this scene, and now, in 1933, she has gone back to her own early work to help her evoke the mood of Elvira's evening. Though the details of the description are very much the same, Woolf as a mature writer has added the insight that explains the motivation for Elvira's effort. It is only now that Woolf can look back and see that those pretty little essays were more than practice exercises; they were a way of authenticating her own existence.

By introducing a writer as a character in her novel, Woolf created a figure with whom she could identify and gave herself a vehicle for commenting on the technical and aesthetic problems of her work in progress within its pages. The artist Lily Briscoe plays a similar role in *To the Lighthouse*, but Elvira's involvement in making pictures with words rather than paints makes her connection with the author even clearer. The exclusion of this aspect of Elvira from *The Years* meant

[9]Virginia Woolf, Unpublished Diary, 30 June–1 Oct. 1903, "A Dance at Queen's Gate," 1–8. These little notebooks precede the continuous journal which Woolf began in 1915. I am indebted for this reference to John Hulcoop, who noted the source for the "1907" scene. Hulcoop, rev. of *Mrs. Dalloway's Party* in *Virginia Woolf Miscellany*, Spring 1975, 4.

that most of her literary comments would have to be deleted from the published novel.

Woolf rewrote the opening of the 1907 chapter several times, and in her second version she added a new element. As Elvira painstakingly records the details of the room's appearance, the sound of music floats in through her open window and interrupts her catalogue of facts. "It was full of (sadness, joy melancholy) other emotions Pleasure, yes; sadness; yes; & what else?" (*TP*, III, 112). Elvira realizes that her record must contain all of these emotions if it is to tell the whole truth. But capturing everything at once proves much too difficult; nothing stays in place long enough—things change before they can be grasped and expressed in words.

Then Elvira sees a couple wandering out of the party to stand together under the trees, and she tries to listen to what they are saying to each other. "She tried to put words to the inarticulate sounds. But what could be beautiful enough, passionate enough, she thought?" (*TP*, III, 119). The inarticulate sounds, the rhythms of speech heard from a distance, hold some meaning that is lost when they are reduced to mere words. Elvira, like Woolf, is continually struggling with the impossibility of rendering the ineffable into words.[10]

Elvira is at home alone because her sister and parents have gone to a party. She has been told to lie straight and still, like Antigone in her tomb, in order to rest her twisted back. Elvira's deformity has excluded her from ordinary social life; She has been placed in the position of an outsider, an observer who asks questions and takes notes. Her special perspective is like that of the writer Woolf described in "Professions for Women," whose professional detachment allows her to see the significance behind the events of daily life.

---

[10]Allen McLaurin has noted Woolf's interest in the effect of words that are heard but not understood. He writes: "The rhythm of a phrase can have an effect even when the phrase itself has no meaning. The repeated cry of the street hawker in *The Years* is unintelligible; the rhythm persists, but the words are 'almost rubbed out.' (*TY*, 175) This lack of meaning can also free the phrases and allow them to become pure pattern. If exact words and phrases to some extent falsify, then the truth might be contained in the modified repetition, the rhythm of language." McLaurin, *Virginia Woolf*, 109.

When Maggie comes into her sister's room after the party, Elvira questions her closely, trying to find out what the party was like by making her sister recount all the details. But her questions keep missing the essence of the experience, and Elvira realizes that she must develop some subtler method of finding out what she wants to know; "it was a case that would need not these wild, these silly these rather exaggerated questions: but a much subtler method; just as an explorer, if he sees a lump, in the sand, makes first a deep trench all the way around it; & then slowly digs & digs & digs . . . (*TP*, III, 126–27). Whenever Woolf has written about her writing method, she has pictured it as a kind of digging, tunneling, or fishing, all images that convey the idea of a search beneath the surface of life to find its hidden springs.[11] Through Elvira she is suggesting yet another approach, that of circling around the subject rather than confronting it directly. Elvira is voicing the need for subtlety that Woolf had expressed in her diary when she decided that this novel should contain "millions of ideas but no preaching" (*AWD*, 25 April 1933, p. 198). Woolf was evolving a way to present her ideas by circling carefully around them and digging in deeply.

Elvira acts as a mouthpiece for Woolf's attempts to deal with her material, a way of talking to herself as she goes along, and as a personification of the philosophical position of the deliberate outsider. One way of seeing *The Pargiters* is as a kind of Menippean satire, in which the characters act out the implications of the social and intellectual stances they take.[12] Elvira is a person who is governed by an inner law, the law of feeling, who regards the law of society as

[11]While writing *Mrs. Dalloway*, Woolf had discovered what she called "my tunneling process, by which I tell the past by instalments, as I have need of it" (*AWD*, 15 Oct. 1923, p. 61). In "Professions for Women" she compares a girl who is writing a novel to "a fisherman lying sunk in dreams on the verge of a deep lake with a rod held out over the water. She was letting her imagination sweep unchecked round every rock and cranny of the world that lies submerged in the depths of our unconscious being." *Collected Essays*, II, 287.

[12]According to Northrop Frye, "The Menippean Satire deals less with people as such than with mental attitudes . . . . The Menippean satire thus resembles the confession in its ability to handle abstract ideas and theories, and differs from the novel in its characterization, which is stylized rather than naturalistic, and presents people as mouthpieces of the ideas they represent." Frye, "Rhetorical Criticism," in *Anatomy of Criticism*, 309. The kinship with this genre is more evident in *The*

something external that does not apply to her. Thus she takes on the
persona of Antigone, the Greek heroine whose tragedy she is reading
as she lies in bed. Like Antigone, Elvira is an extremist who openly
expresses her repudiation of social law and refuses to compromise
despite the personal cost. Maggie, like Antigone's sister, Ismene,
sympathizes with her sister's position but does not cut herself off from
conventional life. The frequent references to the Antigone legend in
both versions of the novel provide a mythic analogue for the
confrontation between a feminine system of ethics based on feeling
and personal relationships and the masculine rationale of power and
conformity to an external social code. Moreover, the legend of the
Greek sisters serves as a model for the intimate relationship between
Maggie and Elvira. In *A Room of One's Own* Virginia Woolf pointed out
that literature has seldom adequately portrayed relationships between
women, for women are usually seen primarily in their relationship to
men as lovers, wives, and mothers.[13] In this novel, Woolf shows
women as friends, sisters, cousins, and nieces, learning from one
another and communicating freely.

In the first scene between Maggie and Elvira, Elvira learns about
social life vicariously, through Maggie's experience. Maggie tells her
about the man dressed in gold braid who sat next to her at dinner and
told her that power was what counted.[14] The sisters compare the
world of politics and competition he represents with the way boys
behave at school. When, as children, they had gone to a cricket match
with their brothers, they saw all the boys cheering fiercely for their
team, and the sisters, who did not care who won, realized that what
mattered at school was to pick a side and identify with it, in order to
belong. To them the masculine domain is just a continuation of the
cricket match, and they resolve to find some other way of life.

Pargiters than in *The Years*, where Woolf struggles to clothe her characters in human
traits and disguise their function as "mouthpieces." Nevertheless, especially in the
conversational scenes, the particular ideological stance of each character can often be
discerned.

[13]*A Room of One's Own*, 142–43.

[14]In *Moments of Being*, Woolf describes going to dine with Ottoline Morrell and
meeting Winston Churchill there: "very rubicund, all gold lace and medals, on his
way to Buckingham Palace . . ." ("Old Bloomsbury," in *Moments of Being*, 177).

Elvira decides, after her sister and mother leave, that she will
dedicate her life to the quest for truth. She is just beginning to realize
how difficult that task will be.

> Even after Maggie had gone she lay still in the dark. It was only
> (then by) shutting out sounds lights, by (lying still) that she could
> hope to deal with the tremendous number of things (half-realised
> ideas) which in the last hour. . . .
> . . . .
> She was only 17, moment would add itself to moment. . . .
> And perhaps, by using immense care, not chattering so much,
> but (carefully devising more powerful means of) never sleeping,
> never drowsing—following with extreme daring each indication
> that was revealed, in (the end, at seventy,) without this blur of
> chatter that often misled, she would have . . . cleared the whole
> the complete truth.   (*TP*, III, 153)

The next time Elvira and her sister Magdalena appear in the novel it
is 1910. By then the girls' parents are dead and they are living alone in
a rather disreputable section of London. As the scene opens in *The
Pargiters*, Elvira is reading Shakespeare and commenting to herself
about how he handles the technical problems of his play. Elvira is a
critic now, as well as an imaginative writer. She is impressed by
Shakespeare's handling of transitions and his use of contrasts,
concerns that Woolf was dealing with herself at this time.
Shakespeare is particularly relevant here because Woolf was
beginning to see that the techniques of drama might be useful to her
in the "Elvira" scenes, which tended toward dramatic form, with
much dialogue and little narrative description (*AWD*, 20 July 1933,
p. 209).

Earlier, when Woolf began her work on the "1907" chapter, she
had already come to realize how challenging and problematic the
novel was going to be. It was then that she formulated her plan: "The
thing is to be venturous, bold, to take every possible fence. One
might introduce plays, poems, letters, dialogues: must get the round,
not only the flat. Not the theory only. And conversation: argument.
How to do that will be one of the problems. I mean intellectual

argument in the form of art: I mean how give ordinary waking Arnold Bennett life the form of art?" (*AWD*, 31 May 1933, p. 208). In the holograph and in the final version of the "Elvira-Sara" scenes, we can see Woolf working out the techniques with which she would attempt to solve these problems.

In the "1910" chapter, cousin Rose's arrival provides the occasion for an "intellectual argument" that Woolf would later attempt to transform into art. Rose also adds interest to the structure of the scene, for, as Elvira observes in her role as critic, a triangle is a more interesting form than a line between two points. Rose will provide a foil for Elvira and Maggie, presenting a point of view based on a different kind of life experience.

Rose serves several functions in this chapter. By recalling scenes from her childhood at Abercorn Terrace and stimulating her cousins to remember incidents from their common past, she recreates the bond of family; in this way she conveys the sense of doubleness, of looking back and commenting while still marching forward, that Woolf was aiming for.[15] Maggie and Elvira's shabby little flat is furnished with fragments salvaged from their past, and Rose recognizes an elegant old chair and a spotted mirror that she remembers from their mother's home.[16] They are familiar, yet different in this new environment. As Rose looks back on herself as a little girl running home from the store, and Maggie thinks of the blue and gold necklace her Uncle Abel once gave her, they begin to see the past refracted from a new angle. This perception is found in both *The Pargiters* and *The Years*; in *The Years* it is Rose who is most aware of what is happening:

> They talked, she thought, as if Abercorn Terrace were a scene in a play. They talked as if they were speaking of people who were real, but not real in the way she felt herself to be real. It puzzled

[15]"I must somehow comment; Lord knows how—while keeping the march of events" (*AWD*, 25 April 1933, p. 197).

[16]Lucio Ruotolo's slide show of Monks House, the Woolf's country home, presented at the 1976 MLA convention, included a picture of a large red chair much like the one that appears frequently in *The Years*. The chair is still part of the furnishings of Monks House—a "solid object" that has survived. Ruotolo believes that it once belonged to Leslie Stephen.

her; it made her feel that she was two different people at the same
time; that she was living at two different times at the same
moment. She was a little girl wearing a pink frock; and she was
here in this room, now.   (*TY*, 167)

In *The Years* the cousins' conversation is mainly personal, and
political and social questions are suggested only indirectly. Children
scream in the road, and pubs filled with drunken men are near by, but
Rose does not refer to the problems of the poor, nor does she talk to
the two young women about what interests *her* most, the women's
suffrage movement. In *The Pargiters* these subjects are examined in
much detail, but the way they are presented has not reached the level
of "intellectual argument in the form of art"; the dialogue is wordy
and didactic, though it does indicate quite clearly what the issues are.

For example, in *The Pargiters*, Rose, who is older than her cousins,
is shocked by the frankness with which Elvira speaks of her family.
Elvira says that she hated her father, and Rose responds that it is
wrong to speak that way. Elvira interprets Rose's answer as meaning
that lies are necessary to the continuance of the family:

> You see Rose says one mustn't say one hates one's father. One
> mustn't tell the truth about anything. why not? I say; because,
> says Rose, the bloom of the family, the continuance of Abercorn
> Terrace and the great round tea table . . . the maid all depend
> upon lies; she says; or rather upon a kind of forbearance and
> respect: whereupon I look down in her mind & see the Pargiters
> crossing the desert; & the stars. this I think is all life taking its
> way from the end of time: a sort of reverence fills me: helpless,
> small, tenacious as they are.   (*TP*, IV, 22–23)

Here Elvira has caught the two conflicting images of the family that
are present throughout the novel. Sometimes it is described as a kind
of hell, a stuffy prison where people are forced to lie to one another. At
other times the family takes on the dignity of a little caravan bravely
crossing the desert, a group of human beings who have banded
together for protection against the terrors of isolation and savagery.[17]

[17]At one point Woolf thought of calling the novel *The Caravan* (*AWD*, 11 Jan.
1935, p. 237). A caravan crossing the desert as a metaphor for the family appears
frequently in the holograph.

In Virginia Woolf's dual vision, both truths have equal validity and do not cancel one another out. The family exists because the human condition requires it, and it shares in all the contradictions of the beings who created it.

But what Rose questions is whether these two healthy young women have the right to live as they do, cut off from their family and ignorant of the poverty and suffering of the people who live around them. The sisters live in social isolation and are unaware of the problems of the poor. They do not understand why people go on having children that they cannot care for, instead of going to a physician for contraceptive help, as Maggie has done. When Rose points out that poor women do not have the three guineas to pay a Harley Street physician, Elvira proposes to write a letter to the *Times*, suggesting that birth control devices be made available to all. (This passage may contain the germ of the idea for the title and the epistolary form of *Three Guineas*.)

Elvira's suggestion amazes Rose, for she realizes that Elvira does not know that it is illegal to disseminate birth control information in the England of 1910. And Elvira, in her turn, is shocked to learn that such an absurd law exists. "'It seems to me that you live in a very odd world,' she tells Rose, who holds the same opinion of the 'ivory tower' her cousins inhabit" (*TP*, IV, 27). Maggie and Elvira, who have lived abroad for years and have never gone to school, have not been indoctrinated with the mores of English society. To them the social codes of England are like the peculiar rituals and taboos of an unknown tribe.

During this conversation, Maggie and Elvira notice that Rose blushes whenever sexual matters are discussed. They cannot understand the importance she places on chastity, since to them it is an artificial concept that has prevented women from developing their potentialities. They can see no reason why a young girl should not walk alone wherever she pleases, but Rose's own experience as a child makes her feel quite differently: "'I did' said Rose 'But I wouldn't allow a child of mine to do it. You talk as if these things weren't complicated. But they are tremendously'" (*TP*, IV, 30).

Because Rose is immersed in the day-to-day struggle for women's votes, she is aware of all the compromises and contradictions that are part of any political movement. Elvira and Maggie, as outsiders, can be iconoclasts, since from their vantage point they can see through to the hypocrisy at the heart of the entire moral code. Though Rose opposes some of the laws of her country, she accepts its Victorian morality, and once her specific grievance has been corrected she will take her place proudly in the ranks of England's defenders.

That evening, when Maggie and Elvira sit together summing up the events of their day, Maggie tries to break through her sister's vagueness to find out about the meeting where Rose had taken Elvira that afternoon. In *The Years* we are given two perspectives on the meeting, which is attended by many of the Pargiters. First we see it through Eleanor's experienced eyes as she places it in the context of the myriad similar meetings she has attended. Later on, we are given Sara's impressions. In *The Pargiters* we have only Elvira as a guide, and she tells Maggie that what impressed her was not the substance of the discussion but the feeling that these people had come together to be part of something larger than themselves, an eyeless, ego-less embodiment of their collective will.

Elvira tells her sister that she had chosen a seat at the window, and when the window was opened the noises of the street, the calls of the hawkers and the cries and coos of cats and pigeons created a kind of broken music that had a most curious effect. As in the earlier scene in her bedroom, when the waltz music and the nightingale's song broke in upon her thoughts and added the emotional dimension that had been missing, the sounds Elvira heard from outside the meeting room lent a spiritual quality to its rather bloodless atmosphere. Elvira does not mention the purpose of the meeting to her sister, though it had been called to decide whether the group will join the militant wing of the suffrage movement or whether it will eschew such violent tactics. Their purpose is important, surely, but Elvira's dreamy perspective places these concerns in the context of what is eternal; pigeons will coo and cats will cry long after the group's weighty deliberations have been forgotten.

In 1935, when she was rewriting her manuscript, Virginia Woolf was to see "that there are four? dimensions: all to be produced, in human life: and that leads to a far richer grouping and proportion. I mean: I; and the not I; and the outer and the inner . . ." (*AWD*, 18 Nov. 1935, p. 259). In the novel Elvira is often the intermediary who brings the different levels in touch with one another, for to her the inner and the outer, the I and the not I, are not as separate as they are for other people. In her mind the barriers are always breaking down, and the felicity of her peculiar way of looking at things is often shared with the reader, as here when she gives her impressions of the meeting.[18]

As Elvira's account continues, Maggie begins to question the purpose of the group. To Maggie the idea of fighting for the vote seems pointless: "But suppose (we had votes) then we should be Englishwomen. Do we want to be Englishwomen? I don't" (*TP*, IV, 56). Maggie sees the role of women in English politics as that of prostitutes; she says that every patriarch has his prostitute, a charming woman who comforts him after his hard day's work and wheedles favors from him. If this is the only way to get the vote, she will have none of it.

The only thing that Maggie thinks women can do to end corruption and change the system is to refuse to take any part in it. "Whereas what Rose says is . . . give me a vote and I'll be like you" (*TP*, IV, 56). Like Woolf, Maggie realizes that men and women were reared in different traditions, the men working only for pay and the women trained never to earn a penny. She hopes that women can retain the selflessness and integrity of their tradition even though they may need to support themselves. She thinks that they should earn only enough to live modestly, eschewing ambition.

The sisters decide that they cannot share Rose's political goals. Nevertheless, she fascinates them, for many aspects of her personality are puzzling.

This is a most curious & interesting woman, Elvira said at length

[18]In her novel, Woolf seemed to be trying to achieve the multileveled effect she had admired in Turgenev's work: "We look at the same thing from different angles, and that's one reason why the short chapters hold so much; they contain so many contrasts. On one and the same page we have irony and passion; the poetic and the commonplace; a tap drips and a nightingale sings. And yet, though the scene is made up of contrasts, it remains the same scene; our impressions are all relevant to each other." "The Novels of Turgenev," *Collected Essays*, I, 249–50.

because her powers of expression have obviously been atrophied by
some early & painful I should venture to say hideous experience:
(which she doesn't want to talk about) Just as a tree you know
Maggie, if you put a ring round its root all the apples on one side
are bitter (small); wrinkled . . . bitter, and about the size of a
(halfpenny) . . . but on the other side dipped in golden
lustre.   (*TP*, IV, 51)

Elvira, who is physically deformed, senses that Rose too is maimed in
some way. Though Rose had felt the impulse to tell her cousins about
the strange man who had frightened her as a child, she had been
unable to bring out the words. And as they had noticed earlier,
whenever sexual matters came up, she blushed and hesitated.

In light of Bell's account of Woolf's childhood trauma, it is
possible to conjecture that this passage reflects the author's attempt to
come to terms with her own past experience and its effect on her
ability to deal openly with sexuality in all its manifestations. Since the
intention of this study is to focus on Woolf's writing process, what is
especially important here is the idea that because of her experience
Rose's "powers of expression" have "atrophied." This remark becomes
even more meaningful when it is juxtaposed with earlier parts of the
same conversation with Maggie and Elvira.

In her attempt to understand her cousin, Elvira had used her
imaginative sympathy to conjure up a picture of Rose as a young
woman. First she imagined her in the arms of a young man, lying in a
flower-strewn meadow. But Maggie had disagreed. "'Besides if Rose
loved anybody . . . it was (obviously not) a man' said Maggie
. . .('Then the story will have to be completely different.') said
Elvira" (*TP*, IV, 69).

Maggie's suggestion is so upsetting to Elvira that it is some time
before she can speak again. Maggie, on the other hand, cannot see
what difference it makes whether one loves a man or a woman. Elvira
explains,

"But whereas . . . I could think of Rose with equanimity in the
arms of a man . . . the other thought is loathesome; just for ten
seconds. But in the one case, you see Maggie I covered them with
syringa petals. In the other—I didn't cover them (at all)—I saw
them, naked; which seems to prove Maggie, that (the nature) of

the act itself is a mixture of the ridiculous & the repulsive, or am I wrong? (*TP*, IV, 69–70)

Woolf may be suggesting here that heterosexual love, which has been idealized and sentimentalized in our art and literature, has been made an acceptable subject, while homosexual love has usually been deprived of such treatment and so appears to us naked of the trappings of legend and romance. In its nakedness it appears ridiculous and repulsive to those who have not experienced it, while the same act between opposite sexes has been clothed in flower petals.

By opening up this subject, Elvira begins to feel that she is getting in touch with a mystery, with something buried deep in human history; she tells her sister, "My feeling was this: when you said Rose flung herself into the arms of Mildred in a greenhouse, a shock; horror; terror. . . . Something that lights up the whole of the dim pale past of the human race . . ." (*TP*, IV, 70). For a moment, it seems that Woolf is about to allow her character to explore human sexual history, but the moment passes, and the conversation moves on to other things.

This passage raises the question that Woolf had posed in "Professions for Women" when she had wondered how long it would be before women could speak the truth about their bodies. When she began the essay that became *The Pargiters*, it had been her intention to write about women's sexuality, yet even in the draft manuscript she never really tackled the subject directly. Although several major characters are openly homosexual, Woolf never explores that part of their lives. It seems that Woolf, whose "powers of expression" on almost any subject were prolific, found herself nearly as tongue-tied as Rose when she tried to deal with sexual behavior. One feels in reading these conversations in *The Pargiters* that her attempt to introduce the subject there is a first tentative step toward overcoming this inhibition.

The discussion of Rose's sexual nature that appears in the MS is not included in *The Years* in any form. Its deletion is part of a pattern of exclusion in which almost all the sexual material in *The Pargiters* was ultimately excluded from the novel.[19] The only exceptions are the

[19]See below, ch. VII, 118–19.

story of Rose's childhood experience and a brief discussion of
Nicholas' homosexuality. While Rose's lesbianism is strongly suggested in the holograph, the published novel presents her as simply a
strong, rather mannish woman who has "felt many passions, and done
many things" (*TY*, 166).[20]

Woolf had written that she wished Elvira to be "seen only in
relation to other things" (AWD, 25 April 1933, p. 197), so that first
we found her looking out her window at a neighborhood party, then
at a suffrage meeting, and finally, in 1913, on the steps of St. Paul's.
In each instance she is an observer: of social gatherings, political
meetings, and religious devotees.

She is at St. Paul's, we learn, because she has quarreled with
Maggie, who is too busy with her baby now to spend time with her
sister. Elvira is seeking consolation elsewhere, and she has gone to
church for the first time in years, after reading the book of Job as she
lay awake at night. But she finds that religion has lost its meaning for
her.[21] She tells her cousin Bobby (Martin in *The Years*), when he
comes upon her on the steps of the cathedral, that "ten years ago I felt,
let me see, something dusky, dim. And it's all gone, Bobby'" (*TP*,
IV, 119). Bobby understands what she is saying: "'You don't get a
thrill any longer. We're an odd generation, aren't we? The grandsons
of bishops.'" They had been brought up to believe in the moral
authority of the Church and State, but, he says, "'it doesn't work any
longer, flags the British army—St. Paul's no longer thrill you'" (*TP*,
IV, 120).

Elvira tells him that she has been trying to find some connection
between the stark words of the Old Testament and the dim
respectability of St. Paul's. "'And then, out I came onto the steps, &
thought to myself. What remains of all this?—whats the meaning? It

[20]It is possible that Woolf avoided labeling Rose as a homosexual in the
published novel out of consideration for Ethel Smyth, who was a model for Rose.

[21]While revising *The Pargiters*, Woolf began reading the Bible, perhaps
prompted by the same impulse that led Elvira to explore the origins of Christianity.
"I must buy the Old Testament. I am reading the Acts of the Apostles. At last I am
illuminating that dark spot in my reading" (*AWD*, 1 Jan. 1935, p. 236).

always escapes me, Bobby. (The book) of Job. There should be lions roaring, & yellow sand: its a savage religion'" (*TP*, IV, 123). Elvira tries to understand what people feel when' they shut their eyes and pray, but for her something fundamental has been lost.

Now the only heaven Elvira believes in is physical pleasure, like the rapture that spreads through her body when she eats "perfect meat, perfectly cooked" in the restaurant Bobby takes her to (*TP*, IV, 124). Without any system of belief, she and her generation can judge only by their feelings. Even when Bobby tells her that his brother Edward prefers young men to women, she is not as shocked as she was earlier when she learned about Rose. "I don't feel it. she spread her hand out. (You see) that's the only test after all. (one's body) You can't say (this is right that's wrong)" (*TP*, IV, 124).

Nevertheless, they have both been brought up to make judgments from a moral point of view. Neither one of them can pass a noseless beggarwoman on the street without having tears come to his eyes, without feeling that something must be done for those who are unfortunate. Elvira's ability to put herself in another's place enhances her response to the beggarwoman, but she fears that acting on emotion can be dangerous, for "'it's a beastly sentimental feeble emotion'"(*TP*, IV, 14).

The sight of the beggarwoman introduces an idea that Woolf will develop further when Elvira and Bobby encounter the soapbox orators in Hyde Park. The genuine sympathy that the cousins feel for the poor and wretched, which makes them long for a more humane society, can be exploited by demagogues whose solutions lie in rigid ideologies that will destroy individual freedom. As Elvira puts it: "There are two people (yourself and me) alive with emotion. spouting with emotion, who can't walk along the street without the tears starting to our eyes & (our bodies) burn with the beauty of the spring . . . & then they take that emotion & down comes the stamp. An ugly stamp. & a lying stamp. What is left of (that emotion?) Hatred (or merely laughter) . . . or nothing at all" (*TP*, IV, 146). It does not matter whether the authoritarian "stamp" is that of an established church or state, or of some new religion or political system; the genuine emotion that generated it will be perverted or destroyed once power is solidified.

When Woolf wrote of this novel that it should contain "millions of ideas but no preaching" (*AWD*, 25 April 1933, p. 198), she was warning herself against the temptations of the soapbox, the inclination toward self-righteous moralism that she feared she had inherited from her father and his Claphamite ancestors. This concern moulded her style as well as her thinking, for when this series of dialogues between Elvira and Bobby is compared to the meeting of Sara and Martin, their counterparts in *The Years*, the form is strikingly different.

In *The Pargiters* the conversation between the two cousins is extensive and detailed, and, as we have seen, it ranges over many topics. In *The Years*, however, though Martin tells Maggie when they meet her that he and Sara had talked of " 'The whole world. . . . Politics; religion; morality' " (*TY*, 244), this is actually a much better description of the original version of the scene in the holograph. In the "1914" chapter of *The Years*, the cousins have little chance to talk. Sara's words are continually interrupted and drowned out in the noisy restaurant and on the crowded street, and she and Martin agree that it is impossible to have a conversation in a public place. The political, religious, and ethical themes in the scene are now presented indirectly, through a series of images and incidents seen mainly through Martin's eyes.

When Martin reads the words "God is Love" chalked on Apsley House[22] in defiance of the law, or watches an old man feed the sparrows on the church steps, "haloed by a circle of fluttering wings" (*TY*, 227), he knows that the religion of feeling espoused by Christ and St. Francis can only exist precariously now, outside the established institutions. He watches as the tolling of the bells of St. Paul's frightens the birds and puts them to flight and later sees how a frail old woman in the park who is "saying something about sparrows" is mimicked by a chorus of little boys (*TY*, 240). Only the most

[22]Apsley House was the home of the first Duke of Wellington, who defeated Napoleon and went home to become a reactionary political leader. Wellington's house is an appropriate choice as a symbol of the masculine power structure's rejection of the religion of love. It also suggests a connection with Napoleon, whose name comes up in the "1917" chapter. Among other things, Napoleon was concerned with keeping women and their property under male control.

powerful and egotistical speaker is able to hold the attention of the crowd by manipulating their emotions.

The relationship between money and power, another theme in the cousins' conversation in the holograph, is dramatized through incidents in *The Years*. Martin's feelings of guilt about his privileged position are illustrated by his reaction to the waiter who tries to hold back a coin.[23] His anger at being cheated is soon followed by discomfort and embarrassment. And later, in the park, though he is impressed by the argument of the socialist speaker, he knows that as a wealthy, artistic dilettante he would have no place in the society the man proposes. He thinks to himself: "There wouldn't be much justice or liberty for the likes of him if the fat man had his way—or beauty either" (*TY*, 241).

Martin knows that his way of life could not survive under an authoritarian regime, and he is fully aware that his position is founded on money. But Sara is quite naive about the real source of the freedom she cherishes. When Martin takes her to lunch, he brings her into the busy world of the "City Man," an atmosphere as alien to her as was the suffrage meeting. She is out of her element and embarrasses him by talking too loudly and getting tipsy on a glass of wine.

In *The Pargiters*, Elvira is fascinated by the bustling atmosphere of the restaurant, but she clearly rejects Bobby's materialism. Continuing the train of thought that had prompted Maggie to eschew Rose's efforts to gain women the vote, Elvira tells Bobby that she can not understand why Rose would want to join this "corrupt, lying society." Bobby tells Elvira that she too is part of society in spite of herself, since she must pay taxes, and the money is used to wage wars without her consent.

But Elvira prefers to write her check and let others decide what to do with it. She thinks that Rose is a fool to get involved. "('She'd like them to do (another sort of job) or she'd like (to do it herself) Whereas

---

[23]Joanna Lipking has shown how Martin characteristically relates all human situations to cash; he learned this from his father, who rewarded him with sixpence for being top of his class. Lipking points out that Martin's last act, "in the last pages, is an imitation of his father's: 'Speak! Speak!' he commands the caretaker's children. 'Sing a song for sixpence!'" (*TY*, 429; Lipking, "Looking at the Monuments," 144).

once I'm a member of this society . . . I'm committed it seems to me
. . . I've got to sit in an office telling lies'" (*TP*, IV, 130). Martin
disagrees: "'But you're a fool too if I may say so' he remarked. 'A
greater fool than Rose. . . . You don't even know the way your
money's invested. . . . There's nothing you can do . . . you're not
educated . . . (you don't even know how to work a typewriter) (*TP*,
IV, 131).[24] Bobby thinks that Elvira is a parasite, living on her
income of 250 pounds a year. If she lost her money, he tells her, she
would be forced to live with her brother and earn a pittance walking
dogs.

Bobby admires his sister Rose because she and her friends are
working for the vote so that they can get jobs and become self-
sufficient. Elvira is seeking another kind of freedom; she thinks that
because she has accepted no "bribes"—no education, no honors, no
social position—society has no hold on her. If she refuses everything
that society has to offer, she reasons, she can remain uncommitted to
its values. But Bobby's opposition to her stance is more than
economic. He remembers how she sat at the window at Rose's
meeting:

> "No, you know he said. "you can't do it."
> "do what?"
> ("What you do.) Well, (remain outside") Sit on
> a chair in the window taking notes. . . . Well,
> you can't go on doing that all your life."   (*TP*, IV, 37)

This remark goes to the heart of Elvira's symbolic position in the
novel, for the price she pays for her refusal to participate is poverty,
loneliness, and helplessness in the face of impending events.

At the time she was writing these words Woolf was faced with a
crisis that was calling her own detachment into question. She had
long played the role of spectator in public affairs, using her profession
as a writer as an excuse for maintaining her distance and "taking
notes." Woolf's journal shows that this episode was written shortly
after she accompanied her husband to a Labour party conference in

---

[24]Anyone who has seen samples of Virginia Woolf's typing might suspect that
she is poking a little fun at her own ineptitude here.

Hastings (*AWD*, 2 Oct. 1933, p. 212). This was in October 1933, when opposing factions in Britain's left were struggling to overcome their differences in order to forge a common opposition to the growing threat of fascism. Both of the Woolfs were beginning to realize that the future of civilization might depend on the commitment of people like themselves.

Virginia Woolf had always used her writing as a way of transforming everyday life into problems of form and language. Now, in *The Pargiters*, she was using her writing as a way of exploring the implications of her own beliefs and re-examining her position on the relationship between the artist and politics.[25]

The full effect of these manuscript passages cannot be conveyed through quotations and paraphrases, but it should be evident that the originals of the "Elvira" scenes are more like a series of dialogues than a fully developed fiction. Elvira appears as a restless, querulous spirit whose oddities never quite coalesce into a recognizable human being. Though she had seemed so alive in the author's mind, she eluded translation into print.

This difficulty persisted as Woolf began going over her original draft, for though the episodes centered on Eleanor and Kitty flowed easily, the more experimental sections where Elvira appears were revised again and again. While working on these scenes in February 1935, Woolf commented that

> Sara is the real difficulty: I can't get her into the main stream, yet she is essential. A very difficult problem; this transition business. And the burden of something that I won't call propaganda. I have a horror of the Aldous novel: that must be avoided. But ideas are sticky things: won't coalesce: hold up the creative, subconscious faculty; that's it, I suppose. I've written the chophouse scene I don't know how many times.   (*AWD*, 20 Feb. 1935, pp. 238–39)

[25]In 1936 Woolf would write an article for *The Daily Worker* which would further explore the relationship of the artist and society. By that time Woolf was ready to argue that the artist must leave his "ivory tower" in a time of political crisis in order to insure the survival of himself and his art. "Why Art Today Follows Politics," *The Daily Worker*, 14 Dec. 1936, reprinted as "The Artist and Politics" in *Collected Essays*, II, 230–32.

A month earlier Woolf had been reading Aldous Huxley's *Point Counterpoint* and had found it "raw, uncooked, protesting" (*AWD*, 23 Jan. 1935, p. 238); her greatest fear was that *The Pargiters* would resemble it. She too was writing a novel of ideas with an element of protest, and she was engaged in a struggle to transform this recalcitrant material into art without losing sight of what she meant to say.

In January 1935, as she continued her revision of the encounter with the soapbox orators in the park, we find the first mention of an essay to be called "On being despised" (*AWD*, 1 Jan. 1935, p. 236). The title suggests Woolf's idea that women have both benefited and suffered because of their ignominious position in society. This idea for an essay seems to be a revival of her original plan for the feminist essay which became the "Essay-Novel." Now, as she struggled to free her novel from "the burden of something that I won't call propaganda" (*AWD*, 20 Feb. 1935, p. 239), it appears that she was beginning to feel that her ideas on women might be better expressed in a pamphlet that would serve as a complement to the novel. Soon she would find herself "plagued by the sudden wish to write an anti-Fascist pamphlet" (*AWD*, 26 Feb. 1935, p. 239); eventually her ideas on women's status and on the roots of fascism would coalesce to form the basis for *Three Guineas*.[26]

Unfortunately, when Woolf began to delete some of the dialogue and soften the argumentative edge of the Elvira/Sara scenes, they lost some of their significance. In *The Pargiters*, Elvira represents a particular point of view—the repudiation of society with all its bribes and rewards. She is visionary and poetic, but she is also argumentative, though her responses are intuitive and sometimes irrational. She regards the world from the vantage point of an outsider who is more concerned with her own emotional reactions than with objective meaning.

[26]Earlier titles for the projected essay, such as "A Tap on the Door" and "On Being Despised," suggest that the status of women was to be her main subject; here for the first time she mentions antifascism. In October 1935 she mentions "a book on women and fascism"; apparently her feminist and antifascist concerns had merged by that time (*AWD*, 15 Oct. 1935, p. 257). The Woolfs' encounters with anti-Semitism and Nazi demonstrations during their trip through Germany in May 1935 may have increased her desire to write on this subject. See *LVW*, V, 389–91.

But in her discussions with her sister and with Rose and Martin, Elvira can be long-winded and shrill, and as a fictional character she lacks dimension; she is more of a mouthpiece than a human being. As we have seen, giving her substance was a problem for Woolf. In January of 1935 she hit upon the idea of having Elvira (called Theresa at this point) sing, "and so lyricise the argument" (*AWD*, 23 Jan. 1935, p. 238). This device is used effectively in *The Years* to convey the dreamy, whimsical way Sara speaks, moving from one image to another with the rhythm of music. (In "1907" Sara sings her thoughts along with the music coming in from the street; in "1910" we find her at the piano.)

Although the Sara of *The Years* does not write in a notebook as Elvira does, she displays her imaginative powers in the series of images which is her response to her reading of *Antigone* (*TY*, 135–36) and in the continual making up of stories that occupies her. Woolf tries in many ways to give her definition, having her mother call her "that imp, Sally," in the opening of the "1907" chapter, revealing her first through her own thoughts as she lies in bed, and then through the impressions of Maggie, Rose, and Martin. She is described as sallow, angular, and plain, and is compared to an ungainly bird as she hops about. She is clumsy, she talks to herself, she embarrasses her cousin by getting tipsy in a restaurant. We begin to see her sitting there, swinging her leg and asking, "Shall I, or shan't I?" yet she remains elusive.

Perhaps it is her eccentricity that makes it so difficult to envision her. She remains more a presence in the novel than a character, and her peculiar manner of speaking is hard to follow. Her quick flashes of perception are meant to convey some of the most important ideas behind the novel, but they are presented so indirectly that they can be overlooked by all but the most careful readers.

In retrospect it seems that the decision Woolf made early on, that "Elvira is to be seen only in relation to other things" (*AWD*, 25 April, 1933, p. 197), made it extremely difficult to use her as a vehicle for the author's poetic vision. It is only in the "1907" chapter that Elvira's thoughts are revealed, and the same is true in *The Years* when she becomes Sara. In both the holograph and the novel after the "1907" chapter, she is presented objectively, through the eyes and ears of others. In this way *The Years* is very different from Woolf's earlier novels, where a nonrational, visionary perspective is present throughout in the thoughts, dreams, and hallucinations of characters like Rachel in *The Voyage Out*, Septimus Smith in *Mrs. Dalloway*, and Rhoda in *The Waves*. Because Sara is allowed such a limited role in *The Years*, Woolf's imaginative freedom is given less play.

IV

1917

.

That very difficult much too crowded raid chapter. . . .

(*AWD*, 21 March 1935, p. 241)

SYNOPSES

1917   *Eleanor goes to visit Maggie and her husband, Renny. It is a cold, dark winter night during the wartime blackout. At Maggie's Eleanor meets Nicholas, a Pole. Sara comes in, and Eleanor realizes that Sara and Nicholas have a special relationship. Sara tells the others that she has just been with North (Morris' son), who has enlisted. Sara voices her disapproval of North's decision, and they discuss her attitude. An air raid begins and they all go down to the cellar. After the raid they go back upstairs, and Nicholas tells Eleanor about his theory of the human soul and its evolution. They all drink a toast to the "New World" after the war. When Sara tells Eleanor that Nicholas loves other men Eleanor finds that this does not disturb her deeply. Sara, Nicholas, and Eleanor depart, going their separate ways.*

.

If the evidence of the holograph and of Woolf's own journal can be accepted, writing the "1917" chapter was the most difficult task in the entire construction of *The Years*. Perhaps this was because this chapter was where Woolf tried to work out a way to present intellectual conversation as art—to have her characters express their views on war and peace, men and women, reality and dreams, and yet somehow remain characters in a novel not lecturers on podiums. The task was difficult, at times impossible, and after many revisions Woolf had nearly given it up; by the time the novel was published, many of the ideas discussed in the chapter had been excised, or made vague. Often all that remains is a fragment or a phrase here and there in the text.

The handwritten draft of "1917" begins with a series of scratched-out pages that are among the most disconnected in the entire MS. Woolf's journal entry of 18 February 1934 explains that a headache overtook her as she began writing this important episode, so that "It has gone—the talk during the Raid—running all over the place, because I was tired; now I must press together; get into the mood and start again" (*AWD*, 18 Feb. 1934, p. 215).

Though she stuck to her resolve and began again more than once, none of the MS versions of the dinner party scene have much coherence. The drafts are long strings of speeches in which the characters debate nearly all the major themes of *The Pargiters*. Its abundance of ideas is what makes this episode central to the novel, but it did not take Woolf long to realize the impossibility of embodying all of them in a fictional structure. A year later, when she was faced with the task of revising "that very difficult much too crowded raid chapter," once more the prospect helped bring on a headache (*AWD*, 21 March 1935, p. 241).

The problems that afflicted Woolf as she attempted to revise this episode make it equally difficult to describe and explicate. Because the material is so loosely structured, I will not follow its sequence but will consolidate its major themes in some sort of coherent order. And rather than contrast each passage with its specific counterpart in *The Years* as I have done previously, I shall examine the material in the MS version as a whole and then explain how it was transformed to become the chapter in *The Years*.

Earlier we saw how the two separate strands of the novel, the factual and the visionary, had been developed in alternating, contrasting scenes. Now, in 1917, they were beginning to converge. Since Eleanor and Elvira are cousins they presumably know one another, but their first meeting in the pages of the novel takes place in this chapter. Though they meet here as guests at an intimate family dinner, they have little to say to one another, and the distance between them symbolizes the split in the novel between their modes of perception, a split that will not be fully resolved until the final chapter.

Though Eleanor and Elvira do not communicate directly as yet, they are linked through Nicholas, who loves Elvira and will become Eleanor's friend. Nicholas Pomjalovsky is a foreigner, and a philosopher of sorts.[1] When Eleanor is introduced to him, she realizes that he is a man who has a compulsion to explain everything, to put everything into words. She thinks to herself that he seems likeable but fears he may become a bore. (This observation may reflect the author's own fear that too many long speeches by Nicholas will be deadly unless she can find some way of breaking them up.)

Nicholas fulfills an important function in the novel. In the MS, Eleanor sees him as someone who can "fill in the gaps" for her (*TP*, V, 72), who will articulate the vague, rambling thoughts that she has mused over for years. She hopes that he will break through her solitude. As he puts it in *The Years*, "We all think the same things; only we do not say them" (*TY*, 282). Because Nicholas lacks the reticence of his English friends, he says whatever he thinks. At least this is true in *The Pargiters*, where he is allowed to give the substance of the speech that is always being interrupted in *The Years*.

When Eleanor enters Maggie's living room, she finds that Elvira has not yet arrived, and Renny and Nicholas are in the midst of a conversation about the war. Renny explains that though they are discussing Napoleon now, they have been searching for the origins of the war: "That was how we came to Napoleon. What the Allies should have done at the end of the Napoleonic Wars" (*TP*, V, 73).[2]

Elvira finally arrives, late and disheveled as usual. Eleanor notices that her cousin has changed, that she seems less crooked than she was, and more grown up. After watching them together, Eleanor realizes that Nicholas and Elvira are in love. It seems that the war has brought many changes, breaking down barriers between different kinds of

---

[1]Avrom Fleischman has suggested S. S. Koteliansky as a model for Nicholas. Fleischman, *Virginia Woolf*, 173. "Kot," as he was known to his friends, was a Russian-Jewish émigré who was a friend of the Woolfs. He and Virginia collaborated on several translations of Dostoevsky and Tolstoy, a relation that may have been the model for the way Eleanor supplies words for Nicholas. Like Nicholas, Kot was a utopian. He carried on a long correspondence with D. H. Lawrence in which they planned their escape to a mythical paradise named Rananim, where they would build a new society. Leonard Woolf, *BA*, 247–53, and "Kot," in *The New Statesman and Nation*, 170–72; Lawrence, *The Quest for Rananim*.

[2]How the settlement terms for one war can lay the groundwork for the next was becoming clear to Woolf and her contemporaries as they began to realize that the Versailles settlement at the end of World War I had created the climate which led to the rise of Hitler.

people, so that unorthodox relationships like that between Elvira and Nicholas are now possible, and family life has become more relaxed and natural. With the absence of servants, husbands and wives have been brought closer to each other; Renny helps Maggie with the washing up and with the children, which would have been unthinkable for Eleanor's parents. Marriages like theirs, Eleanor thinks, could not have existed in her day.

As the guests settle down to talk, the conversation becomes a symposium on attitudes toward the war and toward human suffering, and an exploration of the far-reaching social changes that must take place if the future is to be better than the past.

To Nicholas the war is just a symptom of the distorted values that pervade their society and afflict even its most decent members. Elvira tells of the scorn and ridicule she heaped on Eleanor's nephew George (North in *The Years*) when he came to tell her he had enlisted, but Nicholas points out that George's decision was a perfectly logical result of the kind of education he had been given as a barrister's son and a student at Rugby and Oxford.

> "How can you expect a boy who has been educated like that, who is in no way remarkable, who sees his friends go to the war, who is rather bored by his profession, a nice ordinary English boy—was he that?"
>
> Eleanor nodded: it struck her that Nicholas spoke of him as if he were dead—"to take up an attitude that requires a great deal of courage?"   (*TP*, V, 79)

For Nicholas and Elvira, George's enlistment is an act of conformity, and, conversely, refusal to fight would signify real courage. But by calling George "Eleanor's nephew" Elvira has identified him with Eleanor and her point of view, and now Eleanor comes to George's defense. Eleanor thinks it is perfectly natural to want to defend one's country, since she too has a deep love for her native land and would fight for it if she could. Renny, who makes shells for the army, agrees with Eleanor; the Germans have invaded his native France and burned his uncle's farm; for him the war has a grim reality.

As usual, Maggie and Elvira, the "outsiders," take an extreme position. They refuse to see that it matters who claims Alsace-

Lorraine, or England, for that matter. Elvira, who had been reading Job in 1914, has apparently been continuing her study of religion; she tells them what Jesus said, that the only freedom is "not to own." The two sisters are still so removed from an understanding of what the war really means that they can discuss it in abstract terms. They have no feeling for their country and cannot understand patriotism in others.

> "That's very interesting" said Nicholas. "You get two women like Magdalena & Elvira" he continued; "who are absolutely uneducated; they have received nothing from their country from the institutions of their country; they cannot practice professions, they are kept purely as slaves for the breeding of children: & that system it seems (has) abolished all feelings of patriotism." (*TP* 5, 100)

But the others feel that Nicholas' explanation is an oversimplification. Eleanor is a woman, but she does not share her cousins' detachment, and she points out that Rose, who had been so militant in her fight for suffrage, has volunteered to drive an ambulance at the front. The war has provided Rose with an outlet for the energy and aggressiveness that had made her restless and dissatisfied in peacetime. The war has broken down barriers and allowed her to express her personality.

When Nicholas describes how the sexes have been forced to develop in different ways and the limitations this has placed on women's lives, he reiterates a theme that has been developed all through the earlier chapters of *The Pargiters*. As the dinner guests see it, the resulting difference in the way women act and think has both negative and positive aspects. Earlier, when Elvira described her rather emotional reaction to George's enlistment, Maggie had commented, "It's very difficult, being a woman, Elvira behaves in a (very) silly irrational, undignified & sentimental way; but its partly her training" (*TP*, V, 83). And Eleanor defends her own lack of interest in the kind of education men are given; though she has been denied much opportunity she has been able to retain a kind of integrity that men, who must make careers for themselves, cannot afford. As the conversation continues, the guests begin to wonder whether the overspecialized roles forced on both men and women have contributed to the sorry state of the world they live in.

As the guests sit down to dinner, they hear a siren announcing an air raid and adjourn to finish their meal in the shelter of the cellar, just as Leonard and Virginia Woolf had done during World War I.[3] Here Woolf uses the atmosphere of the cellar to create an aura of primitive mystery around the little group. She writes that they are "like old men round a campfire or a circle of witches brewing some midnight potion" (*TP*, V, 97). In the flickering candlelight beneath the stone arches, Nicholas looks priestlike, and Eleanor resembles an old abbess in a dressing gown she has donned for warmth.

Ignoring the shells falling outside, they turn their thoughts to the future, after the war. Nicholas explains that according to his philosophy the war is just an interruption; what matters is the overall direction in which society is moving. This shocks Eleanor at first, because she cannot see how the suffering of millions of people can be dismissed as unimportant. But Nicholas points out that human suffering has gone on for centuries, without receiving very much attention. "As we did not find it in the least terrible until August the 4th 1914; as we all enjoyed ourselves in perfect comfort while (people) in millions were suffering far more terribly than they suffer on battlefields . . ."(*TP*, V, 98). Then Eleanor recalls her experiences working in the slums and realizes that Nicholas may be right.

> "Yes," said Eleanor, "I have always thought that . . . in a poor district—up in Notting Hill . . . I've always thought the lives people live there; the women always having children; never enough to eat; & not for three four five years, but all their lives, in rooms where you wouldn't keep a dog; that's far worse and infinitely worse . . . that's why . . . war is possible. It's so much better for most people than the lives they are leading, the women can feed their children. The men get excitement." (*TP* V, 98)

As Nicholas and Eleanor talk they realize that the war has been made

[3]Before beginning to write this chapter, Woolf read through her old diaries to "freshen my memory of the war" (*AWD*, 17 Dec. 1933, p. 214). Her diary entry on 17 Dec. 1917 tells of a dinner party during an air raid at which Bob Trevelyan was a guest. He apparently talked so loudly that it was impossible to hear the guns. The same journal entry describes Leonard sitting on a box in the coal hole reading the paper. Like Maggie and Renny, the Woolfs retired to their cellar during raids. *DVW*, I, 93–94.

possible by the conditions in which people live and that important changes must be made to prevent a repetition of what they are living through.

Nicholas suggests that if no honor were accorded to soldiers, there would be no more wars. He thinks that no man would care to fight without parades and medals and pretty girls to spur him on. But Eleanor wonders whether, in the absence of rewards and recognition, anyone would do anything worthwhile, since there seems to be so little disinterestedness in human nature. She has seen young men go into public life out of a genuine desire to serve their fellow men who are soon forced to compromise their principles and end by seeking privileges and patronage like all the rest.

As Eleanor considers the lives men lead, she begins to understand her own reluctance to fight for the right to imitate them: "Perhaps that's why—one always tries to find excuses for oneself—but I never felt so strongly as my sister felt; & so did Bobby my brother—about politics: (votes for women) And I remember thinking, when there was all that talk about education . . . a man's education is all mixed up with money. That's wrong." (*TP*, V, 110). Eleanor realizes that most men, who have always had to earn their living, have never known the luxury of doing something for the love of it, for its own sake. For them everything has always been "mixed up with money."

Nicholas explains: "'The nineteenth century was the age of the specialist: The men were educated in one way; to make money; the women in another, to bear children. The result is war . . . [I'll] tell you what matters; It is to develop not this faculty which makes money, not that faculty which breeds children;—it is to develop the whole soul. the whole being'" (*TP*, V, 111). The present system, with its separate roles for men and women, gives its rewards to those who conform; this distorts and impedes the growth of the soul.[4] Nicholas uses the term "soul" to stand for all of the faculties of the brain and body, for they are mixed:

the soul grows by spreading in rings like those you see in water

---

[4]In this, too, Nicholas resembles Kot. In her diary Woolf commented, "There's a good deal to be said for Kot. He has some likeness to the Russians of literature. He will begin to explain his soul without preface." *DVW*, I, 108.

when a stone has fallen. The only way in which we can educate
ourselves at the present moment (when we are so immature—so
barbaric, killing ourselves as Renny says for a bit of land)* is not
to impede those rings: to let them spread; when we (interrupt the
soul & say)** this is right, not knowing what is right . . . when
we give a prize to the soul—say a peerage, say a don perhaps at
Edinboro & Oxford University; and the soul repeats the same
rhythm again & again & again: like . . . the needle of a
gramophone which has stuck.   (*TP*, V, 112)

Thus the encouragement given a child or an adult to specialize his
interests, to repeat activities that win him praise and rewards,
stultifies growth. In addition, too much emphasis is placed on the
"I," on the narrow, individual ego. Nicholas gives a little demonstra-
tion: "'we . . . sit like this,' he drew himself up, primly '. . . in our
separate cubicles, each with his own little cross, or holy book—each
mending his own sock'" (*TP*, V, 114).

According to Nicholas, it will take centuries to break down these
separate selves; the evolution of the soul is the evolution of the race,
and it is almost indiscernible in the individual. Yet he believes that
even now people can sense that their way of life is an outrage to the
soul—they can feel this in their bodies. Hatred causes a sensation
which is harsh and painful, while there is a sensation of pleasure at the
base of the spine when the soul expands. Like Elvira, Nicholas
believes that what the body tells us is the only reliable guide. If being
open and loving feels good, it follows that freeing the soul from all its
strictures will allow the development of a higher form of human being
and an ideal society.

But at the present time, since the milennium has not yet come,
men are afraid to tell the truth to one another about their bodies.
Nicholas adds: "'We all (conceal) have things we dare not say, I
myself' he smiled" (TP, V, 123). Eleanor realizes that Nicholas is
trying to tell her that he is a homosexual. At first she shrinks from his
confession, not wanting to be told so much about another's private
life. Then she begins to see that opening up what has gone unsaid is

*VW's parentheses.
**My parentheses to show crossed-out words—G.R.

the beginning of the new kind of life they are hoping for, where honesty and trust will be possible.

> Eleanor again thought she ought to go. and yet if people wanted to talk, if they tried to say what they thought, if in spite of all the lies, the exaggerations, the foolishness of their language, they tried to set free the secret within them, and it is not necessarily a little foolish confidence she added. It does not matter whether Nicholas & Elvira are 'in love' or not. but the state of mind, the true balance, the living thing which makes them themselves; if they are to try to communicate that to me that is generous; humane; & I must annihilate little timid defensive self-protective warding off—hoarding up. . . .   (*TP*, V, 126)

By allowing herself to listen to what Nicholas is saying, Eleanor has opened herself to a kind of communication that she has never experienced before. Nicholas suggests that she is able to do this because her education has been of a very special kind. By visiting the poor, by pouring tea and caring for her family, she has developed compassion and sensitivity. Because she has not had to harden herself to make her way in a competitive profession, she has retained the ability to grow and learn. Her creed has been that of the Victorian gentlewoman: "'Not to earn money; not to have power, not to be famous—obscurity, inferiority, to be despised—not to possess; that's the finest education in the world'" (*TP*, V, 132–33). There is a suggestion in this description that some women are like members of a religious order, taking vows of poverty, chastity, and humility in imitation of Christ. Like Elvira, Eleanor has been able to retain her integrity by refusing to be "bribed" by worldly possessions and acclaim; Elvira quotes her Bible and Eleanor reads Renan's life of Jesus to find a model for their way of life.[5]

But Eleanor realizes that the obscure life that has been satisfying for her would mean misery for a different kind of woman. She points out

_____

[5] In the "1908" chapter, Eleanor is reading Renan because "She had always wanted to know about Christianity—how it began; what it meant, originally" (*TY*, 154). She is probably reading Ernest Renan's *Vie de Jésus*, written in 1863, which approaches the story of Christ from an historical, humanistic point of view. In 1935, while working on revisions of *The Years*, Woolf read Renan and the Apostles and was planning to buy an Old Testament.

that one must not gloss over "the bitterness of the woman who feels all her gifts wasting within her. who is compelled to fritter her life away" (*TP*, V, 133). She hopes that the younger generation, Maggie and Elvira, will never have to live with that sense of waste. Even for Eleanor there is a new freedom now, for, as Nicholas tells her, " '(Now that you have learned to give up) to own nothing . . . now you must learn to enjoy. Cigars, love, wine, knowledge' " (*TP*, V, 134). This is the new adventure awaiting women, the chance to experience what only men have known in the past. Maggie's mother, always married to one man, could not experience the varieties of love; now women will be free to explore all aspects of life.

On this note of optimism the manuscript version of the chapter ends, having traveled far afield from the guns of war that sounded ominously over their heads. By now the raid is over, and the dinner guests depart.

When we turn to the "1917" chapter of *The Years* we find that a remarkable transformation has taken place. The pages and pages of long drawn-out exposition which I have summarized here have been reworked into a fictional representation of the atmosphere in which people lived their lives during the war.

The description of the "very cold winter's night, so silent that the air seemed frozen" (*TY*, 279) that begins the chapter appears only in the published novel, since these descriptive passages were apparently an afterthought added after the first proofs were pulled.[6] In the "1917" chapter the brief description is particularly effective, since it suggests the frozen darkness of a country at war, "congealed in the stillness of glass" (*TY*, 279). In the midst of the frozen night, Maggie and Rennie's home is an oasis of light and warmth. The people who are gathered there are trying to keep the flame of civilized discourse alive and to kindle hopes for the future. When Eleanor comes in, dazed and cold, she is able to warm herself at their fire. "It was a real fire; wood blocks were blazing; the flame ran along the streaks of shiny tar. A little trickle of feeble gas was all that was left her at home" (*TY*,

[6]*The Years* was set in type in March 1936, and again in December of that year. The circumstances surrounding the final revisions will be the subject of ch. VII of this study.

280–81). Images like that of the fire and of the searchlight at the end, contrasted with the frozen night and the falling shells, embody Woolf's belief that it is through the continuity of human relationships that man will overcome isolation and death.

But imagery alone could not adequately express all the ideas that were crowded into the original air raid chapter. Many had to be discarded and others expressed so they seem more like the way people really talk to each other. In 1935, when Woolf was struggling with the revision of this difficult chapter, she hit upon a new method of handling the long discourses. On March 25 she wrote: "And this morning, in spite of being in a rage, I wrote the whole of that d--d chapter again, in a spasm of desperation and, I think, got it right, by breaking up, the use of thought skipping and parenthesis. Anyhow, that's the hang of it. And I cut from 20 to 30 pages" (*AWD*, 25 March 1935, p. 242). The parentheses that she mentions seem to have been dropped later, for only one appears in the chapter, in Maggie's brief aside about her children. By "breaking up" and "thought skipping" she may have meant the way she has one character pause in the middle of a sentence only to have his thought completed by someone else who understands what he is trying to say.

This device, which lends naturalness to the discourse, is used most frequently between Nicholas and Eleanor. In the MS it is Eleanor who feels that Nicholas puts her thoughts into words, but the Nicholas of *The Years* is less fluent and sometimes relies on Eleanor to supply him with the right words. In one passage, as Nicholas struggles to explain his theory, Eleanor helps him out and, in so doing, makes sense for herself of what he is trying to say:

> "and if we do not know ourselves, how then can we make religions, laws, that—" he used his hands, as people do who find language obdurate, "that—"

> "That fit—that fit," she said, supplying him with a word that was shorter, she felt sure, than the dictionary word that foreigners always use.

> . . . .

> ". . . that fit." she repeated. She had no idea what they were talking about. Then suddenly, as she bent to warm her hands over

the fire, words floated together in her mind and made an
intelligible sentence. It seemed to her that what he said was, "We
cannot make laws and religions that fit because we do not know
ourselves." (*TY*, 281–82)

Merely hearing Nicholas' words had not made Eleanor understand
him; it is only through her own participation that she is able to grasp
his real meaning. This device of Woolf's is more than a literary
technique; it is a transformation of Nicholas' sterile, one-sided
speech-making into a creative interaction. Woolf is trying to show
how people kindle and stimulate one another, how the sharing of
ideas can create a sense of community, of being among people who
think as we do.

Aside from his hesitant speech, the Nicholas of *The Years* is much
the same character we met in *The Pargiters*, and his theories are
presented sympathetically, though their reception is somewhat ambiguous. The attitude toward "Elvira-Sara," however, has undergone
a decided shift. Even her appearance is described differently. In *The
Pargiters*, Eleanor thinks that Elvira looks happier and less crooked. In
The Years, she sees Sara as having become "older, more worn; though
she laughed, she was bitter" (*TY*, 285). In the original version of the
chapter, when Elvira tells of the scorn and ridicule she heaped on her
young relative because he has enlisted, she is supported in her opinion
by both Maggie and Nicholas, and Nicholas justifies the sisters' lack
of patriotism as a logical result of the oppression of women. When
Sara tells the same tale in *The Years*, her attitude is repudiated
immediately, not only by Eleanor but by Nicholas as well: "'How
unfair you are,' Nicholas was saying to Sara. 'Prejudiced: narrow;
unfair,' he repeated, tapping her hand with his finger. He was saying
what Eleanor felt herself" (*TY*, 286).

In the holograph we learned that Nicholas thought Elvira unfair to
North because the boy had been raised to be patriotic and could not
help responding as he did. As this explanation does not appear in *The
Years*, the reader can easily assume, with Eleanor, that Nicholas
admires North for enlisting when in fact he agrees with Elvira-Sara
that war is absurd. And without Nicholas' comments or his explanation of why Elvira-Sara and Maggie feel no loyalty to their country,
Sara's ridicule of North appears capricious and pointless.

The deletion of expository passages like these changes the tenor of the novel. Where in the holograph one finds straightforward presentation of many radical and unorthodox ideas, in *The Years* the same ideas, if presented at all, are treated as rather absurd notions. It is almost as though Woolf wished to hold them up to ridicule herself, before her critics could do it for her.

Though the political debate that makes up most of the content of the original chapter is much attenuated in *The Years*, one theme that the published version does cover is the way the war changed the fabric of daily life. In addition to the more obvious changes—the lack of servants, eating in the basement—there is the suggestion that objects themselves seem to have lost their edges, to be merging. Eleanor notices this: "A little blur had come round the edges of things. It was the wine; it was the war. Things seemed to have lost their skins; to be freed from some surface hardness; even the chair with gilt claws, at which she was looking, seemed porous; it seemed to retain some warmth, some glamour, as she looked at it" (*TY*, 287). This is the same chair that Rose had recognized in Maggie and Sara's little flat when she visited them:[7] it is a remnant of Aunt Eugénie's furniture, part of their common past. Perhaps the warmth and glamour emanate from Eugénie's remembered personality, transferred to the object that has long outlived her; the heightened atmosphere of wartime has made Eleanor receptive to these associations.

As in *The Pargiters*, the feelings of the dinner guests in *The Years* change dramatically when the bombing begins. The shells interrupt their conversation, illustrating the way in which the war, in Nicholas' theory, interrupts the evolution of mankind to a higher state of being. Eleanor's perception of the raid is that "She felt as if some dull bore had interrupted an interesting conversation" (*TY*, 288). The colors seem to fade; even the red chair looks as if "a light had gone out" (*TY*, 288).

In rewriting this chapter Woolf was concerned about how she might bring in the different layers of life, using music and painting together with certain groupings of people, as well as conveying the way the mood changed during the raid: "This is what I want to try for

[7]See above, ch. III, 49n.

in the raid scene: to keep going and influencing each other: the picture; the music; and the other direction—the action—I mean character telling a character—while the movement (that is the change of feeling as the raid goes on) continues" (*AWD*, 16 Oct. 1935, pp. 257–58).

The sense of relief at the end of the raid is more marked in *The Years* than in the holograph, and it is made the occasion for a toast to the "New World," signifying the guests' hopes for a better future after the war. The toast leads naturally to Sara's call for a speech from Nicholas, but as at Delia's party in the final chapter, Nicholas is not allowed to make his speech in full. It is not until the end of the chapter that Eleanor, who wants to understand him, asks the question that draws him out. As she and Nicholas talk together softly, he is able to express some of his favorite ideas, until Renny's cynicism interrupts them with his exclamation that "it's all damned rot!" (*TY*, 296). Though it is unclear whether Renny is referring to the paper he is reading or to what Nicholas has been saying, his remark undercuts Nicholas' theories, just as Nicholas' criticism had called Sara's views on patriotism into question earlier in the chapter. The insertion of Renny's remark continues the characteristic trend of the revisions, which balance visionary and radical ideas with opposing points of view, creating a deliberate ambiguity. It is difficult to understand why Woolf went quite so far in this direction, since a reading of *Three Guineas* shows that the positions that Sara and Nicholas take bear a close resemblance to her own views.[8] In *The Years* she seems to have been so concerned with avoiding a one-sided polemic that she ended by burying some of her ideas in obscurity and circumlocution.

The ending of the chapter illustrates another, more successful result of the revision process: the embodiment of ideas in human situations and symbolic images. Nicholas' theories about the changes in the relations between the sexes are given human form in the happy marriage of Maggie and Renny, and in the strange yet loving relationship between Sara and Nicholas. And, as Eleanor leaves the

---

[8]It should be noted, however, that while Elvira in *The Pargiters* takes a pacifist stance in the midst of World War I, Woolf in *Three Guineas* strongly opposes fascism while suggesting ways of avoiding future wars by changing society. Woolf's is not nearly as controversial a position.

house, all that she has been thinking and feeling becomes transformed into a broad fan of light, the light of the searchlight sweeping the sky over the now peaceful city. "It seemed to take what she was feeling and to express it broadly and simply, as if another voice were speaking in another language" (*TY*, 299). The hopes and dreams that the dinner guests have tried to share through the recalcitrant medium of speech have found another form.[9]

[9]A detailed examination of the galley and page proofs of the "1917" chapter appears in ch. VIII of this study.

V

"Two Enormous Chunks"

.

In the holograph the "1917" chapter does not stand alone as a representation of how the Pargiters lived during World War I. It is preceded in the draft by an episode centering on Eleanor which reveals her thoughts about the war. This scene was deleted before *The Years* was published, as was another complete episode set in 1921 which followed the "1917" chapter in the MS. These excluded episodes, along with the essays of the original "Essay-Novel," constitute the most dramatic differences between *The Pargiters* and *The Years*.

Our sources indicate that the two canceled episodes were retained in the text through several years of revision, since they can be found in nearly their original form in the galley proofs that were pulled in March of 1936, just a year before *The Years* was published. Evidently Woolf made her decision to delete them during that final year. The circumstances surrounding her decision to exclude these scenes from *The Years* will be described in Chapter VI as part of my discussion of the proofs and final revisions of the novel. In this chapter, I will examine the episodes as they appear in the holograph and try to see what their presence added to the shape and meaning of *The Pargiters*.[1]

The first question that arises from the discovery of these unpublished episodes is how a novel could survive such an amputation and still retain its integrity. This becomes possible because the continuity of *The Years* is not achieved through a causal relationship between what takes place in one episode and its effect on what happens in the next. The structure of the published novel is reverberative; phrases and situations repeat themselves, the same, yet a little different, and scenes are connected by the reminiscences of

---

[1]In this chapter, I will quote from the holograph version of the two deleted episodes. The galley proofs of these episodes are reproduced in the appendix of this book.

family members who share a common past.[2] Since there is little
continuing action, the deletion of entire episodes can go unnoticed.

Yet these cuts do have their effect, for they cause a shift at the center
of the novel, throwing its balance askew. If one projects the deleted
scenes back into the text, their presence changes the meaning of the
work as a whole, for both scenes describe experiences that are grim and
even terrifying, and their reinsertion further deepens the tone of the
work that is already regarded as Virginia Woolf's darkest novel. And
since Eleanor Pargiter is a major figure in both episodes, the effect on
her of what she experiences in each of them adds significant
dimensions to her character.

Eleanor Pargiter, as we come to know her in *The Years*, is a
cheerful, capable woman whose enthusiasm for people and good
works carries her buoyantly through life. Though given to intro-
spection when alone, she is usually able to find some justification,
however vague, for her faith in humanity. But in the episodes Woolf
deleted, Eleanor is shown beginning to realize that her absorption in
her family and charities has prevented her from coming to grips with
the destructive forces that are overtaking her society. And when she is
exposed to experiences that shake her faith in ordinary people, she is
shocked to find herself regarding them with fear and revulsion. She is
forced to question her values and her idea of herself, to wonder if all
her good deeds have been nothing but a pose and a meaningless
pastime.

The first unpublished episode is set in the same period as Maggie's
party and may have been intended as the opening scene of the "1917"
chapter. As the scene opens, Crosby, the Pargiter maid whom Eleanor
has pensioned off, is taking her landlady's grandchildren to the park.
On the way they pass marching soldiers and newsboys hawking the
latest news of the war. (Although we are not told the year, World War
I is apparently still going on.)

The scene soon shifts to a crowded London train, where an
unknown man catches sight of the headlines blazing from the news-

---

[2]In the final chapter, Eleanor asks, "Does everything then come over again a
little differently? . . . If so, is there a pattern; a theme, recurring, like music; half
remembered, half foreseen?" (*TY*, 369).

papers being read around him: three British cruisers have been sunk. He looks at the other passengers:

> He fixed his eyes on the swarthy fat face of the woman in a shawl; (she was not to blame; she was) impassive, indifferent; . . . but she was (respectable) innocent compared [to] the men: & he (again attacked) the usual (people:) the statesmen, English, French, Germans: . . . They were the criminals: they were the plotters; educated men. And the newspapers puffing up these poor half educated defenceless bodies with their swollen words. Everybody looked bloated (and) enlarged in his eyes—the atmosphere was thick with a kind of uneasy gloating excitement; something uneasy moved down the carriage; there was the suppressed excitement that comes when everybody is thinking the same thing.   (TP, V, 52)

He thinks that he alone feels differently; he wants to cry out, to protest, but knows that he is powerless to change anything.

A young couple boards the train, an officer and his girl, and the other passengers look at them sympathetically, admiring their air of decorous resignation. An elderly lady imagines that this is the couple's last night together before he goes to the front. "She sighed, perfunctorily. But it was right; it was inevitable. English people always behave like that, she thought to herself, crooning over in the depths of her mind the stock phrases . . . She had a touching & moving feeling that they all belonged to one family, were moving on, united to (one high goal) victory" (TP, V, 53). Caught up in the spirit of patriotism, for a moment she forgets her own loneliness and her petty concerns.

Here the scene shifts to Eleanor, who is walking home alone after a play. She overhears two men arguing about how the war got started and begins to ask herself what she might have done to prevent it. If, she thinks, she had started a society, had marched on Whitehall in protest—but no, that was absurd. She had no education; she had become absorbed in building her houses for the poor and caring for her father. Yet she realizes she might have done more. Eleanor becomes more and more disturbed by her own apathy. "She had no strong convictions. . . . She did this & that; often she forgot about the war for hours together. (But then she thought) And it was for that reason that there was war" (*TP*, V, 55). She has come to feel that people's lives are governed by vast forces that individuals cannot control, that the day when a leader like Gladstone or Parnell could change history through the force of individual character is over.

Then Eleanor boards a bus, hoping to find relief from her solitary thoughts in the company of other people. "She had a queer feeling that she wished to give up her solitary attempt to find something solid . . . perhaps other people would help her—her own individual effort started valiantly, then it faded" (*TP*, V, 60). The passengers on the bus have little to offer her, but later, at Maggie's party, she will meet Nicholas, who will share his thoughts with her and give her his friendship.

Now that her father has died, Eleanor lives alone in a flat. As she arrives at her door, she cannot help feeling happy at the thought of her peaceful room, where no Crosby awaits her, where heat and light and boiling water for tea are available at the flick of an electric switch. Time and technology have brought her a freedom and independence she had never dreamed of.

Her mood is quickly broken as she picks up the newspaper lying at her door and reads of the disaster at sea. Among those drowned she recognizes the name of a young man she had met at her brother's house:[3]

> For a second the scene appeared quite clearly: The calm swaying
> waves; For all she could do to stop it she could not help seeing his
> face, politely smiling up at the moon; & then she looked &
> realized it was a dead face, quite helpless, drifting away,
> something like anger guilt terror rose in her; (But) I didn't ask it
> (of you) she said, as if she had been telling him not to hold the
> door open for her. He was the first person to die in the war that
> she knew.   (*TP*, V, 65)

In her mind she makes a connection between the courtesy with which the young sailor had held the door for her in Morris' drawing room and the sacrifice of his life. It was not she who had asked it of him, but his upbringing had taught him that men must die for their women as

---

[3]This incident may be based on the drowning of Charles Fisher, Virginia's cousin, who went down with the *Invincible* in 1916. *LVW*, II, 98.

gallantly as they held doors for them and took their arms as they crossed the street.

These scenes of England at war are based in part on Woolf's rereading of the diaries she had kept during the last years of World War I (*AWD*, 17 Dec. 1933, p. 214). The draft was written in 1934, but by 1936, when she was revising her proofs, Woolf may have felt that her attitude was too critical of the heated patriotism of World War I to be published at a time when Hitler was gaining power and England was facing the possibility of attack. Both Leonard and Virginia Woolf were struggling in those years to reconcile their commitment to peaceful solutions with their growing horror of fascism. Though Woolf would deal incisively with the roots of war in British society in *Three Guineas*, she chose to soften the antiwar impact of *The Years* by deleting this episode.

But in the tempering process an important turning point in Eleanor's personal development was obscured. It is here in her little flat that Eleanor first questions the assumptions that have guided her all her life. She is beginning to wonder whether her charitable efforts had been mistaken because they had diverted her energies and prevented her from confronting the real issues of her time. She had accepted a limited role in her society, concerning herself with her family and her tenements and leaving politics to the men.

It is with these questions in her mind that Eleanor makes her way to the house of Maggie and Rennie, hoping, perhaps, that her cousins will help her find that "something solid" for her to grasp that the strangers on the bus could not provide. In *The Years'* version of the "1917" chapter, the only comment that might refer to the canceled episode preceding it appears when Eleanor responds to Nicholas' philosophizing with a vague remark: " 'Coming along in the omnibus tonight,' she began, 'I was thinking about this war—I don't feel this, but other people do. . . .' She stopped. He looked puzzled; probably she had misunderstood what he had said; she had not made her own meaning plain" (*TY*, 282). What had been a dramatic representation of the consequences of Eleanor's detachment from the political issues of her time has been reduced in this final version to an example of another major theme of this novel, the difficulty of communication.

In this case, Virginia Woolf, like Eleanor, has not been able to make her meaning clear.

The second unpublished episode is set in 1921. The war is over now, and life is beginning again. Kitty, whose husband has died, meets her cousin Edward for a stroll in the park. She has heard that Edward may be appointed Master of his college, to live in the house where she had grown up. To her discomfort, she realizes that he is about to propose marriage to her again, and she quickly distracts him with idle chatter. Now, as before, neither Edward nor Oxford is what she wants, and since as a widow she must relinquish her London house and her beloved country estate to her son, she plans to buy a little house in the north, where she can cultivate her garden.

Kitty leaves Edward and hurries to her home, where Eleanor is waiting for her. As the two middle-aged women drink their tea, they talk of the freedom to live as they choose that has finally come for them. Kitty invites Eleanor to join her in the country, but Eleanor says that she cannot imagine leaving the city because people interest her so much.

Eleanor tells her cousin how in recent years she had made new friends like Nicholas, to whom she can talk more openly than she ever could before. "I can say to Nicholas things I never dreamed of saying to my own brother. Why I was never in love; for instance. . . . And his feelings are so interesting; he's always loved men, not women; how Rose loves women & not men. (And) Life's more interesting than it was when I was a girl" (*TP*, VI, 4). Eleanor and Nicholas have initiated a new kind of communication between a man and a woman, but even Nicholas has not been able to relinquish his masculine need to dominate; she recalls that Nicholas has all sorts of theories about creating a new world but will not let her pay the bill at dinner.

After their talk about Nicholas, the two women begin to conjecture about how Kitty might educate her boys to be different from the men they have known. Eleanor warns Kitty not to bring them up to seek power, for power will make them barbarous.

> But it sounded a little silly in that room with the manservants coming in & out—Two men, just to clear away tea.

. . . .

"Power," Kitty repeated. "Yes," she said But it has an
extraordinary fascination. I find it quite difficult to give up the
little bit of power I had: now I'm pensioned off like an old
servant.   (*TP*, V, 5, 12)

Kitty's remark creates a parallel with the earlier scene when Eleanor
"pensioned off" her old servant, Crosby. Kitty's little bit of power
was derived from her husband's social and financial position. Now
that he is gone, even the house she lives in is passing on to the male
heir, and she has been pushed aside. In the holograph version of the
suffrage meeting in "1910," Kitty had argued against the use of force
to attain women's rights and offered to use her position and
connections with those in power to further the women's cause. Later,
at her dinner party, watching women use their wiles to wheedle jobs
and favors from men, she remembered a slogan a girl had once shouted
at her: "Every patriarch has his prostitute!" Then she had asked
herself, "What else am I?" (*TP*, V, 17–18). Now Kitty realizes that
her power was illusory. Like the prostitute and the old servant, Kitty
has been discarded once her usefulness is over.

After tea Eleanor leaves Kitty's elegant house and wanders through
an unfamiliar, rather dingy part of the city. She passes stalls hawking
the racing news and prostitutes parading. She wonders whether
women would be like men and have no shame about sexual passion if
they could prevent themselves from having children. She glances
"rather furtively at a shady little shop with red rubber tubes in the
window"—probably some form of contraceptive device (*TP*, VI, 14).
Such things could not be openly displayed in her youth, she realizes,
and her thoughts turn to the plight of unwed mothers and to the fears
her own mother must have had after bearing five children. Though
her mother was not poor, she too must have dreaded another
pregnancy, and this must surely have affected her feelings about sex.
The frank, wide-ranging talks Eleanor has been having with Nicholas
have led her to examine aspects of life she had known little about when
she was young, and she finds herself asking questions she had never
asked before.

When she realizes that she is getting hungry, Eleanor decides to
dine out alone, since it is too late to make plans to meet a friend. At

first this seems an exciting adventure. She enters a restaurant that is
bright and gaudy—not expensive, yet pretentious. Sitting alone, she
observes the other diners. She realizes that they are working people,
hairdressers and manicurists, playing at the game of leisure. When
her food finally comes, it is tasteless and unimaginative, and the tired
waitress is rude. Yet all around her people are acting as if they are
enjoying themselves. "Why was this their dream? Did they like it or
were they afraid because they were supposed to like it? Nothing could
be more passive than their faces . . . they seemed under a spell,
(drugged hypnotized)" (*TP*, VI, 22–23). Yet she senses an energy
here, a potential for something more than dreary imitation of the rich.

Leaving the restaurant, Eleanor passes a moving-picture house,
where larger-than-life-sized, red-lipped images embrace, enticing the
work-sodden people to enter a false dream world. "Common lust she
thought would be better" (*TP*, VI, 30). Then she remembers the men
at the next table winking at the waitress and recalls that even at her
age she must avoid certain streets at night. "Then the world was
nothing but a (jungle) men and women remained beasts; veneered,
covered over, suffused with pink light from cheap lamps; she looked
at the faces— . . . when they were not sodden and passive, the
expression was (hard, rapacious insolent)" (*TP*, VI, 30).

Eleanor remembers telling Kitty how she enjoyed people, found
them so interesting. "And that was a lie she said (to herself) the kind
of lie she hated most; (the becoming pose) —she who said that she did
not pose. The lie that makes one out a lover of one's kind" (*TP*, VI,
24). She asks herself whether in fact she has been a hypocrite, serving
on her committees and visiting the poor because she enjoys her little
bit of power and the sense of her own importance.

All that she had worked for and believed in seems to dissolve in the
harsh light of the common street. As she walks along, a group of
young men lurches drunkenly toward her, "bawling a coarse, defiant
song, so that she stepped off the curb to avoid them—." She seems to
be walking into a nightmare.

> One of the big shops was being pulled down, a line of scaffolding
> zigzagged across the sky. There was something violent and crazy
> in the crooked lines. It seemed to her as she looked up, that there

was something violent and crazy in the world tonight. It was
tumbling and falling, pitching forward to disaster. The crazy
lines of the scaffolding, the jagged outline of the broken wall, the
bestial shouts of the young men, made her feel there was no order,
no purpose in the world, but all was hurtling to ruin beneath a
perfectly indifferent moon.   (*TP*, VI, 31)

Throughout *The Years* Eleanor has struggled to find order and
meaning amidst the confusion of proliferating events. In this canceled
episode Woolf has allowed her character to experience the terror and
violence of the postwar world and forced her to confront her own
helplessness when faced with brutality and unreason. In the restaurant
and the street Eleanor has begun to see that the civilization she
believed in is crumbling, that it is at best a thin veneer over
unthinking bestiality. The poor people she had worked all her life to
help, whose energy and openness had given her hope for the future,
have been manipulated into aping the upper classes or drugged into
passivity with alcohol and movies. Eleanor's innate generosity and
sympathy cannot withstand exposure to the reality of life amidst the
violence of the modern city.

This final scene reflects an experience of Woolf's that she had
recorded in her diary in 1932. At that time she recalled a walk she
took with her husband shortly after the death of Lytton Strachey and
the suicide of Dora Carrington, who loved him.

A saying of Leonard's comes into my head in this season of
complete inanity and boredom. "Things have gone wrong
somehow." It was the night C. killed herself. We were walking
along that silent blue street with the scaffolding. I saw all the
violence and unreason crossing in the air: ourselves small; a
tumult outside: something terrifying: unreason—shall I make a
book out of this? It would be a way of bringing order and speed
again into my world.   (*AWD*, 25 May 1932, p. 181)

The jagged skyline with its scaffolding was one of the seminal
images that set Woolf's mind working on the idea for this novel, and
it seems strange that she should have eliminated this significant
passage from its final version. But the scaffold image belongs at the
climax of this episode, and it would undoubtedly have lost a great deal

of its impact if it had been inserted somewhere else. Some of the images and ideas in this scene were later transferred to the "Present Day" chapter, but evidently Woolf could not find a way of using this powerful passage elsewhere.

Even in its final form, *The Years* was longer than any of Woolf's novels since *Night and Day*, and, as was noted earlier, Woolf made her decision to delete these episodes only months before the novel was published, probably because when Leonard Woolf read her proofs, he suggested that the novel was too long, especially in the middle.[4] The text had already been cut and compressed a great deal as Virginia had worked on it over the years, and it may have seemed advisable at this point to omit entire episodes rather than try to pare them down. But deletion of the two episodes in which Eleanor's lonely self-questioning is revealed weakens the impact of her moment of revelation in the final chapter. Without the reflective passages, Eleanor's character lacks complexity; her optimism seems naive. With their inclusion, she would have been seen as a woman who had struggled through her own doubts and fears to arrive at a reaffirmation of faith in the future of the human race, the kind of reaffirmation Woolf herself hoped for when she decided to write *The Years* as a way of "bringing order and speed again into my world" (*AWD*, 25 May 1932, p. 181). The Eleanor of *The Years* has less of Woolf's self-awareness than the Eleanor of the earlier version had and as a result is a less interesting character and less able to carry her weight as the central figure of the novel.

[4]*DAW*, 155.

VI

The Final Chorus

·

The last chapters must be so rich, so resuming, so
weaving together. . . .

SYNOPSES

Present Day
Eleanor is at her flat with a group of friends, including Nicholas and her
nephew North (Morris' son). North has just returned from Africa. Then
North leaves Eleanor and goes to dine with Sara. Meanwhile, Peggy (North's
sister) arrives at Eleanor's to accompany her aunt to the family reunion Delia
has arranged. Eleanor calls Sara's apartment to remind her to come to the
reunion. Peggy and Eleanor leave for the party, and Maggie and Renny stop
at Sara's to bring her with them.

In the final scene of the novel the entire family, including Nicholas, Delia's
Irish husband Patrick, and Milly and her family gather at the party.
During the evening Eleanor falls asleep and dreams of happiness. Maggie,
Renny, and Peggy advise North on how to live his life. Peggy and North
quarrel and are reconciled. Nicholas tries to make a speech but is continually
interrupted. When dawn comes the guests depart.

The final or "Present Day" chapter of the holograph is a reprise and
summing up of all that has come before. In a manner reminiscent of
Proust's *Le Temps Retrouvé*, all of the major characters reappear at the
party and the lives they have lived serve as a commentary on human
nature, and on what time and history have wrought. And even before
the party begins, as the cousins prepare for the gathering, questions
are raised about what their lives have meant and what the future
holds.

Throughout the novel the characters have been questioning one another about whether things are getting better in the world, whether human nature can change, whether solitude is good and society bad, whether it is possible to lead a better life. Now, as Woolf prepared to write her concluding chapter, she asked herself once again how she could give these dialogues substance without resorting to long passages of exposition. She found herself thinking of musical forms as a way of developing a structure for her final chapter. In her diary she noted: "But I am thinking all the time of what is to end *Here and Now*. I want a chorus, a general statement, a song for four voices" (*AWD*, 7 Aug. 1934, p. 221). In these last scenes she would try to bring the rhythms and structure of music and poetry into her prose.

The opening scenes, which take place simultaneously at the homes of Eleanor and Elvira, can be regarded as a fugue for four voices that alternate, contrast, and develop their themes in counterpoint. The milieu in which they meet and talk takes on the aspect of an opera, with the noises of the city streets as chorus. As in contemporary music, street cries and the sounds of technology—the ringing of telephones and hooting of car horns—are integrated into the action and meaning of the scenes. The telephone becomes especially important as a link between the four main actors in the drama, allowing them to interrupt one another and share each other's thoughts, though they are far apart. As Woolf uses it, the telephone is a manifestation of the invisible network she believed existed between those who love one another.

The idea of using musical forms came to her as she contemplated writing the first draft of the chapter, and her initial attempts at working out this technique are more visible there. The effects are more awkward and obvious in the holograph, for by the time she had completed her revisions she had found ways of making the transitions smoother. In general, however, the published chapter follows the same form as the holograph, though it is less detailed, and many long explanatory passages have been cut. In my interpretation of this material, I will endeavor to point out the difference between the two texts as they occur, and I quote passages from the holograph wherever they add new dimensions of meaning.

In both versions of the interlocking opening scenes, we meet Eleanor and Elvira once more, each flanked by a younger relative who will provide a new perspective. According to the MS, what *The Years* calls "Present Day" is the year 1927; ten years have passed since the dinner at Maggie's where they drank their toast to the "New World" after the war. (In *The Years*, "Present Day" is undated.) Now the "New World" has arrived, and with it the new generation. Peggy and George (North in *The Years*) are now adults who are trying to find their own way of life, turning to their older relatives for help in understanding the past.

Peggy, who is Morris' daughter, is at Eleanor's apartment, waiting to accompany her to the family party. As she listens to Eleanor's talk, she finds herself imagining how she would describe her aunt to a friend. In earlier scenes it was Eleanor who carried on imaginary conversations, turning her solitary musings into dialogues. Now Peggy's thoughts serve as a distancing device; instead of responding to Eleanor she tries to place her, to type her as a typical Victorian spinster, and to use her to make some generalizations about the past.

Similarly, George finds himself regarding Elvira as a stranger might, after his ten years abroad. (George is Peggy's brother, whom we first met as a young boy in 1911. He has returned to England from Australia, where he had gone to raise sheep after serving in the army during the war). The holograph describes how he comes upon Elvira on her little island, the shabby little flat in which she is "living on the outside of the real world" (*TP*, VI, 101). Like Peggy, he tries to find words to describe his relative, and when prose fails he turns to poetry, since he had once tried to be a poet himself. He thinks to himself that poetry may suit Elvira better than prose, for its rhythms convey the movement of her body as she sits swinging her leg, saying, "I shall, I shan't, I shall, I shan't" to life. Elvira, in her turn, sees George as a young man in an old portrait, holding his hat. It is only after they have been together for a while that they can pick up the threads of their old relationship and piece together the fragments of the years gone past.

As the scene shifts back to Eleanor and Peggy, they begin to ask each other whether the world has improved since the days when Eleanor was young, raising a question that will be repeated in many forms throughout the chapter. Eleanor praises the advances of science, the shower baths and electric lights that have made her life more comfortable, and Peggy tells her that little is known about how things really work. While Peggy questions her aunt about her childhood, thinking that Victorian women were "suppressed" but admiring the vigor and strength of character such an upbringing has produced, Eleanor extols the excitement and freedom of the modern age.

An ominous note is struck when Eleanor, the "fine old Prophetess," sees a picture of a fat, gesticulating man in the newspaper. Doubtless he is one of the fascist dictators that have recently appeared on the scene. Just before picking up the paper, Eleanor's mind had wandered for a moment. In *The Years* we are told that her thoughts had turned to the night at Maggie's party during the raid, but in the MS her mind's eye had seen the grey head of the dead sailor bobbing in the water. This image from one of the deleted episodes makes a powerful connection with the picture of the politician in the paper— they are both death's heads, one from the past and one soon to come. The MS has Eleanor explaining her sudden anger by saying, "when I read the paper, when I saw that man's face:—& you can't help seeing it everywhere—then I do ask myself, haven't people forgotten, haven't they gone crazy? What is wrong with men?" (*TP*, VI, 96). As she recalls the horrors of the last war, her instincts tell her the world is preparing for the next.

In her scene in the MS, Elvira also sees the dictator's picture and comments on it to George, whom she has been reminding of his role in the war. She asks him scornfully if he "didn't mind shooting the (tops of their) heads off and finding bloody hands" (*TP*, VI, 103). Her remarks, when coupled with Eleanor's thoughts, create an atmosphere of grim foreboding in the MS that is lost in *The Years*.

The counterpoint between pessimism and optimism that is expressed in George and Elvira's dialogue is echoed in the sounds they hear. When George arrives at Elvira's house, he hears the voice of a soprano paralleling his movements as he mounts the stairs; her scales move upward, slowly but inexorably. Against her confident voice another is heard, the wail of a trombone, crying for all the sorrow and suffering in the world. In *The Years* Woolf underlines the meaning of this passage, commenting that "They sounded like two people trying

to express completely different views of the world in general at one
and the same time. The voice ascended, the trombone wailed" (*TY*,
316).

As the cousins talk, the holograph tells us more about Elvira's
relationship with Nicholas. George questions her about why they
have never married and why she has chosen to live as she does. She tells
George that she loves Nicholas, but that he had become too pos-
sessive. He had wanted to pin her down, to control her: "'First you
shall explain to me he would say your conduct. As if I were there; I in
one place, I nothing but one person'" (*TP*, VI, 38). Elvira wants the
freedom to be fluid, to grow and change; she does not want to solidify
into a single identity. She says that if she married Nicholas she would
no longer be able to live as she pleases and eat underdone lamb in her
shabby flat. Nicholas would want everything well-done. (In the MS,
Elvira and her way of life are presented in a more attractive light than
they are in *The Years*—even George overcomes his dislike of
undercooked meat and discovers it is quite succulent served that way.)

Nevertheless, Elvira tells George, she has been forced to deal with
life outside her door, despite her wish to keep herself separate. As
Bobby had predicted, she has not been allowed to go on sitting in her
window "taking notes." She tells George that the money needed to
buy "Johnny's pop-guns"—to pay for the weapons of war—has raised
the taxes on her little income, so that now it cannot sustain her unless
she is willing to share a bath with a Jew who leaves a line of grease
around the tub. From her window she has seen the unemployed
singing for a handout and has watched the mourners carrying wreaths
for the war dead. One day, in despair, she ran out to the river bank and
watched the rushing hordes of workers and asked herself—must she
join this company "And sign on to this damned humbug & crouch
under idols & serve a master; and make thirty bob a week all because of
a Jew in my bath?" (*TP*, VI, 119).[1]

[1]The disgust Elvira expresses at sharing a bath with a greasy Jew sounds
anti-Semitic. Such an attitude would not be uncommon among young women of
Elvira's background, and it may well have been Virginia Stephen's own attitude
before she came to know Jews like Leonard Woolf and S. S. Koteliansky. It is only
one of several references to Jews in the novel, in many different contexts. There are
the Levys, "who enjoy themselves more than we do" (*TY*, 30); the "clever little
Jew-boy from Birmingham," who is vying with Edward for honors at the university

Elvira has been forced to compromise, but she still refuses to mix love and money. She decides that she will write for pay, but not about the literature she loves. Instead, she will write about practical things—how to remove stains from tablecloths and fry fish. But the woman who edits the women's weekly she goes to for work tells her that what are wanted are articles with the personal touch. She wants Elvira to report on the parties of fashionable people and to write as if she were talking to her sister about a mutual friend.

As George listens to his cousin's tale, he realizes that she is trying to keep her commercial writing separate from her creative work in order to protect what is vital to her self. He recalls how her physical defect had affected her childhood, making her the object of other children's ridicule. He sees her writing as a kind of defense: "Probably people who have been bullied when they are young, find ways of protecting themselves. Is that the origin of art he asked himself: (phrase making singing) making yourself immune by making an image?" (*TP*, VI, 104). Once more we see how Woolf uses the characters of Elvira as a way of exploring her own need to write; here she has George realize that Elvira uses her pen as a defense against the world.[2]

Sara's story of her job hunt and North's perception of her are conveyed differently in *The Years*. The MS of this section rambles on while Elvira goes into great detail about her visit to the editor's office,

---

(*TY*, 49); and Nicholas, who is half-Jewish in the holograph, as was S. S. Koteliansky. Margaret Comstock suggests that "Sara begins by thinking of Jews in a voice like Eliot's, perhaps expressing and confronting her own anti-Semitism, but by remaining in her shabby flat she chooses to live in the poverty that has always been the condition of the ghettoized Jews." Comstock quotes *Three Guineas*, where Woolf tells men that the dictators are now doing to them what they have always done to women: "You are feeling in your own persons what your mothers felt when they were shut out, when they were shut up, because they were women. Now you are being shut out, you are being shut up, because you are Jews, because you are democrats, because of race, because of religion." Comstock, "The Loudspeaker and the Human voice," 273; *Three Guineas*, 102–3. In the holograph, though not in *The Years*, Elvira will decide to remain in her apartment and learn to live with her Jew, as Virginia did with Leonard, on even more intimate terms.

[2] In *Moments of Being*, Woolf writes that when she experiences a shock she deals with it by putting the experience into words: "It is only by putting it into words that I make it whole; this wholeness means that it has lost its power to hurt me; it gives me, perhaps because by doing so I take away the pain, a great delight to put the severed parts together" ("A Sketch of the Past," 72).

but in *The Years* the same story is presented through a few vivid
images, as when Sara remembers how on the day she saw the mourners
with their wreaths she thought, "this is Hell. We are the damned?"
(*TY*, 321). And when she goes to the river in despair she encounters
an upper-class couple in a Rolls Royce and sees the woman polishing
"that spade, her mouth"[3] (*TY*, 322). When North remembers Sara as
a child, he recalls that when she visited them she wore her skirt the
wrong way 'round, and he and Peggy had laughed at her crookedness.
Some of these incidents and phrases can be found scattered through
the several versions of this scene in the holograph, but in *The Years*
Woolf has brought them together to create a powerful effect.

Sara's job hunt is mentioned in *The Years*, but only in the sketchiest
terms. Sara's flights of fancy make her story almost unintelligible, and
North interrupts her repeatedly, trying to establish the facts of the
situation. In the end, whether or not it really happened is left in
doubt, for he asks her, "How much of that was true?" (*TY*, 342).
Sara's life is much more shadowy in *The Years* than Elvira's is in *The
Pargiters*.

In the "1917" chapter, Eleanor and Elvira had appeared together
for the first time. Now, in the final chapter, they seem to be
converging on a deeper level. Eleanor is becoming more like Elvira;
Peggy notices that she is beginning to wander in her talk as her mind
wanders, instead of carefully reserving her wayward thoughts for
solitude as she did when she was younger. Now Eleanor speaks in
discontinuous phrases like her cousin, and now she too is
characterized as a bird, a "queer old bird, venerable and funny at one
and the same time" (*TY*, 328). (In earlier chapters it was always Elvira
who was described as a bird and associated with birds.)

And it is Eleanor who calls Elvira to remind her to come to the
party, trying to pull her back into the family fold. First George, then
Eleanor, and later Maggie and Renny try to awaken Elvira from her

[3]Marcus notes that "Pargetting as painting to hide ugliness is used in Ben
Jonson's *Silent Woman*: 'She's above fiftie too, and pargets.' Peggy is well under fifty
and she pargets; Eleanor says that lipstick would make her feel 'bedizzened.' The
American professor's wife in the Oxford section pargets, and Sara in an
extraordinary metaphor tells North how angry the sight of a wealthy woman
painting her face made her." Marcus, 281.

dream and bring her back to family and society. In the *MS* this theme
is reinforced by images from *The Tempest* used to suggest the dreamlike
slumber in which Elvira has been living. Like Ferdinand, George
comes to her little island of a flat from a faraway land, and as they sit
together George picks up a copy of Shakespeare and begins to read the
play to himself. Elvira watches him and tries to imagine the scene he is
reading: "the storm was over: there was music in the air . . . the
shipwrecked crew rubbed sleep from their eyes" (*TP*, VII, 14). At
that moment Maggie appears in the doorway, and Elvira asks, " 'Who
is this spirit that has come among us . . . what is this vision? Do I
wake or dream?' " (*TP*, VII, 15).

With Maggie's entrance, a spirit of reconciliation and reunion
takes over, and Elvira is persuaded that she must come to the party
after all. In the holograph we learn that Renny too is hesitant about
going, for he hates family affairs. The others accuse him of coldness
and ask how he can be so concerned about the plight of the suffering
peoples of the world yet care so little about the feelings of his relatives.
This discussion revives another important theme, the link between
public and private life, the importance of family relationships as the
basic unit and model for society as a whole. This linkage is reiterated
when Eleanor and Peggy arrive at the rooms that Delia has rented for
her party. They recognize the house as the place where political
meetings were held in the past. Here Rose's suffrage meeting was held
and Delia met with her Irish sympathizers. [4] Now they are meeting
once more, and memories of all those forgotten causes will be revived
in their conversation.

In the holograph, when Maggie, Renny, George, and Elvira reach
the building, they hesitate outside the door. "Come in! Come in!"
their cousin Delia calls from the window, but Elvira still hangs back.
The others pause too, George still talking of Africa and the charms of
solitude, Renny hearing the voice of duty urging him to enter. Elvira
hears "The voice of the nightingale singing out of time in the wastes of

---

[4]The building described here resembles the one that housed the leftist 1917
Club, which Leonard Woolf helped to found. It was located, he recalled, "in
Gerrard Street, in those days the rather melancholy haunt of prostitutes daily from
2:30 P.M. onwards" (*BA*, 216). It was a gathering place for artists and politicians,
and Virginia often met friends there for tea.

the heart" (*TP*, VII, 58). The call of the spirit is pulling her away from
the others, for she is still reluctant to relinquish her separateness. She
stops to read the names of all the societies to free the slaves or help the
poor, all the well-meaning organizations that have held their
meetings here. They symbolize the good that can come from common
effort and suggest that her isolation is selfish. As she continues to hold
back, "Renny put his arms round her; she was about to lag behind &
give them the slip he knew" (*TP*, VII, 58).

Finally Elvira enters the room.

> "Come and sit beside me, Elvira" said Eleanor, stretching out her
> hand. We won't dance. We'll watch the others dancing."
> "Like sitting in the stalls at a play" said Elvira sitting down on a
> stool beside Eleanor . . . Elvira laid her hand on Eleanor's
> knee.   (*TP*, VII, 63–64)

Though she still tries to fall back into her role of observer, by joining
the party Elvira has moved away from her solitary stance. But Elvira's
reluctance, which is underlined in a rather obvious way in the
holograph, is absent from the published version of the scene. There
the whole group pauses before entering the party, until Renny cries,
"Come! . . . Come. We must" (*TY*, 363). Thus in the published
novel the significance of Elvira's move from separation to reunion with
the family is lost.

The Pargiters describes how, as the family group forms, Eleanor
becomes its center. The "old prophetess" is now the matriarch of her
clan. Each in turn comes to her and touches her in some way, as if she
were a talisman. Even Peggy, the skeptic, will momentarily
relinquish her separateness and enter Eleanor's world; late in the
evening she will go to sit at her aunt's side and lean her head against
Eleanor's knee "with a feeling that she was for the moment shutting
her notebook, giving up her attempt to check to count to analyse.
Perhaps what George said was true—sometimes it was better to
enjoy, to feel, to have done with probing and dissecting" (*TP*, VII,
99). Eleanor has come to symbolize the life of feeling, of family
warmth. As she has grown older she has expanded, freeing herself
from worries and constraints, becoming aware of her inner life and
that of others.

Nicholas arrives and begins to tease Elvira about her unmatched stockings. She had dressed in the dark, still immersed in her dream, and though she has finally come to the party she wears motley. Dressed as a fool, she retains her right to ridicule and mock, to be different. But as the music starts she decides to join the dance, saying to Nicholas, "I will dance with you," echoing Emma's words to Mr. Knightley.[5]

As Eleanor watches, she thinks of the two couples—of the happy marriage of Maggie and Renny, and of Elvira and Nicholas' strange alliance: "Eleanor had long given up wondering what their relationship was. They kissed each other's hands. They abused each other. He scolded her—she railed at him. It did not seem to matter any longer . . . (if [one] married) or did not marry.[6] Except now & again a marriage like Rennys and Maggies seemed (different), to matter" (*TP*, VII, 74). Even the married couple, though more conventional, are living differently. Maggie, a pacifist, has persuaded Renny to give up his job making munitions, and they are trying to live as simply as possible. This is an aspect of their relationship that is not discussed in *The Years*. The holograph, like *Three Guineas*, suggests ways in which women can influence men to abandon their warlike pursuits.

As the family members make their appearance, alone, or in couples, their demeanor forms a commentary on the question of how best to live one's life. Except for Maggie and Renny, with their new style of marriage, those who are single appear to have fared better. Rose is proud of her lifelong fight for "Justice and Liberty," Elvira has found her moments of truth, and Eleanor has had her share of happiness. Even Edward, though somewhat desiccated, has retained

[5] As Lipking has noted, these are Emma's words as Woolf quoted them in her essay "On Not Knowing Greek," where she called them a moment with "the whole weight of the book behind it." This is the quotation as Woolf gives it; Austen actually has Emma say, more submissively, "With you, if you will ask me." Jane Austen, *Emma*, 290; Lipking, 142.

[6] Eleanor's thoughts about Sara and Nicholas' relationship do not appear in *The Years*. In January 1934 she wrote to her nephew, Quentin Bell, "I am writing about sodomy at the moment and wish I could discuss the matter with you; how far can one say openly what is the relation of a woman and a sod? In French, yes; but in Mr. Galsworthys English, no" (*LVW*, V, 273).

his integrity. The couples, Delia and Patrick, and Milly and Hugh, provide dire examples of the pitfalls of marriage, for Patrick is a far cry from the noble Parnell that Delia dreamed of and the Gibbses are more like cows than human beings.

But even those who have not married have failed to achieve wholeness. Peggy, the emancipated professional, has lost some of her humanity in the process of entering the male domain. She is narrow, bitter, and repressed. As North puts it in *The Years*, "She was neither one thing nor the other" (*TY*, 396). She uses her analytic mind to shield her from the horrors of personal relations. Like Elvira, she takes notes, but her mental note-taking is quite unlike Elvira's imaginative flights:

> Her imagination was not creative it was analytic: she was very
> good at collecting facts; but not good at combining them. She
> had a fair visual imagination; if she said to herself "an anodyne
> sold at the chemists" she instantly saw a packet covered in shiny
> green paper: but the visual imagination is not the other kind of
> imagination. . . . She did not like messing about with he feels
> that, she feels this. She got things wrong. . . . She could make
> any number of lists of qualities; but she could not make of it
> Delia. . . .   (*TP*, VII, 41–42)

Her mind is not synthetic, only analytic; she cannot combine.

When George becomes entranced with a pretty girl, Peggy can only see this as a potential disaster. She feels that she and her brother have been warped and maimed, he in one way and she in another:

> I so suppressed I can feel practically nothing: George all sex. So
> we go on; breeding—producing. . . . But perhaps it was better to
> produce Gibbses than to be, as she was, so sexless, so inhibited, so
> aware of all the things she mustn't do, mustn't be, so abused from
> childhood for any breach of the conventions that she could never
> let herself go in any relation without a sense of guilt.   (*TP*, VII,
> 130–31)

Here in the holograph the theme of sexual repression and its source in childhood experience is raised once again, as it was in the "1910" chapter when Elvira and Maggie discussed Rose. Like Nicholas, who believes that the soul is warped and distorted by pressures to conform,

Peggy realizes that their upbringing has forced both her and her brother into an unnatural way of life. As she looks around the room, she thinks that someone could write a novel about all of them and call it "Warped Souls." "Warped Souls" could well be another alternate title for *The Pargiters*, since all of its characters are shown to be maimed, handicapped, or warped in some way. This idea is clearly a part of *The Years* as well as *The Pargiters*, but the sexual effects of such distortions are treated less openly in the published novel.

The draft tells us that Peggy is particularly disgusted with her own generation, which seems to have produced a crop of effeminate, egotistical young men. Only the servants, stealing kisses in the doorways below, are capable of real passion. Peggy's attitude toward homosexuality differs markedly from the tolerance exhibited by Elvira and Eleanor. It reflects her own fear of any form of sexuality, and it is also a reaction to a younger group of homosexuals who are unlike Nicholas and Rose. Since the war, she has noticed, young men have become the object of too much attention, perhaps because their older brothers had been lost. "How could young men be other than pretty girls nowadays, being as they were the centre of all the sentimenal adoration of the old?" (*TP*, VII, 51). Peggy wonders whether the reason she has never married might be that there are no men for her. The new era has brought a further separation of the sexes, not a coming together, as far as she is concerned.

In *The Years*, Peggy's bitterness and isolation are still evident, but they are not associated with sexual difficulties. She continues to play the role of devil's advocate as Eleanor sings the praises of progress and describes her vision of happiness. But instead of reflecting on her private experiences, the Peggy of *The Years* opens a book and reads a pessimistic passage in French, asking herself how anyone can proclaim his happiness in a world bursting with misery. There is still some suggestion that her unhappiness is rooted in her own personality, but since less attention is given to her personal life, her role as skeptic has more validity in *The Years*.

The other young person in the family, George, becomes the center of interest when he asks the others for help in choosing a way of life for himself. After ten years abroad, the "nice cricketing boy" who had gaily gone off to the war has changed greatly. He has had his taste of

war and empire, and now wants to live differently. Like the young
Leonard Woolf, who returned from Ceylon in 1911 and gave up a
government career to marry Virginia and earn his living as a writer
and journalist,[7] George decides that he does not want to work at a
conventional office job. He has saved some money, and his cousins
decide immediately that they must draw up a budget that will allow
him the freedom to live as he chooses. They all agree that money is the
determinant of freedom, for to have enough for basic needs and not
want what one cannot afford is seen as the only way out of the morass
of ambition and greed that can poison one's life. (In the MS, a passage
added to this scene in a later revision has Elvira give George a piece of
paper to write his figures on. It is the paper she had brought in order
to take notes on the party for her article, but she decides not to write
it, declaring that pehaps the Jew is not such a bad fellow after all. She
will not sacrifice her integrity for the sake of a private bath.)

The prerequisite for a decent, self-respecting life for George, the
cousins decide, is a moderate income, enough to provide for a little
house and one servant, for theirs is a profoundly middle-class notion.
Then he will have the freedom to find whatever occupation he likes.
Renny, ever practical, wonders if many people could be happy living
that way. He reminds the group that men often die within two years
of retirement, unable to live without regular work. But Eleanor
thinks that George will find his new way of life a challenge: "Oh but
he'd have to work much harder than he's ever worked in his life, if you
didnt allow him to kill & you didnt allow him to have a career. . . .
He'd have to be a really imaginative man. Liking things for
themselves; music art, books. . . . Not in order to make money out of
them. that's the hardest work there is" (*TP*, VII, 95). Their pre-
scription for George will require exceptional courage on his part.

In *The Years*, the discussion of George-North's future is treated
very lightly. Instead of drawing up a budget, Maggie draws a picture
of her older brother as a fat man in a white waistcoat, a caricature of
the British imperialist that North has refused to become. And when
North tells her that he does not know what he wants to do, Eleanor
feels very happy, for he has suggested that the future is open and full of

[7]*BA*, 47–70.

exciting possibilities: "It seemed to her that they were all young, with the future before them. Nothing was fixed; nothing was known; life was open and free before them" (*TY*, p. 382). The sober little group in *The Pargiters*, plotting George's future with pencil and paper, has been transformed in *The Years* into a gay company full of laughter and hope.

In both versions, George-North soon drifts away from his cousins and finds a pretty girl who suddenly gives him a new purpose in life. This is the incident that brings on Peggy's outburst, for she sees her brother falling into the same trap that has snared Delia, and Kitty, and has kept Morris, her father, penned in the law courts day after day to support his family. "All the talk had become to her perfectly meaningless. How to live? What to live on? Ideals. A life in common. Tush, she echoed Renny's word. He would marry a pretty silly girl & the usual thing would begin all over again" (*TP*, VII, 104). Peggy continues to be the voice of pessimism, for she foresees no fundamental change in the way people live. She tries to speak to George, to warn him not to allow himself to be captivated by youth and sex, but the words come out all wrong; she only succeeds in angering him.

Writing about Peggy's outburst struck a deep chord in Woolf's own psyche, according to her diary: "I wrote like a—forget the word—yesterday; my cheeks burn; my hands tremble. I am doing the scene where Peggy listens to their talking and bursts out. It was this outburst that excited me so. Too much perhaps" (*AWD*, 2 Sept. 1934, p. 223). Peggy's emotions seemed to serve as a release for Woolf, as she lived through the experience with her character. The directness of Peggy's anger, and the pain it causes her when she realizes that she has alienated her brother, may express Woolf's own difficulties with anger and criticism, and her fear of being misunderstood.

But in the novel all is not lost. When Peggy and George go down to supper together, their memories of a common childhood bridge the gap of time and misunderstanding. George senses the concern for him behind Peggy's criticism, and they are reconciled. With her reunion with George, Peggy's isolation is broken and, like Elvira, she rejoins the family. She too has been converted to a belief in the bonds of kinship and the importance of common human experiences that can break down the barriers between people.

Meanwhile, all evening long, Eleanor has carried her knotted handkerchief and clutched the coins with which she wished to pay her own way. She is holding on to both the money that has given her independence and the concern for others that has given her life meaning. Woolf's diary indicates that she originally pictured Elvira holding the coins, but Eleanor seems a better choice for this role, since the freedom she had won so late in life is so important to her (*AWD*, 17 Aug. 1934, p. 222).

When Eleanor asks Edward to help the porter's son go to college, he asks what examinations the boy has passed, for this is what is important to him—not the desire for learning but the ability to pass exams, as he had done.[8] Eleanor does not know or care about exams; what she sees is a boy whose parents want a better life for him than they have had, and her own role as one who will help the poor realize their aspirations.

Eleanor's good deeds are only the outward manifestation of the inner peace that has come to her. Earlier in the evening she had fallen asleep, to waken with an ineffable feeling of happiness. In the holograph, Elvira is so closely united with Eleanor now that she can tell her what she had dreamed; Eleanor remembers only the feeling, but Elvira tells her that she had dreamed she was a young girl standing on the edge of a cliff above the water, with all her life before her. Her dreams have made Eleanor believe in some new capacity in human nature: "'Renny says people cant make use of freedom. But why not? when dreams are so full of extraordinary emotion! Just falling asleep for a moment one seems to be in another universe . . .'" (*TP*, VII, 101).

In earlier chapters, it was Elvira who seemed to be always between sleep and waking, by the Round Pond, where she fell asleep against a tree after drinking too much wine at lunch, and in the scene with George in her apartment, with its dreamlike *Tempest* ambience. Now

<hr/>

[8]Nevertheless, as Comstock points out, "Edward is doing what Woolf calls for in *Three Guineas*, seeing to it that his profession is not closed off by reason of class." *Three Guineas*, 80; Comstock, 256.

it is Eleanor who drifts off while the others talk and wakens with a feeling that she has seen a vision.[9] Harvena Richter, in her study of modes of perception in Woolf's work, speaks of the "hypnagogic state" between sleeping and waking when "things simplify themselves" so that complex structures are reduced to blurs or single lines.[10] In Eleanor's reverie, the complexity of conflicting events and forces that she has struggled to understand all her life is reduced to a single image of herself as a young girl, looking into the future, and a single feeling, unexplainable happiness.

When the porter's children come in and sing their song, Eleanor is able to see their innate dignity despite their shrill, unintelligible Cockney accents. Like the boy who wants to go to college, they are part of a new generation, full of strength and determination. She realizes that in many ways the time to come will be both alien and incomprehensible to her, but she believes it will have its own strange beauty, like the children's song.[11]

The image of the strange children blends into the final moment of the party. Eleanor sees the harsh new light of day falling on their pallid faces, bringing them back to reality. She goes to the window:

> She looked at the square. She thought how she had walked round it, all those years ago. how she had explored the back streets: how she had felt rather afraid. how the people had seemed to her alien and hostile; And then she must have been young, almost a girl; the sleeping street seemed for a moment the grave; & the pigeons were crooning a requiem for her past; for one of the selves that had been; for one of the many million human beings who had walked, who had suffered, who had thought so intensely. . . . And now a new moment was coming into being . . . made of the dust of

---

[9]The description of Eleanor's unconscious state may be based on Woolf's fainting spells, which occurred during the period when she was working on *The Years* (*LVW*, V, 75, 78, 89, 94).

[10]Harvena Richter, *Virginia Woolf*, 35 and 178–79.

[11]Lipking suggests a further interpretation of the children's song: "Their hideously discordant song is at once a triumphant answer to this raw act of class condescension and a suggestion of something beyond, outside history, some unknown and more authentically divine spirit borne in through a speaking in tongues. (As St. Paul says, 'If any man speak in an unknown tongue, let it be by two.')" Lipking, 144.

generation upon generation: . . . "I have enjoyed myself," she said to Delia.   (*TP*, VIII, 12–13)

In the holograph, the novel ends a few lines later. After Eleanor's words to Delia, Morris gets her coat and they say good night. These lines are dated 30 September 1934, which is the day that Woolf announced in her diary that "The last words of the nameless book were written 10 minutes ago, quite calmly, too" (*AWD*, 30 Sept. 1934, p. 225).

In the pages of the holograph notebook that follow, Woolf has written some brief revisions of the final scene, ending this time with Delia exclaiming, "And the sun has risen!" (*TP*, VIII, 20). These words can be said to be the last in the first complete version of the novel, for in the next few pages, dated 15 November, Woolf has returned to the opening of the "1880" chapter to begin rewriting the text. This attempt at revision dwindles away on page 23, and the rest of notebook VIII is blank.

The scene Eleanor sees through the window in *The Years*, the young couple getting out of the cab, does not appear at all in the holograph; it must have been added at a later time, as was the expansion of Delia's announcement of the sunrise into the vision of "extraordinary beauty, simplicty and peace" with which Woolf ends *The Years* (*TY*, 435).

In "Present Day" Woolf has evoked all the motifs of the novel once more: the themes of love and marriage, money and power, integrity and conformity have been re-enacted as the family members repeat their childhood quarrels and cousinly debates. Woolf repeats key phrases and images until they become a kind of litany: the lost flower in Mrs. Pargiter's portrait, the owl that flew over Peggy's porch, the Jew in the bath, the teapot that would not boil, all reappear as memories out of the past.

Her diary tells us that when Woolf was preparing to write the last chapter, she tried to recreate mentally the scenes and events that made up the rest of the novel:

The last chapters must be so rich, so resuming, so weaving together that I can only go on by letting my mind brood every morning on the whole book. There's no longer any need to forge ahead, as the narrative part is over. What I want is to enrich and

stabilise. This last chapter must equal in length and importance
and volume the first book: and must in fact give the other side,
the submerged side, of that. I shan't, I think, re-read; I shall
summon it back—the tea party, the death, Oxford and so on—
from my memory. (*AWD*, 22 May 1934, p. 219)

Because she remembered rather than reread, the moments recalled
from the past are blurred and dreamlike, and slightly inaccurate, as
memories often are, so that Eleanor is remembered fraying the wick of
the flame under the teapot with her hairpin, when it was Delia who
had this habit. (Eleanor does do this once later in the book, and the
recollection merges the two sisters into one figure presiding over the
tea table; *TY*, 151).

Initially, Virginia Woolf had seen her last chapter as a series of
"very intricate scenes: all constrasting; building; . . ." (*AWD*, 11
June 1934, p. 219). Intricate and contrasting they are, but whether
they "build" to a satisfying climax is another question. Did she
achieve the rich "weaving together" that would orchestrate into a
resounding finale, or do the thousands of details militate against the
effect? For me, at least, the chapter that appears in *The Years* does not
quite come together as a whole.[12]

Perhaps it fails because, unlike the earlier episodes, which are
shorter and are focused on a few characters at a time, "Present Day"
attempts to include too much, moving so rapidly from one voice to
another that the sense of continuity is lost. The first scenes, set in the
cousins' flats, have a more coherent structure, if only because fewer
people are involved. But once the guests arrive at the party they
wander about and engage one another in conversations that seem
nearly as aimless as the talk at most real-life parties, despite Woolf's
deliberate introduction of her themes and motifs. The structure is
overwhelmed by her attempt at verisimilitude, for the party is so
much like "life" that it has little semblance to art. As I have shown,

[12]Many critics, including several who have a low opinion of *The Years* as a
whole, disagree with my estimate of this chapter. These include Edwin Muir and
W. H. Mellers, both of whom regard "Present Day" as the best part of the book.
Edwin Muir, rev. of *The Years* by Virginia Woolf, *The Listener*, 31 March 1937, p.
622; W. H. Mellers, rev. of *The Years* by Virginia Woolf, *Scrutiny* [June 1937],
rpt. in *The Importance of Scrutiny*, ed. Eric Bentley, 382.

108   Virginia Woolf's *The Years*

some sense of pattern was suggested in the MS by the way the family gathered around Eleanor, making her its center, but this effect is almost lost in *The Years*.

Apparently Woolf was well aware of the problems the chapter posed, for while revising she remarked, "I think I see that the last chapter should be formed round N.[icholas]'s speech: it must be much more formal . . ." (*AWD*, 17 July 1935, p. 252). Most readers of *The Years* are under the impression that Nicholas' speech is never given, but a careful reading of the last section of the chapter shows what Woolf was about. Nicholas says he will speak "in the name of all" but, of course, he can only speak for himself, out of his own sense of "I," like the soapbox speaker; therefore each character must have his own say, stepping forward to do his turn. The speech becomes an expression of all of them, rather than any single individual.

Thus, when Nicholas speaks of gratitude, Renny, ever the skeptic, asks, "What for?" while Sara pokes her hand up from under the table to scatter petals on Rose, who has fought for women's liberation. Then, as Martin proposes a toast to "Pargiter of Pargiter's Horse," Kitty insists, as usual, that Force is always wrong. Peggy is asked to speak for the younger generation, but she had already said her piece when she warned North of the pitfalls of marriage. Now North takes up what she said, that they must live differently. Maggie too is asked to speak, but all she can do is laugh, "as if possessed by some genial spirit," and North hears the words "No idols, no idols, no idols" chiming in her laughter: if they wish to change themselves and their society, he realizes, they must follow no leaders and worship no gods—their future lies in themselves. As they turn once again to Nicholas, he asks them to drink to "The human race, . . . which is now in its infancy, may it grow to maturity!" (*TY*, 426). Nicholas is reasserting his belief in human evolution and in the potential of the new generations; when he puts his glass down it shatters, as in the Jewish marriage ritual that symbolizes fertility.[13]

[13]Delia remarks at this point that this is the thirteenth glass broken that night (*TY*, 426). Since the thirteenth year marks the beginning of manhood for the Jewish male, this remark may also relate to Nicholas' hope that the human race will

As if on cue, the Cockney children appear and add their peculiar chorus. But we are still left feeling, as Kitty did, that we want "something—some finish—some filip—what she doesn't know" (*TY*, 425). But to have an ending, to tie the novel together in a neat bundle, would violate the meaning of *The Years*, for though it dwells on the past, it looks toward the future and so must remain open-ended. As James Hafley puts it in *The Glass Roof*, Eleanor's vision is of the future and what it will hold for mankind:

> Furthermore, although she knows now that she will not disappear into "the endless night; the endless dark," it is not the sense of her own immortality that most impresses and satisfies her, but rather the sense that life is improvable as well as everlasting, that good can triumph over and annihilate evil. *The Years* is not a triumph of consciousness over the past so much as it is a consciousness of triumph in the future. *To the Lighthouse* concludes when Lily Briscoe, exhausted but triumphant, says, "I have had my vision" and puts aside her paintbrush. *The Years*, on the other hand, concludes with Eleanor reaching out, asking, "'And now?'" The present moment is no longer simply an end in itself; it is at once an end and a means.[14]

The contrast between the ending of *To the Lighthouse* and the ending of *The Years* points to a significant difference between the two novels. *To the Lighthouse* is an artist's vision; it captures a particular group of people in a particular time. It is an attempt to encapsulate experience and present it whole. As Woolf neared the end of *The Years*, she seemed to feel the same urge to enclose and complete her work, to bring its disparate elements together in a final moment of resolution. But while the world of *To the Lighthouse* could be placed in perspective through the artist's eyes of Lily Briscoe, there is no figure in *The Years* who can fulfill this role.

We have seen how in her first draft of the chapter Woolf attempted to place Eleanor at the center and to create a circle of family around

---

grow from infancy to maturity. (As noted above, in the holograph Nicholas is half-Jewish).

[14]Hafley, 143–44.

her, and then how she tried to make Nicholas' speech into a final chorus. But in both *The Pargiters* and *The Years* the center does not hold.[15] A novel which "includes everything" can hold its focus only for a moment, and the final chapter, like the rest of the novel, becomes a series of separate moments. When an eccentric spinster joins the party, when an old lady falls asleep and awakens filled with a strange happiness, when a brother and sister understand one another across the barrier of years, the novel rises to a peak of intensity and then falls again like a wave that has crested. Each of these moments quickly dissolves in the maelstrom of voices, phrases, incidents that slow to a halt only as the party ends and the sun rises on another day.

This examination of the "Present Day" chapter completes my study of the holograph version of *The Years*. That version fills seven bound manuscript notebooks and overflows into an eighth, and in this brief survey I have been able to discuss only a small portion of what a reader can find if able to read through them himself. I have tried to choose excerpts from *The Pargiters* for quotation and discussion that clarify the intentions behind the writing of *The Years* and provide a basis for understanding the way Woolf worked from draft to published novel. But the record shows that the completion of this long MS did not mean that her work was nearing its end. *The Pargiters* was completed in September 1934, and *The Years* was not published until March 1937. What happened in the years between will be the subject of my final chapters.

[15]Comstock has suggested that the lack of a central figure in *The Years* is an expression of Woolf's rejection of a hierarchical, tyrannical social structure: "From this point of view, *The Years* may be said to be written on aesthetic principles that are the opposite of fascist. It has no center or central figure around which subordinate elements are arranged. The reader cannot possibly surrender to the glamour of a life that seems more elevated than one's own." Comstock, 254. This view is supported by the documentation, which shows that Woolf deliberately suppressed the tendency to center the final chapter first on Eleanor and then on Nicholas' speech.

VII

The Proofs

.

Once we reach the end of the holograph draft, the novel's development becomes more difficult to trace. Between the completion of the holograph notebooks, whose final entries are dated 15 November 1934, and the first set of galley proofs pulled in March 1936, there is no substantial documentation of the revision process. We do know from Woolf's diary comments that most of the chapters were rewritten many times, but we cannot be sure just when many important decisions about the direction of the novel were made. Although it is clear that Woolf abandoned the "Essay-Novel" format very early in the writing of the first draft, we do not know exactly when she made the decisions that led to the diminishing presence of political and sexual content in the text as a whole. What *is* evident is that when the first proofs were pulled the text still included many political and sexual references that cannot be found in the published novel. We can see that their excision was part of a process that continued to the very end, a process that paralleled and seemed closely related to Woolf's efforts to make the novel more dramatic, concise, and readable.

To examine this process we will have to review the history of the novel as it evolved and gather what evidence we can from the documents that survive. We know that Woolf completed the first draft on 30 September 1934. On that date she wrote that "The last words of the nameless book were written 10 minutes ago, quite calmly too. 900 pages: L[eonard] says 200,000 words" (*AWD*, 30 Sept. 1934, p. 225). Though her diary records the many vicissitudes of those first two years, in retrospect she felt that the draft had gone at a "greater gallop than any of her other works, owing to the ease with which the objective, representational episodes flowed forth" (*AWD*, 30 Sept. 1934, p. 225). (This is attested to by the greater legibility of those sections of the holograph, where even the penmanship is more flowing than in the more fragmented episodes.) But she realized that the extreme length of the draft meant that the work of revision would have to be extensive if the novel were ever to be cut to a manageable size. Many of the diary comments of the next two years document this concern, for she writes repeatedly of the need to cut and compress, and worries that she may ruin her work in the process (*AWD*, 27 Mar. 1935, p. 242).[1]

The comments in her diary and letters are almost all the documentation that survives for this period. A few days after writing the last words of the first draft, which ends on page 13 of notebook VIII of the holograph, Woolf started to revise her first chapter in the same volume, but soon stopped. She began to write in the notebook again in November, resolving to write ten pages a day for ninety days, and "to contract: each scene to be a scene: much dramatised: contrasted: each to be carefully dominated by one interest: some generalized" (*AWD*, 14 Nov. 1934, p. 232). Comparison of the holograph and the published novel shows that this was indeed the direction in which she was working, but detailed evidence of how she continued the process is not available because the revisions in the notebook soon dwindle away, ending on page 23. After that, she went on with her work somewhere else, probably on her typewriter.

The only remnants that might possibly date from the period that followed are eight sheets of typescript with the author's handwritten revisions. The haphazard typing technique and Woolf's own handwritten corrections make it seem more than likely that she typed these pages herself, but they are not dated and could have been written earlier. Since we know that Woolf often spent afternoons typing up what she had written in her holograph notebook in the morning, they may be part of what she called the "first wild retyping" which she completed in July of 1935 (*AWD*, 17 July 1935, p. 252). These fragments cover the part of the "1910" chapter in which Sara and Maggie talk together at the end of the day. They correspond approximately to pages 186–89 of the Harcourt, Brace edition of *The Years*, although they contain a great deal of material that cannot be found in the published novel. One important change that was not in

[1]In February 1935 she wrote to Ethel Smyth, "what a labour writing is: re-writing; making one sentence do the work of a page" (*LVW*, V, 369).

the holograph is that we are told that Maggie and Sara are sisters of Eleanor and Edward, rather than cousins. This idea was dropped, but a hint of it remains in *The Years* in Maggie's suggestion to Martin that since his father was in love with her mother, they might actually be brother and sister (*TY*, 247).

By 17 July 1933 the first retyping was completed, despite the interruption caused by a trip to Europe and the temptation to break off and begin writing "On Being Despised," which would become *Three Guineas* (*AWD*, 9 April 1935, pp. 243–44). The retyped version was still 740 pages long, and it was clear that more cutting would be necessary. Revision would continue for another two and a half years, and *The Years* would not be ready for publication until March of 1937.

The final stage of revision began in March 1936; by that time Woolf had decided that what had become a seemingly endless process must be brought to some conclusion. She began sending pages to her Scottish printer with instructions to send back galley proofs. Woolf usually had her manuscripts set in pages the first time she sent them to the printer. This time she departed from her usual practice and requested galley proofs because, according to Leonard, "Virginia was in a state of despair about the book and wanted galleys so that she would be free to make any alterations she wished in proof" (*DAW*, 153).

Leonard had always been the first reader of his wife's novels, and he usually read them just before they were set in type.[2] In this instance he did not begin to read until April, when the proofs started coming back from the printer.[3] He made no comment as he read the first batch, but Virginia fancied "a certain tepidity in his verdict so far; but then it is provisional" (*AWD*, 9 April 1936, p. 268).

Sadly, even this hint of disappointment was enough to tip the balance of her already precarious mental state. The diary entries lapse

[2]Ibid., 347.
[3]These galley proofs were sent directly to Donald Brace of Harcourt, Brace, in New York. Brace was very enthusiastic about publishing *The Years* in America as soon as the author had corrected her proofs, and sent an advance of $1,920. Brace's correspondence with Leonard Woolf concerning *The Years* can be found in folder 15 of letters and telegrams from Harcourt, Brace to the Hogarth Press (Berg).

at this point, and when they resume on June 11 they tell us that she had spent the past two months in the grips of "almost catastrophic illness." In her own estimation, her collapse had brought her closer to the edge of insanity than she had been in many years.

In June, Woolf felt confident she had recovered and set to work immediately on yet another complete revision of *The Years*. But her optimism proved premature. Later she was to recall that experience: "I wonder if anyone has ever suffered so much from a book as I have from *The Years*. Once out I will never look at it again. It's like a long childbirth. Think of that summer, every morning a headache, and forcing myself into that room in my nightgown; and lying down after a page: and always with the certainty of failure" (*AWD*, 10 Nov. 1936, p. 273).

When it became clear that the effort was too much for her, the Woolfs retired to their country house at Rodmell, where she rested for three and a half months. According to Leonard, she was unable to write, or even look at her proofs, during that time (*DAW*, 154).

If Leonard's memoirs are correct, this would mean that Virginia spent only nine or ten days in June revising her proofs and did not begin work again until November. But a letter of Leonard's to Donald Brace contradicts his later recollections. On 7 July 1936 he wrote: "My wife has been ill off and on, the whole time, and has not been able to work for any connected period on the novel. She is, at the present moment, working on the first proofs, but altering them considerably."[4] Virginia's own journal breaks off on 23 June and does not resume until 30 October, so we do not have her record of what transpired that summer, but in the November diary entry which I quoted above she talked about working "that summer" with "every morning" a headache, which suggests a more continuous effort than Leonard recalled. This discrepancy is important because, as we shall see, the work done on the galley proofs was phenomenal: the entire text was carefully revised and all the descriptive preludes and interludes were added. If Leonard's later recollections are accurate, all of this work must have been done in ten days in June and six weeks in November and December, since the revised proofs had already been pulled by 15

[4]Letter from Leonard Woolf to Donald Brace, 7 July 1936. In folder 15, Berg.

December 1936. This seems almost impossible, no matter how assiduously Virginia worked.

Whatever the true course of the summer's events, Virginia did recover by fall. Leonard recalled:

> Toward the end of October she seemed very much better and we decided that I should read the proofs of *The Years* and that she would accept my verdict of its merits and defects and whether it should or should not be published. It was for me a difficult and dangerous task. I knew that unless I could give a completely favourable verdict she would be in despair and would have a very serious breakdown. (*DAW*, 155)

For the first time in their relationship, Leonard was less than candid in his appraisal of her work. He was relieved to find that the novel was not as bad as she had feared, but he thought it too long, especially in the middle, and not really as good as her other major novels. To Virginia he praised the book more than he would have done if she had been well, but he told her exactly what he thought about its length.

> This gave her enormous relief and, for the moment, exhilaration, and she began to revise the proofs in order to send them back to the printer. She worked at them on and off from November 10 until the end of the year, sometimes fairly happy about the book and sometimes in despair. . . . She revised the book in the most ruthless and drastic way. I have compared the galley proofs with the published version and the work which she did on the galleys is astonishing. She cut out bodily two enormous chunks and there is hardly a single page on which there are not considerable rewritings and alterations. (*DAW*, 155–56)

The "two enormous chunks" referred to are, of course, the two unpublished sections dealing with Eleanor's experiences during and after the war that have been included in the appendix of this study. The altered proofs, minus the "two chunks" and carefully revised, were set in page proofs by 15 December 1936. After further, less drastic revisions the text was set in page proofs at least one more time and published in March of 1937.

The major documentation we have for the final painful stages of the novel can be found in the Berg Collection of the New York Public

Library. The Berg's holdings include a nearly complete set of the
March 1936 galley proofs, unmarked, plus a few galleys with the
author's handwritten revisions. (One of these hand-revised galleys
will be reproduced and examined below in Chapter VIII.) The Berg
Collection also owns thirteen sheets of page proofs dated 15
December, 1936. Since the extant page proofs differ in some details
from the Hogarth Press first edition and the contents of the pages do
not correspond, we can assume that the novel, or at least part of it, was
reset in type after the December 15 page proofs were pulled.

Our most comprehensive single source of information about what
took place from the end of the holograph to the publication of the
novel is the set of unmarked galleys. These proofs contain complete
versions of six of the seven chapters of *The Years*, with only nine
galleys missing. Of the final, or "Present Day" chapter, only
fragments remain. As would be expected, these 1936 galleys bear a
much closer resemblance to the published novel than to the
holograph, which had been completed a year and a half earlier. By this
time, many of the changes I have described in my comparison of the
holograph and the published novel had already been made; the long,
rambling chapters had been compressed and brought into focus, and
the strings of dialogue had been dramatized.

The structure and content of the scenes in the existing galleys
corresponds to what one finds in *The Years*, with two important
exceptions. The two unpublished episodes have not yet been
removed—they appear in the galleys in the same places as in the
holograph and, though the writing has been smoothed, the content is
very much like that in their holograph versions.[5] The other major
difference between the holograph and *The Years* is quite surprising. As
noted above,[6] the brief descriptive passages that open each chapter of
The Years and the similar passages that serve as bridges between scenes
within the chapters do not appear in the galleys at all.

The existence of the galley proofs makes it possible for us to see just

<hr />

[5]Some of the material covered in this chapter can be found in slightly different
form in my article "'Two enormous chunks': Episodes Excluded during the Final
Revisions of *The Years*," 221–51.

[6]See above, ch. VII, p. 114.

what Woolf was working with during these final months. For this reason, the main focus of this chapter will be a comparison of the galleys with the published novel to see what these changes entailed. Since the galley proofs are an intermediate stage between *The Pargiters* and *The Years*, they can be compared with either, and comparison to *The Pargiters* will also be brought in wherever it seems relevant.

The galleys are, of course, much smoother and more coherent than the original holograph draft, and, more important, there is a noticeable difference in tone. As I have noted, Woolf often used the holograph as a vehicle for personal expression—in its private pages she felt free to express a great deal of anger, and resentment, and a fearfulness that is sometimes irrational.[7] The galley proofs, which were at least tentatively prepared for publication, express many of the same feelings, but in a much more controlled manner. An example of this kind of change was cited earlier in one of the unpublished episodes, where she is describing the reaction of an unknown man to the patriotism of the other passengers on the train. The holograph version of his thoughts is almost hysterical in tone:

> They were the criminals: they were the plotters; the uneducated men. And the newspapers puffing up these poor half educated defenseless bodies with their swollen words. Everybody looked bloated (and) enlarged in his eyes—the atmosphere was thick with a kind of uneasy gloating excitement; something uneasy moved down the carriage; there was the suppressed excitement that comes when everyone is thinking the same thing.   (*TP*, 52)

The proofs describe the same atmosphere, but quietly, with building tension.

> They were all of the respectable classes, save for a flower-woman with a basket at the door. . . . Nobody moved or spoke. Everybody seemed to be gloating; to have fed on the garbage in the newspapers; and to be passively chewing the cud. He felt that if this went on he must get up and cry out.   (*G*, 182)

It is difficult to generalize about the contents of eighty-three galley sheets, but it does seem that the overall tone of the proofs is blander

[7]See above, ch. I, p. 4.

than either the first draft or the published novel. *The Years* is less wordy than the proofs and more dramatic; Woolf was successful in her effort to sharpen and heighten the impact of her scenes. Detail of one kind, that which simply reinforces what has already been said in another way, has been eliminated, while detail of another kind, that which brings color and drama to a pallid passage, has been added.

But though the text had been improved considerably, the cutting and compressing does entail some loss of clarity, particularly in the delineation of character and situation. For example, some references to Delia's ambition to be a violinist are still to be found in the galley proofs, but not in *The Years*, where, as I noted in my discussion of the "1880" chapter, her unhappiness seems vague and baseless.[8] In this, as in many other instances, a pointed social comment in the holograph is reduced to a more casual reference in the galley proofs, and is either eliminated altogether or obscured further in *The Years*.

All the details eliminated from the final version are not as ideologically pointed as the discussion of Delia's career, but many of them did add complexity to the characters and provided specific social and economic motivations for their behavior. The galley proofs tell us, for instance, that Edward is not in fact a first-rate scholar; his main reason for wanting to do well in his exams is so he can avoid spending his life working in an office (G, 31). This detail lends credence to the later impression of Edward as a "hollow man" when he speaks of his "wasted life" (*TY*, 135 and 405). Martin, too, is treated in greater depth in the galleys: we learn that he is a snob when he hesitates to greet his cousin on the steps of St. Paul's because she is wearing a shabby coat (G, 147). And an insight into the circumstances that have created this middle-aged dilettante is provided in the galleys when he muses on the way he had been coerced into a military career: "It was an abominable system. . . . How can a boy of fifteen know what he wants to be? So they shove you into the Army, he thought walking down Picadilly. There's the polo and the pig-sticking and by the time you're seen through the humbug it's too late in the day . . ." (G, 146).

Other episodes that come through with greater clarity and depth in

[8]See above, ch. II, p. 8-19.

the galleys are the scene between Abel Pargiter and Mira that opens the novel and the depiction of Rose at her luncheon with Maggie and Sara. Colonel Pargiter's liaison with Mira is treated with greater sympathy in both the holograph and proofs than it is in *The Years*. It is shown to be a necessary escape for him from the depressing circumstances of his family life, and the relationship between the colonel and his mistress reveals that there is real affection between them.

A freer treatment of sexual themes is also evident in the way Rose's lesbianism is handled in the galleys of "1910." In *The Years*, her sexual nature is barely touched on, aside from the account of her childhood trauma, save that as an adult she is described through Maggie's eyes as "handsome, in a ravaged way; more like a man than a woman" (*TY*, 170). We can surmise that she has had some sort of love life, because she remembers as she nears her cousins' house that she had cried one night because a loved one had become engaged. In the published version of this chapter, there is no indication of the sex of the person she had loved, but in the galleys she tells her cousins that she had lived in the neighborhood with a friend, presumably a woman. "A friend who married," she adds with a sigh (G, 183). She had cried at the engagement, she remembers. In *The Years*, a deliberate ambiguity is created by the deletion of this passage and by the insertion of the cryptic remark that she had "lived in many places, felt many passions, and done many things" (*TY*, 166).

Although Woolf apparently felt free to present Nicholas, an overt homosexual, as a sympathetic character, she seems more constrained when dealing with female homosexuality. The deletion of Rose's experience with her friend is unfortunate because, in addition to limiting the novel's exploration of the variety of human relationships, it obscures the parallel between Rose's feeling for her friend and Sara's attachment to her sister. Later in this scene, Sara's realization that her sister will soon marry and leave her will sadden her (*TY*, 189–90), and when we meet her again she will be alone, seeking comfort at St. Paul's (*TY*, 228).

Another theme that is presented more fully in the galleys is Eleanor's attitude toward being excluded from those areas of life that have been reserved for males only. In the "1913" chapter, when

Eleanor leaves the dinner table with her sister-in-law Celia, the galley proof includes these thoughts:

> As she left the room, Eleanor felt that the men were glad to be free to talk about politics uninterruptedly. She felt for a moment shut out; rather as she did in one of the Greek churches when the guide refused to let her step on a sacred spot; or at Pompeii when a picture had been too indecent for ladies to look at. It did not make her angry, as it made Rose; it amused her rather. After all, she thought, as they went out, she did not want to step on a sacred spot, or to look at an indecent picture. But she wanted to see the owl. . . .   (G, 133)

Eleanor's tolerant acceptance of the way things are is more consistent with her character than was the slightly paranoid feeling that the men are in a "conspiracy" that is ascribed to her in the holograph version of this passage.[9] But Eleanor's acquiescence will become a cause for regret later on, when, in one of the deleted episodes, she will realize that she might have done more to prevent war if she had gotten involved in politics.

The deletion of the two episodes, the wartime London scene and the one set in 1921, created several problems for Woolf, since she could no longer use incidents from these scenes as recollections in the later chapters. This difficulty arises early in the "Present Day" chapter of *The Years* when Eleanor is momentarily distracted while talking to Peggy (*TY*, 329–30). In the proofs, Eleanor's mind forms a picture of the dead sailor's head bobbing in the water, the same image that had haunted her in the first deleted episode. Because that scene did not appear in *The Years*, Woolf had to substitute a memory from another chapter, and she chose the night of the air raid when Eleanor had dinner with Maggie and Renny. Thus, in the final version of "Present Day," what Eleanor recalls is not the dead sailor but the hope with which she and her cousins had drunk together to a "New World" (*TY*, 329–30). This happier memory contradicts Peggy's impression that what Eleanor is recalling is a "painful thought; which she had

---

[9]In the holograph, when Eleanor left the table it seemed to her that "the men were all drawing up at the end of the table to talk about politics in a conspiracy" (*TP*, IV, 96).

once concealed. . . ." (*TY*, 329). The first image, the sailor's death-head, created a parallel that has now been lost between the head of the dictator which she will see grinning at her from the newspaper and the image of the drowned young man. The earlier juxtaposition of images seems more apt, although the association of 1917's hopes with 1930's realities creates an irony of its own.

In this case, the deletion of material related to one of the unpublished episodes softened the political content of the "Present Day" chapter. In general, it can be said that the galley proofs retained more of the antiwar commentary from the holograph than can be found in *The Years*. Despite the evidence that Woolf's plans for *Three Guineas* were well under way at this time, she apparently did not envision as sharp a dichotomy between the two works as later emerged. If more of the galley material had remained in the text, the connection between the novel and the essay would undoubtedly have been clearer.[10] Although we cannot know how much influence Leonard Woolf had on the changes his wife made, it is worth noting that he had told her earlier that "Politics ought to be separate from art" (*AWD*, 2 Oct. 1935, p. 256). According to Leonard's own account, all of these changes were made after his reading of the proofs.

But not all the changes made between March and December of 1936 were deletions or substitutions. Passages and phrases were added throughout, and although fewer words were added than were subtracted, especially when the "two enormous chunks" are taken into account, the additions did have their significance.

One interesting addition to the novel involves the introduction of a much broader range of perspectives. In the galley proofs, most scenes are presented from a limited point of view, with the narrator providing insight into the thoughts of only one or two major characters. It is only in the published novel that one finds what contemporary television viewers might call the "Upstairs,

---

[10]Woolf regarded *The Years* and *Three Guineas* as one book (*AWD*, 3 June 1938, p. 295). This connection went unnoticed until after *A Writer's Diary* was published in 1953. Guiguet was the first to note the relationship between the two works, but he devoted little space to tracing their connection. Guiguet, 179, 249n.

Downstairs" aspect of *The Years*.[11] At this late date, Woolf apparently
decided that she wanted to bring in more of the point of view of
servants and working people, which she did both literally and figura-
tively, for she shows us both what they think of their "betters," and
how the upper classes look when seen from below. (Crosby, the maid,
had always been an important if minor figure in the novel; I am
referring here to shorter passages, such as the Italian manservant's
reaction to Colonel Pargiter's arrival at Eugénie's home in 1891 [*TY*,
117], and the caretaker's view of Martin in 1908 [*TY*, 147].) This
innovation was a valuable addition to *The Years*; it rounds off our view
of the major characters and enriches our sense of London life of the
time, with its servants and artisans doing the world's work below
ground level and viewing the gentry as just so many legs passing by.[12]
They are part of Woolf's sense of the great subterranean life of the
city, with its sewers and tunnels and cavelike basements connecting
what seem to be the separate lives of individuals.

The development of multiple points of view goes beyond the
introduction of a servant or lower-class perspective. In passage after
passage throughout the novel, Woolf carefully inserted a phrase here
and there which made an objective description of a scene into
something personal, because the feelings and perceptions of one or
more of the participants had been introduced. (This technique will be
examined further in the detailed study of the "1917" chapter in
Chapter VIII.)

As Woolf revised the galley proofs, she found more and more
opportunities for emphasizing the reverberative structure of the
novel, by introducing instances where the common experiences of the
family are recalled as they meet. One such addition occurs in the
"1908" chapter when Martin, chatting with Eleanor and Rose, recalls
details of his childhood quarrel with Rose: "He turned. Some memory
from his childhood came over him as he saw Rose sitting there at the

[11]I am referring here to a popular television series in which Edwardian family
life is portrayed from both the servant's and master's point of view.

[12]In *Moments of Being*, Woolf explains that "as it is impossible to have every
experience, one must make do with seeds—germs of what might have been . . .
momentary glimpses, like those glances I cast into basements when I walk in
London streets" (116).

tea table with her fist still clenched. He saw her standing with her back to the school-room door; very red in the face, with her lips tight shut as they were now. She had wanted him to do something. And he had crumpled a ball of paper in his hand and shied it at her" ((*TY*, 159).

In her final version Woolf also managed to reinsert some of the powerful images that had been discarded from the holograph as she compressed her text. One such image is that of Rose in her prison cell, being force-fed as she sits on a three-legged stool (*TP*, V, 12). Rose's predicament, which is discussed by Bobby and Elvira in the holograph, was left out of the galleys but reinserted in *The Years* (*TY*, 232).

In this way Woolf was able to recover ideas and themes from earlier versions for the final one. Moreover, she was able to weave some of the material from the deleted episodes into the chapters that remained. Thus we find Kitty telling Martin that she had met Edward and walked with him in the park (*TY*, 261). That meeting originally occurred in the deleted "1921" section, but since Kitty now reports this in 1914, when her husband is still alive, the marriage proposal that Kitty evades in 1921 can have no place in her account. Nevertheless, Kitty's remarks to Martin manage to convey her continuing ambivalence about Edward and Oxford and all they represent.

Of more significance are the insertions Woolf made in the "Present Day" chapter of *The Years* to suggest the grim, gaudy atmosphere of modern London that had been conveyed with such intensity in the description of Eleanor's walk through the streets in the canceled "1921" episode. Woolf was able to bring this material in at two different points in her narrative. As Peggy and Eleanor ride to the party in their cab, a view of the streets that is less ominous than that in the last part of the deleted episode is presented. "They were driving along a bright crowded street; here stained ruby with the light from picture palaces; here yellow from shop windows gay with summer dresses, for the shops, though shut, were still lit up, and people were looking at dresses, at flights of hats on little rods, at jewels" (*TY*, 333). This insertion picks up some of the images from the early part of Eleanor's walk, when she had enjoyed looking in store windows (G, 222–23).

Later in the "Present Day" chapter, Peggy's thoughts will express some of the fear and horror that Eleanor had felt when she went out into the streets again after her disappointing dinner. This passage occurs after Eleanor had described her vision of being "happy in this world, happy with living people" (*TY*, 387). In both versions, Peggy reacts by asking herself how one can be happy in a world that is "bursting with misery." In the galleys, her thoughts are presented briefly: "Happy in this world with living people! she thought. What nonsense, what nonsense, she thought. Happy in this world—in a world that is bursting with misery, she thought. Look at them, she said to herself; there's cruelty, there's pettiness, there's meanness enough. . . . [ellipses in text]" (G, 279). In *The Years* Peggy's words are different, and Woolf has given her Eleanor's feelings from the "1921" episode, when Eleanor saw the scaffolding against the sky, and chaos everywhere. "On every placard on every street corner there was death; or worse—tyranny; brutality; torture; the fall of civilisation; the end of freedom. We here, she thought, are only sheltering under a leaf, which will be destroyed" (*TY*, 388). The fear and foreboding these lines express provide a moment of culmination for the vision of the destruction of civilization that runs through the novel. And the direct image of placards proclaiming death underlines the repeated use of newspaper headlines and placards to punctuate the novel with the deaths of kings and political leaders, the disasters of war, and the rise of tyrants.[13]

Further along in the same passage, Peggy recalls the scene at the movie theater, seeing its sordidness now. Here her thoughts are expressed in almost the same words Eleanor had used near the end of the deleted "1921" episode:

Thinking was torment; why not give up thinking and drift and dream? But the misery of the world, she thought, forces me to think. Or was that a pose? Was she not seeing herself in the becoming attitude of one who points to his own bleeding heart? to whom the miseries of the world are misery, when in fact, she

[13]In her diary, Woolf describes learning of her friend Stella Benson's death from a newspaper placard: "I was walking through Leicester Square—how far from China—just now when I read 'Death of a Noted Novelist' on the posters" (*AWD*, 7 Dec. 1933, p. 213).

thought, I do not love my kind. Again she saw the ruby-splashed
pavement, and faces mobbed at the door of a picture palace;
apathetic, passive faces; the faces of people drugged with cheap
pleasures; who had not even the courage to be themselves, but
must dress up, imitate, pretend. (*TY*, 388)

These thoughts, once Eleanor's, seem more appropriate to Peggy, for
though she is a doctor who heals the sick, she is bitter and
disillusioned. For Eleanor to have reacted as she did in the "1921"
episode was somewhat out of character, but arresting for that very
reason.

Not all of the changes Woolf made between the galleys and *The
Years* involved thematic material; some were made for the sake of
style. Many of the most felicitous descriptive passages were perfected
in the final stages of revision, as is easily demonstrated by the
alterations in Kitty's soliloquy on the hilltop at the end of the "1914"
chapter. The lines that were revised are among the most frequently
quoted passages in the novel. Here is the galley proof version:

Suddenly she saw the sky between two striped tree-trunks,
extraordinarily blue. Then she came out on the rough turf by the
monument which the old earl had built; the mark for ships at sea.
The wind ceased, and the country opened wide all round her. Her
body seemed to shrink and to become all eye. She threw herself on
the ground and looked over the billowing land that went, rising
and falling, away and away till somewhere off it reached the sea. It
was an uncultivated land, seen from this height, an uninhibited
land, existing by itself, for itself. Dark wedges of shadow, bright
breadths of light, lay side by side. Then as she watched, light
moved and dark moved; and light and dark went travelling over
the hills and over the valleys. Yellow, blue, red and deep violet
the land changed as the light and shadow passed over it. It seemed
transient yet everlasting. Whoever comes, she thought, whether I
see it or I don't see it, there it is; and these little bright flowers,
she thought, holding one of the little moor flowers between her
thumb and finger. (G, 177)

The version of the passage in *The Years* has been compressed and
heightened:

Suddenly she saw the sky between two striped tree trunks

extraordinarily blue. She came out on the top. The wind ceased;
the country spread wide all round her. Her body seemed to
shrink; her eyes to widen. She threw herself on the ground, and
looked over the billowing land that was rising and falling, away
and away, until somewhere far off it reached the sea.
Uncultivated, uninhabited, existing by itself, for itself, without
towns or houses it looked from this height. Dark wedges of
shadow, bright breadths of light lay side by side. Then, as she
watched, light moved and dark moved; light and shadow were
traveling over the hills and over the valleys. A deep murmur sang
in her ears—the land itself, singing to itself, a chorus, alone. She
lay there listening. She was happy, completely. Time had ceased.
(*TY*, 278–79)

Despite these internal changes, the structure of the galley proof
version of the novel is quite similar to that of *The Years*. The most
striking difference, aside from the deletion of two complete episodes,
is the addition of the descriptive passages that open each chapter,
which I shall refer to hereafter as preludes and interludes. These
passages make their first appearance in the page proofs of the "1917"
chapter, which are dated 15 December, 1936.[14] The "1917" chapter
is the only one for which a complete set of page proofs is still in
existence, but if the format of this chapter is typical of the novel as a
whole, we can assume that all of the preludes and interludes were
written between March and December of 1936.

The dates as chapter headings also appear first in the 15 December
page proofs—the galleys have no chapter titles and the holograph
chapters are simply headed "Part I" or "Part II." It is likely, however,
that Woolf had intended to use dates as chapter titles as soon as she
decided to call the book *The Years*, a title she was using as early as
September 1935 (*AWD*, 5 Sept. 1935, 253). Indeed, it is difficult to
imagine how the reader could be oriented in the novel without them.

---

[14]Although the descriptive passages do not appear in proof until 15 Dec. 1936,
Woolf may have conceived of them earlier. In July 1935, she noted: "I think I see
how I can bring in interludes—I mean spaces of silence, and poetry and contrast"
(*AWD*, 17 July 1935, p. 252). Woolf had called the descriptive chapter
introductions in *The Waves* "interludes" (*AWD*, 7 July 1931, p. 171), so she may
have been thinking, in 1935, of doing something similar in *The Years*.

It is remarkable that the preludes and interludes were added so late in the evolution of *The Years*, since they seem to be such an important structural device. As early as 1935, Woolf had noted that "The difficulty is always at the beginning of chapter or sections where a whole new mood has to be caught, plumb in the centre" (*AWD*, 13 Sept. 1935, p. 255). She was successful in achieving this aim, for each scene in *The Years* seems to open *in medias res*, as if one were suddenly allowed to focus a camera on an encounter between people and record that segment of their lives detached from any past or future. But these sudden shifts through time and space would seem abrupt and disjointed if it were not for the insertion of the preludes and interludes, which place the scenes and provide a sense of continuity by picking up images from earlier chapters. In some cases, they also provide information about what has transpired in the intervening years.

The scenes of the novel are dramatic and immediate and bring the reader close to one or more of the participants; the preludes and interludes provide a way of stepping back to assume a more impersonal stance, to connect the encapsulated moment with past and future events and with the themes and motifs that form the structure of the novel. It can be argued that these passages are artificially imposed on what had been an organic flow of narrative, and the documentation supports this view because they were added at such a late date. But almost from the beginning, and certainly from the introduction of Elvira, Woolf's conception of the novel was at variance with the naturalist tradition to which many of its early readers thought it belonged.

Woolf's diary comments through these years testify to her preoccupation with finding some means of providing pattern and continuity for the amorphous mass of material she had compiled in her first draft, and it is clear that a far more structured novel was her goal. In my view, what the preludes and interludes signal to the reader is exactly what Woolf intended they should—that *The Years* is not, in fact a *Forsythe Saga* or an *Old Wives' Tale*—it is a carefully organized symbolic structure in the guise of a family chronicle. The conflict between these two literary forms, which is at the heart of Woolf's difficulties with the novel, is nowhere better delineated than

in the contrast between the immediacy of the narrative scenes and the
distanced stasis of the preludes and interludes.

Thus it is not surprising to find the motifs and themes that are
scattered through the novel carefully gathered together in these
passages. In the very first prelude (*TY*, 3–4) we find, within the
course of a page and a half, the following motifs: the contrasting of
city and country life, a metaphor about the march of a caravan, the
song of street musicians, the voices of sparrows and pigeons, a glance
at London's monuments and government buildings, the sight of a
royal princess, servants in basements preparing tea, a reference to the
women who nursed the wounded during the Boer War, the Round
Pond, the Serpentine, a comparison of the moon to a coin, and a
comparison of the passage of time to the rays of a searchlight wheeling
across the sky. All of these themes and images will appear and
reappear throughout the course of the novel.

The preludes and interludes, are not, of course, totally detached
from the movement of the narration: often they serve as connectives,
as when the rain leads us from London to Oxford (*TY*, 47–48). In the
1981 chapter, the prelude tells what has happened to the characters
during the intervening years, information that is necessary because
many of them will not reappear in the novel for some time to come
(*TY*, 80–91). Description of specific characters and their situations
brings this prelude somewhat closer to the narrative than most of the
other inserted passages, for Woolf does not seem to have restricted
herself narrowly in what she can include in them. Many of these
passages, and especially the interludes, which are placed between
scenes within chapters, contain a little action, and some even show a
character arriving at the scene of the next episode. The prelude with
the most narrative development is the one that opens the "1907"
chapter, where Eugénie, Digby, and Maggie are shown traveling and
chatting together in a manner barely distinguishable from the body of
the chapter (*TY*, 129–31). But this prelude does fulfill its structural
function, bringing in mention of the man in gold braid who
symbolizes the lust for power, and the socially knowledgeable remark
that "eight-fifteen means eight-thirty," which will be echoed years
later by Martin as he crosses the Serpentine on the way to a party and

tells himself that "eight-thirty means eight forty-five" (*TY*, 131 and 248).

For the most part, however, the preludes and interludes serve only to provide background and atmosphere for the ensuing scenes. Often the time of day, the season, and the weather they describe complement the mood of the chapter. The hot summer night in 1907 is appropriate to Sara's restlessness, and the bitter cold of 1917 reflects England in a state of siege. The snow that falls everywhere, "all over England," as Eleanor leaves her family home for the last time and dismisses Crosby, buries a way of life that is as dead as the Irish tradition Joyce eulogized in "The Dead," using a similar metaphor.

The weather often foreshadows events, as when the "uncertain spring" described in the "1880" prelude (*TY*, 3) sets the stage for the uncertainties of the Pargiter household, as they wait for Mrs. Pargiter to relinquish her tenuous hold on life. Conversely, the "brilliant spring" of 1914 enhances the excitement of the fashionable "London season," the last flourish of a society that will not survive the events of the coming year (*TY*, 224).

Perhaps the most remarkable of all the preludes are those of the "1908" and the "Present Day" chapters. In 1908 (*TY*, 146–47), the description of the March wind's effect combines Dickensian personification with an evocation of Eliot's *Wasteland*. In this "polluted city," an overturned dust cart scatters objects more sordid than the old bones of *Our Mutual Friend*: "twists of hair; papers already blood smeared, yellow smeared" are sent scudding against lampposts, pillar boxes, and railings (*TY*, 147). (Considering Woolf's reputation for circumspection and delicacy, it is interesting to note that she is probably the first writer in English to allude even indirectly to menstrual blood—a subject that comes up again when she has Peggy remark that the statue of Nurse Cavell reminds her of an "advertisement of sanitary towels"; *TY*, 336).

In contrast to these unpleasant images, the opening of the "Present Day" chapter is remarkable for its translucent beauty. In one paragraph Woolf has captured the essence of an impressionist painting: on this summer evening, everything is transfused with light. An aura of light from the setting sun surrounds each object, and the atmosphere is such that even the ordinary brick houses are incandescent, as if "lit from within" (*TY*, 306). The process that Eleanor had noticed in 1917, when solid objects became porous, "Seemed to radiate out some warmth, some glamour" (*TY*, 287), has advanced to the point where inner and outer space are "permeated" with light. The passage expresses Woolf's metaphor for Eleanor's vision of another world, existing here and now, if we can only see it. Eleanor, whose name means light or sun,[15] is lighted from within by a spirit that has purified itself as she has learned to live without self-consciousness. Eleanor's continuing meditation conveys Woolf's belief in the spiritual dimension of life and in the validity of holding to an ideal vision of society despite all the counter-evidence she has marshaled against her faith. In these preludes and interludes, we have Virginia Woolf's consciousness, unhampered by any need to create character or move events forward. In this final prelude, and in the last sentence of *The Years*, which was also added at this time, we are given a sense of the meaning she wished to leave with us.

Looking back over the galley proofs, it is clear that they are far closer to *The Years* than to *The Pargiters*, as would be expected since they were printed only a year before *The Years* was published. Yet the changes made during that period are a continuation of the process that began early in the writing of the holograph, when Woolf first asked herself how she might write about "intellectual argument in the form of art" (*AWD*, 31 May 1933, p. 208). Intellectual argument, by its very nature, lacks the color and liveliness of fiction, and what we find in the proofs is that as Woolf developed her characters, her scenes, her dramatic contrasts, many of the arguments were reduced to scraps of conversation, half-expressed and barely comprehensible. What Woolf had to decide, as she reworked the galleys to ready the novel for publication, was whether to delete the arguments altogether or to bring back enough explication from earlier drafts to make them clearer. In many cases, it seems, she chose to delete them altogether, or leave them in the text as barely intelligible fragments.

At the same time, the introduction of the preludes and interludes

---

[15]Marcus notes that "'Eleanor' is 'Helen', from Helios, the sun; she puts the sunflower on the houses she builds . . . ." Marcus, 282.

gave her a means of gathering together the symbols and motifs scattered through the body of the novel, so that the chronological narrative would be balanced against a series of static, detached set pieces that create a mood and provide a connective tissue between nearly autonomous episodes. By studying the changes between the first proofs, the page proofs, and the published novel, we can understand the contradictions that Woolf attempted to reconcile as she worked. On the one hand, she was struggling to transform a series of intellectual arguments into a work of fiction; on the other, she was trying to provide a coherent symbolic framework for a novel whose original form was loosely structured and discursive.

Woolf worked toward these goals until the end of 1936, and the extent of the changes she made leaves little doubt as to the intensity with which she could work when she was in full gear. By 31 December, 1936, the corrected proofs were ready for the printer. On that day she wrote, with a mixture of relief and trepidation: "There in front of me lie the proofs—the galleys—to go off today, a sort of stinging nettle that I cover over" (*AWD*, 31 Dec. 1936, p. 274).[16] Woolf's long struggle had finally come to an end.

[16]It is not clear why she calls these the "galleys," since the page proofs dated 15 Dec. 1936 are more likely to be what she was readying for the printer at this time. There probably were a further set of proofs, since the 15 Dec. page proofs do not correspond with the Hogarth Press first edition or the Harcourt, Brace first edition. (Punctuation varies between the Hogarth and Harcourt editions, and occasionally wording varies as well. The Uniform Edition published in 1940 by the Hogarth Press is a second impression of the Hogarth Press first edition, and is identical with it.) See B. J. Kirkpatrick, *A Bibliography of Virginia Woolf*.

VIII

"1917" Revised

.

SYNOPSES

1917   *Eleanor goes to visit Maggie and her husband, Renny. It is a cold, dark winter night during the wartime blackout. At Maggie's Eleanor meets Nicholas, a Pole. Sara comes in, and Eleanor realizes that Sara and Nicholas have a special relationship. Sara tells the others that she has just come from a visit with North (Morris' son), who has enlisted. Sara voices her disapproval of North's decision, and they discuss her attitude. An air raid begins and they all go into the cellar. After the raid they go back upstairs and Nicholas tells Eleanor about his theory of the human soul and its evolution. They all drink a toast to the New World after the war. Sara tells Eleanor that Nicholas loves other men, and Eleanor finds that this does not disturb her deeply. Sara, Nicholas, and Eleanor depart, going their separate ways.*

.

In the preceding chapter I developed some generalizations based on an overview of the proofs, but my study would not be complete without a more detailed examination of at least a part of that document, where the reader can see just how the changes were made. For this purpose I have selected the "1917" chapter, because it brings together the separate threads of the novel and illustrates the methods Woolf used as she attempted to transform intellectual conversation into art. Since I will analyze the proofs of "1917" in detail while making comparisons to both the holograph and the published versions of that episode, the reader will find it helpful at this point to reread chapter IV of this study in conjunction with this chapter, and also to refresh his or her memory of the "1917" chapter in *The Years.*

Since the prelude had not yet been inserted, the 1936 galley proofs of "1917" open with Eleanor searching through dark, unfamiliar streets for her cousin's house. We experience the effect of the frozen night and the searchlight's rays directly through Eleanor's consciousness, rather than through a descriptive prelude that is detached from the action. (In the 15 December 1936 page proofs, the prelude has been added and is identical with that in *The Years* except for the last two words—in *The Years* "fleecy spot" has replaced "suspected spot." This is typical of the minor changes one finds between the only extant page proofs and the published novel.)

The prelude which was added provides a more generalized impression of the night; instead of focusing on the neighborhood where Eleanor is walking, it tells us that the "stillness of glass" has spread all over England, both in the cities and the countryside (*TY*, 279). the eerie conjunction of frozen weather and the dark isolation of a war-besieged society pervades the entire country.

At the very beginning of the galleys, the image that emerges most clearly is that of Westminster Abbey. The galley text reads: "The huge bulk of the Abbey always seemed to brood over the streets here, making them even smaller and darker" (G, 189). In later versions this passage was changed to say only that Maggie and Renny live "in one of the obscure little streets under the shadow of the Abbey" (*TY*, 279). The importance of the Abbey as a powerful institution that dwarfs human beings and invades their very homes will be stressed again later in the galleys when Eleanor notices the cryptlike construction of the cellar of her cousin's house and wonders if it was once "part of the Abbey" (G, 198). In the published text this idea is suggested more subtly when it is remarked that the cellar, "with its crypt-like ceiling and stone walls . . . had a damp ecclesiastical look" (*TY*, 289). In all the versions, the Abbey motif is repeated when Maggie remarks that Eleanor "looks like an abbess" (*TY*, 292).

Westminster Abbey, which is both an important religious institution and the place where English kings are crowned, represents established power, both secular and sacred. And since it is also the burial place of both kings and poets, its presence is linked with the idea of death and burial, a theme that is present throughout the chapter. Death and burial are evoked in the language that describes the bus passengers as "cadaverous," the lamps as "shrouded," and the cellar as cryptlike, and in the Dantesque movement of the chapter, which leads the dinner guests indoors from the frozen darkness to the warmth and light of the life-giving fire and then down into the cellar

depths to wait for death, and finally back tυ the upper level for a kind
of rebirth. In *The Years*, the idea of death is introduced at the chapter's
beginning with the image of the omnibus whose silent "cadaverous"
passengers are like new arrivals venturing across the river Styx to the
land of the dead. In the galleys, the omnibus appears only at the end of
the chapter, but Woolf later re-emphasized this image by inserting it
at the beginning as well, so that in *The Years* the arrival and departure
of the mysterious bus brackets and encloses the scene.

When Eleanor enters her cousins' house and meets Nicholas, she
begins to ask herself what kind of person he is, and whether she likes
him. Most of the phrases describing Eleanor's impressions and her
reactions to Nicholas and the others are found in the page proofs and
in *The Years*, but not in the galley proofs. In the galleys, the scene is
presented objectively through an impersonal narrator, so there is
much less identification with Eleanor and her point of view. In the
published novel, Eleanor puzzles over her feelings for Nicholas and
creates a little drama about the emergence of their friendship that adds
interest to the scene and shows that she is open to new ideas and
relationships. This change is part of Woolf's movement away from
purely intellectual conversation; by adding personal comments, she is
bringing out the emotional connection that makes people want to
share their ideas and reveal themselves to one another.

In the galleys, however, we learn more of the details of wartime
life, for there we are told that Eleanor's appreciation of the wine is
enhanced because she has not tasted it for months, and that all the
guests have brought their own sugar rations. These homely concerns
give a more realistic idea of life during the war, as does Eleanor's
lowering of the blinds to hide the light, another detail which is
missing from the final version.

A sample column from the galley sheets, with Virginia Woolf's
handwritten alterations, can be used to illustrate the way Woolf
revised. The galley's content corresponds approximately to pages
282-83 of the Harcourt, Brace first edition; it begins just as Nicholas
starts to worry about Sara's lateness. I have placed it here juxtaposed
with the corresponding pages of the page proofs.

The Years—192   *Galley proofs*

and looking round her, "having no servants?"

"We have a woman in to do the washing-up,♥" said Maggie.

"And we are extremely dirty," said Renny. He took up a fork and examined it between the prongs. "No, this fork, as it happens, is clean," he said, and put it down.

Nicholas came back into the room again. He looked perturbed.

~~Why is he so much interested in Sara? Eleanor wondered. Are they engaged?~~

"She is not there," he said to Maggie. "I rang her up but I could get no answer."

"Probably she's ~~on her way~~," said Maggie. "Or she may have forgotten and gone somewhere else." *coming*

She handed him his soup. But he sat looking at his plate without moving. Wrinkles had come on his forehead. He made no attempt to disguise his anxiety. ~~He must be engaged to Sara, Eleanor thought; she liked~~ him now that he was silent, ~~and yet he puzzled her.~~ He began ~~gulping~~ his soup in great mouthfuls, making a noise, for he was entirely without self-consciousness. He made no pretence of listening as they talked about servants.

And why did he look this intently... Sara was... on ... to her, ... She wondered.

"There!" he exclaimed, interrupting Eleanor, ~~who was saying~~ something about Crosby. She stopped but ~~she could hear nothing. But~~ as she listened she heard somebody coming rather haltingly down the kitchen stairs.

"Here she is!" said Nicholas. He put down his spoon and sat looking at the door. The door opened and Sara came in. She looked pinched with the cold; her cheeks were white here, and red there; and she blinked a little as if the light dazzled her. She hardly smiled at them, as if she were numb still from her walk through the blue shrouded streets. But she gave her hand to Nicholas as she sat down beside him and he kissed it.

"Yes. We are dirty," said Maggie, looking at her sister. She had not changed; she was in her day clothes. "And I'm in rags," she added, for a loop of gold thread hung down from her sleeve, ~~as she handed Sara her soup.~~

"I was thinking how beautiful it is," Eleanor said, looking at her dress. ~~It was silver with gold threads in it, but rather worn.~~ Her eyes had been ~~rested on it~~ unconsciously with pleasure. "Where did you get it?" she asked.

resting on the silver dress with gold threads in it

"In Constantinople, from a Turk," said Maggie.

"A turbaned and fantastic Turk," Sara murmured,

stroking the sleeve as she took her plate. "~~And that's pretty," she added, touching the golden rabbit, whose head made a boss on the soup tureen, "the golden rabbit.~~" She still seemed dazed.

g/ "~~Yes,~~ and the plates too," said Eleanor, looking at the purple birds of Paradise on her plate. "Don't I remember them?" she asked.

"In a cabinet in the drawing-room at home," said Maggie. "But it seemed silly—keeping them in a cabinet," she added.

"We break one every week," said Renny.

"They'll last out the war," said Maggie.

Eleanor observed a curious mask-like expression fall over Renny's face as she said "the war." Like all the French, she thought, he feels passionately for his country. He was silent. ~~He did something: he was in some works; she could not remember what.~~

Page proofs   05

"But Magdalena," said Nicholas, as they stood in the little low-ceilinged room in which dinner was laid, "Sara said, 'We shall meet tomorrow night at Maggie's . . .' She is not here."

He stood while the others sat down.

"She will come in time," said Maggie.

"I shall ring her up," said Nicholas. He left the room.

"Isn't it much nicer," said Eleanor, taking her plate, "not having servants . . ."

"We have a woman to do the washing-up," said Maggie.

"And we are extremely dirty," said Renny.

He took up a fork and examined it between the prongs.

"No, this fork, as it happens, is clean," he said, and put it down again.

Nicholas came back into the room. He looked perturbed. "She is not there," he said to Maggie. "I rang her up, but I could get no answer."

"Probably she's coming," said Maggie. "Or she may have forgotten. . . ."

She handed him his soup. But he sat looking at his plate without moving. Wrinkles had come on his forehead; he made no attempt to hide his anxiety. "There!" he suddenly exclaimed, interrupting them as they talked. "She is coming!" he added. He put down his spoon and waited. Someone was coming slowly down the steep stairs.

The door opened and Sara came in. She looked pinched with the cold. Her cheeks were white here and red there, and she blinked as if she were still dazed from her walk through the blue-shrouded streets.

o6   THE YEARS

She gave her hand to Nicholas and he kissed it. But
she wore no engagement ring, Eleanor observed.

"Yes, we are dirty," said Maggie,, looking at her.
She was in her day clothes. "In rags," she added, for
a loop of gold thread hung down from her sleeve.

"I was thinking how beautiful . . ." said Eleanor,
for her eyes had been resting on the silver dress with
gold threads in it. "Where did you get it?"

"In Constantinople, from a Turk," said Maggie.

"A turbaned and fantastic Turk," Sara murmured,
stroking the sleeve as she took her plate. She still
seemed dazed.

"And the plates," said Eleanor, looking at the purple
birds on her plate, "Don't I remember them?" she
asked.

"In the cabinet in the drawing-room at home," said
Maggie. "But it seemed silly—keeping them in a
cabinet."

"We break one every week," said Renny.

"They'll last the war," said Maggie.

Eleanor observed a curious mask-like expression
come down over Renny's face as she said "the war."
Like all the French, she thought, he cares passionately
for his country. But contradictorily, she felt, looking
at him. He was silent. His silence oppressed her. He
was a formidable man.

"And why were you so late?" said Nicholas, turning to Sara. He spoke gently, reproachfully, rather as
if she were a child. He poured her out a glass of wine.

Take care, Eleanor felt inclined to say to her; the
wine goes to one's head. She had not drunk wine for
months. She was feeling already a little blurred; a
little light-headed.

Comparison of the March 1936 galley proof and corresponding
page proof pulled the following December show how Woolf made her
cuts, eliminating redundancies and unnecessary details. (In *The Years*
as published, there are only two additions to the page proofs: after
noting that Nicholas was "without anxiety" Woolf added, "he was
without self-consciousness" (*TY*, 283), and after Eleanor's realization
that she is "a little lightheaded," the explanation, "It was the light
after the dark; talk after silence; the war, perhaps removing barriers,"
has been added (*TY*, 284). Otherwise, the only differences between
these page proofs and *The Years* involve matters of punctuation.)

In both the page proofs and *The Years*, deletions and changes in punctuation are used as a way of creating the semblance of casual conversation; by eliminating the final words of a sentence and substituting an ellipsis, the fragmentary nature of ordinary speech is suggested. For example, in paragraph six of the first proofs Maggie says that Sara is probably coming "Or she might have forgotten and gone somewhere else." In paragraph eleven of the page proofs, which corresponds, the last few words have been cut, leaving the end of the remark open. A similar effect is created when Eleanor's remark about Maggie's dress is cut to "I was thinking how beautiful . . ." leaving out "it is."

The most interesting series of revisions on these pages shows how Woolf worked out a method of introducing the idea that there is something special yet rather unorthodox in the relationship between Nicholas and Sara. Before this galley begins, Nicholas had already expressed his concern that Sara had not yet arrived. Now Eleanor notices that he is perturbed and, like any well-meaning relative, she wonders whether they are engaged. As his agitation increases she becomes convinced that she is right. Woolf's initial change was to delete Eleanor's first thoughts and move them down in the text to the place where she sees that he is too upset to eat his soup. By eliminating the description of his table manners, Woolf avoided introducing an element of snobbery and focused attention on Nicholas' unself-conscious interest in Sara's well-being. By the time the passage was ready for publication, Woolf had decided to present Nicholas' behavior without Eleanor's surmise, trusting the reader to pick up its implications for himself. Now it is only after Sara's arrival that Eleanor's thoughts are revealed by her glance at Sara's hand to see if she wears an engagement ring. At this point the reader is as puzzled as Eleanor, and it will be nearly the end of the chapter before the nature of Sara and Nicholas' friendship will be made clearer.

The careful changes Woolf made in this galley are typical of what one finds throughout the chapter. As the scene continues past Sara's entrance, which occurs at the end of this passage, Eleanor's thoughts give her impression of the new arrival. Her response to her cousin is treated more fully in the galley proofs than in the page proofs or *The Years*: "She dramatizes things: Just as Eugénie used to, Eleanor thought. But she liked her better than usual; she conveyed an

impression of bitterness. She had grown older; she was less affected"
(G, 193). Eleanor too, has grown, for bitterness is hardly a quality she
would have admired in her youth.

In the galleys, Sara is more readily understandable than in *The
Years*, and her ideas are treated more seriously. When she tells the
others of the scorn with which she greeted her cousin North's
enlistment, her attitude is given some support by Nicholas. In the
holograph version of this scene, Nicholas is in sympathy with Sara's
attack on patriotism but points out that little else could be expected
from a young man brought up as conventionally as North has been. In
the galleys, some of that original train of thought is retained.
Nicholas asks where North was educated, and Eleanor notes that
Nicholas' manner is like that of a doctor questioning the relatives of a
patient, a simile that suggests that he regards patriotic fervor as a
disease. This is less straightforward than the holograph, where
Nicholas openly sides with Elvira, but it does give the possibility of a
different interpretation of Nicholas' criticism of Sara, when he calls
her "Prejudiced; narrow; unfair" (*TY*, 286). Nicholas says the same
words in the galleys, but there, as in the holograph, it is her lack of
understanding of how little chance North had to do anything but
conform that Nicholas is castigating. This will be reinforced later on
when the Nicholas of the galleys asks why we go to war and theorizes
that governments want war, but people do not.

In the published version, all the other guests including Nicholas
seem to line up in opposition to Sara. Eleanor thinks Nicholas favors
North's enlistment, and since she is strongly patriotic, she believes
that Nicholas feels just as she does (*TY*, 286). The irony of this
misunderstanding is lost in *The Years* because there the complexity of
Nicholas' attitude has been obscured by deletions.

One of the results of these changes is that the antiwar point of view
is presented equivocally in *The Years*, since it is only voiced by a
flighty and peculiar character who is given no support by the others.
Because the section depicting wartime London with its feverish
patriotism has also been deleted, Sara's repudiation of war is given
little support in the final version of the novel. (Since these changes
were all made after Leonard Woolf read the galley proofs, they may
reflect his growing conviction that war against the Nazis was

becoming inevitable, and his fear that his wife would be subjected to adverse criticism for belittling patriotism at this time.)

As the conversation moves on, Eleanor looks at a familiar chair and is reminded of Maggie's and Sara's mother, Eugénie. In the treatment of this passage, comparison of the galleys and the final version provides a fine example of Woolf's skillful revision.

Galley proofs	*The Years* (page proofs are identical here)
"I remember your mother so well," said Eleanor, leaning towards her. "She was—" all her good qualities seemed to come before her, not her bad ones—"so unlike other people," she added, "Everything about her," she said, remembering Eugénie.	"I remember that chair," she said to Maggie. "and your mother . . ." she added. But she always saw Eugénie not sitting but in movement. ". . . dancing," she added.
"She used to dance," said Sara. She drummed on the table, "When I was young" she hummed. (G, 195)	"Dancing . . ." Sara repeated. She began drumming on the table with her fork. "When I was young, I used to dance," she hummed. (*TY*, 287–88)

In the galley version, Eleanor's remembrance of Eugénie is vague and general. In *The Years*, her thoughts move more quickly and vividly, and Eugénie is recreated for them both. Woolf has accomplished this through the use of association and repetition, techniques that she relied on throughout to weave together the disparate strands of the novel. In both versions the sight of the red chair that had once stood in the hall of Eugénie's home brings her to mind, the same chair that Rose had recognized when she visited the two sisters in 1910 (*TY*, 165). In *The Years*, when Eleanor sees the chair, she associates it with sitting but realizes immediately that when she thinks of Eugénie she thinks of her moving—dancing. The word "dancing" becomes a refrain, for Sara repeats it once, and then again, in a slightly different form as part of the song, adding the line, "I used to dance."

As Sara sings, she and Maggie remember the night their mother waltzed for them. The prelude to the "1907" chapter, which opens with this remembered scene, adds the information that the waltz being played all over London at that time was "After the Ball was Over," a song whose lines, "Many the hopes that have vanished/After the ball . . . after the break of dawn" are related thematically to *The Years*. At this point they would be appropriate to the feelings of the gathered guests, for whom the war has destroyed so much. In the galleys it is this song which Sara sings in "1917," but Woolf might have felt that the allusion was too obvious and so substituted the less significant, though equally nostalgic, "When I was young" and moved the first song title back to the earlier chapter.

As Sara sings she is interrupted by a "wrong note," the air raid siren. The guests descend to the cellar as the war comes closer to their lives. Here the galleys are somewhat grimmer in tone than either the page proofs or *The Years*. More attention is paid to the process of bringing the sleeping children downstairs, and Maggie tells the others that she wants them with her so that if they are hit by a bomb they will all die together (G, 197). Eleanor too is more fatalistic in her thinking. As she hears the bombs she looks at the trembling of the stone arches and thinks, "That stone will fall" (G, 198). In *The Years* the line has been changed to "That stone *may* fall" (*TY*, 291: emphasis mine).

Beginning on page 292 of *The Years*, we find an important addition to the text that is missing from both the galleys and the page proofs, so that it must have been brought in just before publication. In the galleys and page proofs, Sara's suggestion that they drink a toast to the "New World" is not taken up and repeated by the others, as it is in *The Years* (*TY*, 292).[1] Nor does Sara suggest that Nicholas make a speech in the galleys; his opening salutation, "Ladies and Gentlemen!" is also missing, and there is no prefiguring here of the interrupted speech in the "Present Day" chapter. In the published version of "1917," Woolf interrupts Nicholas' speech. One clearly sees here how even as the novel went into print Woolf was continuing her efforts to tie its threads together, working backward and forward in the text to turn the novel into a series of echo chambers.

[1]The phrase "The New World" is used here once in the galleys and three times in *The Years*; it is one of the triple repetitions that McLaurin has pointed to as a structuring device in *The Years* (McLaurin, 121–24 and 162–65). This shows that much of the patterning of the novel was worked out in the final stages of revision. Other repeated phrases, "A Speech! A Speech!" and "Ladies and Gentlemen!" which appear both in the "1917" and "Present Day" chapters, were also added after the March 1936 galley proofs.

The idea of Nicholas as a speechmaker, which is brought in here in *The Years*, will serve as an opening for Eleanor, who regrets the interruption. She will question him later about what he had planned to say. Although the designation of his talk as a "speech" is missing from the galleys, they do include more of his opinions as to why the war is not very important than can be found in *The Years*. In the final version, all that is left is Nicholas' remark about "children letting off fireworks in the back garden" (*TY*, 293), which is said to Eleanor in private rather than to the group as a whole. Nicholas' remark sounds facetious and condescending in the context of the air raid, but he is actually alluding to his theory of evolution, which posits that man is now in a primitive or infantile stage of development. It is related to Sara's remark, in 1910, when she predicted that

> "In time to come . . . people, looking into this room—this cave, this little antre, scooped out of mud and dung, will hold their fingers to their noses . . . and say, 'Pah! They stink!'" (*TY*, 189)

Here, in 1917, she repeats this image, calling the cellar they have been hiding in a "cave of mud and dung . . ." (*TY*, 293; the ellipsis is Woolf's).[2] Sara's remark immediately precedes Nicholas' comment about the children playing with fireworks, but it would require a very sophisticated reading of the text of *The Years* to see their connection. In the galleys, these remarks are given more explanation. There, Nicholas' words are preceded by his comment that they are all acting as if "this war were of any importance whatsoever . . ." (G, 199). And Eleanor continues his train of thought, connecting it with her own experiences: "Eleanor was not certain what he meant, but it hitched on to something in her own mind, and, as the usual transitions were broken, as it did not matter much what one said, she hazarded: 'Because people didn't live very nice lives before the War, you mean, so why make all this fuss? I've often thought that myself,' she added" (G, 199). This carefully qualified remark is a vaguer version of Eleanor's speech in the holograph, in which she suggests that one

[2]Marcus notes that "The traditional materials for pargetting were lime and cow dung; Sara calls their houses 'caves of mud and dung.'" Marcus, 281.

reason for the war is that it provided some relief from the dull and impoverished lives most people led in peacetime.

In the galleys, Nicholas follows up on Eleanor's words:

> "We didn't live very nice lives before" he repeated. "No. and even now"—he stretched his hand out; it almost touched the other wall of the cellar—"we don't live very nice lives."
>
> . . . .
>
> "In this cellar," said Sara, "this cave of mud and dung." (G, 199)

The placement of Sara's remark in the galleys clearly ties it to Nicholas' and Eleanor's remarks, while in *The Years* it seems rather gratuitous, except as an echo of her 1910 statement.

In rewriting, Woolf apparently saw a need to cut this passage. In the galleys some of the original sentiments of the holograph are retained, but in such an abridged form that they are difficult to decipher. The further cuts in *The Years* meant that the idea of human evolution, which is given so much prominence in the holograph, receives little attention in *The Years*.

After the group returns upstairs, Rennys sits smoking a cigar. In the galleys, he offers one to Eleanor, and she begins to smoke too. This incident was depicted in the holograph as well, where it played a part in a discussion of women's new-found freedom to explore a variety of pleasures, both sexual and social. Its deletion from the text removes yet another theme from the novel.

In the galleys, this passage is followed by a meditation in which Eleanor reflects on the way people affect her, and on the feelings that lie beneath the surface of ordinary conversation. The removal of these thoughts is justifiable, since its purpose is better met in *The Years* by the insertion of the descriptions of the shifts and changes in Eleanor's responses that are scattered through the published chapter.

When Nicholas begins to tell Eleanor about his theories of the human soul, Eleanor's reaction is to feel a new sense of the possibilities of life, and of her own powers. These thoughts are present in all three versions, but they come through with greater strength and lyricism in the page proofs and the published novel. Also, it is in the final version that the phrase "cripples in a cave" makes its first appearance (*TY*,

297). The image brings to mind Plato's parable of the shadow world inhabited by those who cannot see the light of truth, and also refers back to Sara's cave allusions. Moreover, it gives concrete expression to the theme of crippling and deformity, both physical and spiritual, that runs through the novel.

As Nicholas talks quietly with Eleanor, he expounds a theory of the soul which suggests that without society's strictures it could expand and develop into a higher form of consciousness. Like Plato, he sees the life of the individual as a spiritual quest and a process of development which can lead to the fulfillment of his highest potentialities. But unlike Plato, Nicholas locates truth in this world, not in a higher realm, and believes that full development includes all aspects of human experience, the material and sensual as well as the intellectual and spiritual. Nicholas' philosophy will become the basis for Eleanor's vision at the end, when she will see that happiness exists "in this world . . . with living people" (*TY*, 38). What Woolf has borrowed from Plato is his metaphor of the cave and of the light that is there if only one can see it. His cave dwellers are chained in their positions; hers are too crippled to move. The images derived from these metaphors pervade the last chapters of the novel, as the characters move from the cavelike basement to the light and warmth of the drawing room in "1917," and then, at the end, into the light of sunset and dawn that frames "Present Day."

In her final version of Eleanor and Nicholas' conversation, Woolf has managed to convey more optimism and immediacy than is present in the galleys. There is added conviction in *The Years*, when Eleanor thinks, "We shall be free, we shall be free," a sentence which does not appear in the earlier version (*TY*, 297).

In the galleys it is made clear that Nicholas does not expect that his ideal world will be achieved in their lifetime. He answers Eleanor carefully when she asks him how long it will take for the world to change. When he tells her that it will be five hundred or a thousand years before the change becomes noticeable, she is quite disappointed, as if she expected some miraculous transformation to take place.

"Then we shall never know what it is like," she said. She could not prevent her disappointment sounding in her voice, absurd though it was. "Not in the body," he said. "No." "But I don't

believe in life after death," she murmured, "Do you"—she
hesitated.   (G, 203)

Nicholas strokes his head, but tells her he does not believe in "our life
here on earth. . . . My life, no; our life, yes," (G, 203). Eleanor
thinks vaguely that he must be quoting someone; perhaps she is
remembering the night at Celia's so many years ago when she had
opened an edition of Dante to the words, "For by so many more there
are who say 'ours'/So much more of good doth each possess" (*TY*,
212);[3] these words express the same idea of human life as communal
rather than individual that Nicholas is trying to convey.

Earlier, Eleanor had felt "robbed by the presence of death of
something personal"; the shared danger has broken down the bounds
of the self. In the galleys this idea is repeated when she looks at a
painting on the way upstairs and feels "Immune/. . . from my self in
some way" (G, 200). In *The Years* only the word "Immune" remains,
which suggests a sense of personal safety after the experience that
brought her so close to death. The earlier version is closer to the
feeling the old lady had as she left the train in the first deleted episode,
which would have preceded this chapter, when the sight of the young
officer and his girl made her feel at one with the English people, and
temporarily freed from petty personal concerns. In this scene Eleanor
realizes that the experience they have shared has broken down the
barriers that held them "each in his own cubicle," as Nicholas put it
(G, 203). The possibility of a future with a new sense of community,
of openness and sharing, opens up before them. It is then that the
breakdown of barriers between people makes it possible for Sara to
reveal that Nicholas is a homosexual, to which she adds, in the galley
version, that his honesty about his sexual nature is "The one thing I
respect him for" (G, 205).

As the guests prepare to leave, the galleys describe Sara spilling out
the contents of her purse while looking for her key, so that the coins
scatter, an incident that prefigures Eleanor's fumbling search for a
coin in the "Present Day" chapter. We know from Woolf's diary that
she originally intended to have Sara be the one to clutch her coins at
the end, and this detail may be a relic of that intention, which would

[3]Dante Alighieri, *La Divina Commedia*, Purgatorio (XV, 56–57).

explain its deletion (*AWD*, 30 Aug. 1934, p. 222). Its appearance in
the galleys does, however, provide a parallel between Sara and
Eleanor, and harks back to Eleanor's father, who fumbled in his
pocket for a coin to reward his son (*TY*, 13).[4]

Although the coin incident was discarded, another, Eleanor's brief
encounter with an old man on the bus who is eating his bread and
meat, is included in the galleys, deleted in the page proofs, and
reinserted in the published novel. Without this anecdote we have a
rather melodramatic ending for the chapter, as Nicholas is left
standing alone in the gloom; its insertion adds a humorous and
humanizing touch that seems a fitting end for the episode.

This close examination of the penultimate revisions of "1917"
reveals the meticulous attention to detail, the utter professionalism,
of the way Woolf worked. Even the version pulled in page proof did
not satisfy her; she made enough changes in wording after December
to require another set of pages to be set in type before publication in
March of 1937.

For the most part, the changes documented here were im-
provements on the galley proofs. The final version has more flow and
conveys a feeling of casual conversation between friends. To be sure,
some things were lost, such as the fuller explication of the group's
views on war and Nicholas' philosophy of human evolution, but the
chapter as a whole has been given a more coherent form. Despite the
many years of effort that went into Virginia Woolf's revisions of *The
Years*, these last-minute rewordings make one wonder whether *The
Years* might not have been further improved if she had given it still
more time at the end.

---

[4]See Herbert Marder for an extensive discussion of symbolism in Virginia
Woolf's work, *Feminism and Art*, 98–153.

CONCLUSION

Looking back over the whole course of Virginia Woolf's work on *The Years*, we can begin to understand how her original conception was modified as the novel evolved. She had begun, we recall, with an impulse to write an essay which would explore women's sexuality and their role in society. Then, seeing the value of fictionalizing the biographical material she had been reading as background for her essay, she decided to create a new form, a "Novel-Essay," which would alternate interpretative essays with episodes in the lives of an ordinary middle-class English family.

Though the "Novel-Essay" format was soon discarded, the dual nature of the novel remained. At the outset Virginia Woolf had announced that she intended to write a novel based on "fact," replete with the kind of detailed description of people, places, and objects that she had previously rejected as outdated and antithetical to the spirit of the modern novel. But facts alone could not hold her interest for long; soon Woolf began feeling "the tug to vision," the need to imbue her narrative of "ordinary waking Arnold Bennett life" with a visionary spirit, to lift her reader's eyes from the sordid London streets to the stars above (*AWD*, 2 Nov. 1932, p. 189; 31 May 1933, p. 208). Thus Woolf took on the ambitious task of combining fact and vision, of creating a multileveled novel that would include everything: the personal and the familial, the political and the spiritual.

When Woolf began to search for a structure that could give form to her dual vision, she hit upon the idea of using contrasting, alternating episodes to convey two different perspectives. The two cousins,

Eleanor and Elvira, became the centers of these contrasting sections. Eleanor's scenes are presented, for the most part, with the straightforward narrative technique of the conventional realistic novel, while Elvira's are fragmented and externalized, requiring the reader to make the connections. Elvira, whose peculiarities and circumstances place her outside the mainstream of society, becomes the major vehicle for the visionary impulse in the novel. Her mind soars beyond the concerns of daily life, and her speech incorporates fragments of song and scraps of poetry as it leaps from one image to another. But Eleanor, too, searches for vision in her own prosaic way, trying to find pattern and meaning in the profusion of daily events and searching for a philosophy that will help her see beyond the grim realities of modern society.

As the first draft of the novel progressed, Woolf tried to bring the separate threads together, causing the two cousins to meet in "1917," when Nicholas forms a link between them, through his friendship with both and through his philosophy. He articulates Eleanor's vague yearnings and provides a vision of a future in which artistic spirits like Elvira will not be impeded by social values that constrict and distort their personalities.

The "Present Day" chapter brings the separate strands even closer. It becomes a reprise in which all the themes and issues of the novel are raised once more when all the characters convene at Delia's party, a casual, heterogenous affair that provides a contrast to the stilted Victorian gathering around the tea table with which the novel began. In the holograph version Elvira reluctantly gives up her role as outsider to join her relatives, while all the family gathers around Eleanor, who has become a kind of matriarch. Each family member in turn recalls the important moments of his life, and Eleanor has her vision.

After completing the holograph, Woolf began revising in earnest. When the first draft is compared with the published novel, one becomes aware of the extent to which feminist, pacifist, and sexual themes have been deleted, obscured, or attenuated. This seemed to stem in part from Woolf's desire to avoid one-sidedness or polemic, a concern she expressed frequently in her diary as she revised. And as she rewrote, she tended to undercut the credibility of the two main proponents of radical views, Elvira and Nicholas. Elvira, who becomes Sara, is made to seem even more capricious and fanciful in *The Years* than she is in the holograph, and she is deprived of Nicholas' support for her antiwar stance. Nicholas' philosophical expositions are cut drastically, and his tendency to repeat himself is given more emphasis in *The Years*, making his ideas appear little more than a clever lecturer's stock in trade.

The deletion of most of the discussion of female sexuality is probably indicative of Woolf's ambivalence about exploring this theme in print, but the removal of so much of the antiwar argument is more puzzling, since she had no scruples about presenting similar views in *Three Guineas*. Possibly it seemed easier to argue against war in general while strongly opposing fascism in all its forms, as she does in *Three Guineas*, than to give a sympathetic treatment to a character who is advocating pacificism in wartime, as Elvira does in the "1917" chapter. And since the novel had been started in 1932 and was being revised until 1936, the changing times may have given a different color to the issue.

Aside from these considerations, it appears that the main reason for the deletion of much of the ideological material was the need to cut and compress a long, unwieldy draft, and to embody its arguments and ideas in imagery and dramatic incidents. And in order to express her ideas through her art, as she revised Woolf developed the novel's reverberative structure, using a pattern of repeated motifs and reminiscences to connect the episodes and heighten their significance.

As the lengthy dialogues that can be found in the holograph were compressed and dramatized, Woolf developed a technique for mimicking actual conversation, using interruptions, hesitations, and ellipses. Woolf's diary entries in the months before she began to write *The Years* show that she was carefully noting down the chatter of friends who visited her (*AWD*, 31 Jan. 1932, p. 178). This experiment was probably the source for Rose's comment that "All talk was nonsense . . . if it were written down" (*TY*, 171), and in *The Years* we find talk that can almost be called "nonsense"—conversation that is carefully structured to seem inconsequential, though Woolf has scattered through it the significant phrases that express the themes of the novel.

Some of the ideas that Woolf could not express in conversation were presented as the thoughts of Eleanor, Kitty, Martin, and later, Peggy and North. In *The Years*, these interior monologues provided the best opportunity for developing themes coherently, since the conversation is fragmented and there is little direct action. Yet Woolf chose to delete two of Eleanor's long meditations when she made her final revisions, a decision which further diminished the presentation of antiwar views and limited the reader's understanding of Eleanor's development.

The March 1936 galley proofs, which provide documentation for the final stages of revision, show that as Woolf moved away from her first draft her text became blander and less angry, and that some of the details and ideas that had been cut during revisions were reinserted in the text just before publication. Comparison of the galley proofs and the later page proofs reveals that the descriptive preludes and interludes we find in *The Years* were also added at the very end.

As one compares the holograph and proofs and final version of *The Years*, one wonders whether another novel might have emerged if she had reworked her material differently. The first chapter in the holograph is a fascinating document, a lively portrait of a family and a period that is nearly complete in itself. But as one moves on to the rest of the holograph, the text thins and often becomes repetitious and polemical. It appears that Woolf's imaginative powers began to wane as she left the vivid memories of her childhood behind. The evidence of the holograph suggests that Woolf turned to her techniques of fragmentation and repeated recollection not because of some preconceived intention, but because she could no longer invent with the spontaneity with which she had begun her novel. In one sense, the format Woolf resorted to out of necessity reflects a truth about her own experience.

Despite her talk of drawing on many biographies, it can easily be demonstrated that the source of much of the material for *The Years* was Virginia Woolf's own family life, and as with many people, her memories of childhood were richer and clearer than her recollections of later years. In her case, the death of her mother made a particularly sharp break, which is reflected in the structure of both *To the*

Lighthouse and *The Years*.[1] But while the earlier novel attempts little
beyond a reunion and resolution after the mother's death, *The Years*
continues through many subsequent episodes. What both the form
and content of *The Years* seem to be saying, then, is that later life is a
reliving and reshaping of experiences firmly rooted in childhood, and
that the familial ties based on those shared memories are the most
meaningful we will have in our lives. Although the later episodes of
The Years are less vivid than the first chapter, they are far more
successfully realized than the chapters in the holograph from which
they were drawn. It is here that Woolf's skill as a writer manifests
itself, for she literally transformed her raw material, giving drama and
color to scenes that are mere strings of dialogue in the original. Yet,
despite her skill, it is unlikely that Woolf could have created a fully
integrated novel unless she had completely abandoned her first draft;
the final version is still shaped by the form the holograph took, which
in turn was shaped by Woolf's own special way of experiencing her
life.

The problem Woolf faced in *The Years* when her initial enthusiasm
began to wane was not new to her. She had experienced it before,
notably in 1920, when she had barely begun work on *Jacob's Room*
before noticing a similar falling-off of interest: "It is worth
mentioning, for future reference, that the creative power which
bubbles so pleasantly in beginning a new book quiets down after a
time, and one goes on more steadily. Doubts creep in. Then one
becomes resigned. Determination not to give in, and the sense of an
impending shape keep one at it more than anything" (*AWD*, 11 May
1920, p. 26). But when she was writing *The Years*, the sense of
"impending shape" that had sustained her in the past was never
completely secure. Her first structuring device, "The Novel-Essay,"
proved unworkable, and the techniques of alternation, repetition, and
contrast were never quite comprehensive enough to bring together all

---

[1] In *Moments of Being* Woolf writes: "With mother's death the merry, various
family life which she had held in being shut for ever. In its place a dark cloud settled
over us; we seemed to sit all together cooped up, sad, solemn, unreal, under a haze
of heavy emotion." "A Sketch of the Past," in *Moments of Being*, 93.

the disparate elements in the novel.[2] Even in the published novel the continual shifts from representational narrative to fragmented speech, from static detached description to dramatic scenes caught *in medias res*, from one center of consciousness to another, can easily confuse the reader.

Woolf's comments in her diary as she wrote and rewrote the novel show that she was fully aware of this problem; she was continually preoccupied with the need to shape, compress, and integrate its heterogeneous material. As Jean Guiguet points out, it was unusual for her to focus so exclusively on this problem: "Whereas after each of her books she questions the value of what she has written, we must note that here, contrary to her usual habit, she is preoccupied by one very precise aspect; composition and unity."[3]

It may be that Woolf's failure to unify *The Years* stems from her decision to avoid the use of the extended interior monologues that characterize the novels of her middle period. The flexibility of this technique, which allowed her to move with her character, through a series of associations, from the sensation of the moment to a more abstract level where the thought of the individual becomes a kind of universal consciousness, gave Woolf the ability to connect the one with the many, the moment with the flux of time.[4]

In *The Years* no such fluidity is possible. The soliloquys in this novel are fairly conventional, and moments from the past are introduced mainly through the meetings of relatives and friends who reminisce together, rather than through Proustian associations. As Hafley has noted, in *The Years* it is "social behaviour instead of

---

[2]In Guiguet's view, "the synthesis of the two orders of reality, that of fact and that of vision, to use the author's own terms, remains insecure and intermittent and consequently fails to convince the reader" (312).

[3]Ibid., 308.

[4]Hafley writes: "Beneath the diverse points of view presented to the reader, there is an impersonal narrator—the central intelligence—of which, in and after *Mrs. Dalloway*, the reader is never allowed to become immediately aware, but which extends the idea of a common impulse beneath diversity. . . . The reader moves with confidence from one character to another, always conscious of a single point of view beneath, but never offensively so, since it is completely impersonal; thus he strings his impressions upon the very thread that is essential for their comprehensive significance." Hafley, 74. In *The Years* the central intelligence is much less in evidence, except in the preludes and interludes.

exclusive symbolism, that prompts and explains individual response."[5]

Elvira-Sara, the one character who might have provided a more wide-ranging consciousness, whose literary inclinations and agile mind might have served as an effective balance to Eleanor's rather prosaic musings, is seldom allowed to soliloquize. In "1907," when Sara lies in bed reading *Antigone* and imagining she is a tree, she is able to provide a visionary perspective on the social scene she is observing. In the holograph, where Elvira aspires to be a writer, this role is even more pronounced. But after "1907," Elvira-Sara is seen only from the outside—we can follow her thoughts only by following her spoken words, which are often nearly unintelligible.

Elvira is by far the most interesting character in the holograph, and even as the somewhat more subdued Sara her eccentricity is a welcome contrast to the ordinariness of the others. But Elvira is shrill and angry—her character seems to have its source in the less stable elements in Woolf's own personality. It may be that Woolf was trying to keep these tendencies within herself under control by limiting Elvira's role in the novel.

The holograph hints at other possible solutions to the problem of unity, particularly in the final chapter. There we see Elvira moving away from her separatist position and joining Eleanor, who has absorbed some of her cousins' visionary tendencies. As the family gathers around Eleanor, she becomes matriarchal and prophetic. Later, as Woolf reworked this material, she de-emphasized the movement toward Eleanor and planned to center the chapter on Nicholas' speech (*AWD*, 17 July 1935, p. 252). It is possible that in some interim version of the novel Nicholas was allowed to make his speech, but in the final version he is interrupted by the others, each of whom expresses his characteristic point of view. This is exactly opposite to the tactic Woolf adopted at the end of *The Waves*, where she decided at the very end to "merge all the interjected passages into Bernard's final speech and end with the words O solitude . . ." (*AWD*, 22 December, 1930, p. 162). The decision to create a reverse effect in *The Years*, to break up a single speech into a series of

[5]Ibid., 133.

fragments, suggests a fundamental difference in intention, a move away from unity and closure.

Ultimately, then, the lack of unity in *The Years* is much more than a question of technique. In a novel which attempts to include everything, to face the facts of life in this world, the only possibility for an integrated point of view lies in finding some perspective that transcends daily life. *The Years* describes a quest for such a perspective; in moments of solitude, and in conversation, the characters search for some philosophy, some way of looking at life that can provide a sense of order and meaning in the face of burgeoning events.

At different times, both Eleanor and Sara look to the Christian tradition for some glimpse of meaning. Eleanor puzzles over a passage from Dante and reads Renan to learn about the origins of the faith; Sara reads Job and goes to St. Paul's, trying to understand how people feel when they pray (*TY*, 154–55 and 229–30). We know from Woolf's diary that she herself was exploring Christianity as she wrote *The Years*, reading Renan and the Old Testament and thinking of renaming Elvira after St. Theresa (*AWD*, 1 Jan. 1935, p. 236; 23 Jan. 1935, p. 238). Religious themes are introduced into the novel in many ways: the figure of an old man or woman feeding sparrows, a kind of St. Francis, appears here and there, and Eleanor is described as an abbess as she sits in a cellar resembling a Roman catacomb. Woolf's attitude toward Christianity, if not toward the church, seems to have shifted in the years since *The Voyage Out*, when she wrote, with apparent approval, of Mrs. Dalloway's efforts to make her children think of God as a "kind of walrus."[6]

Woolf's growing interest in Christianity will become even more pronounced in *Between the Acts*, where, as Hafley notes, for the first time in her novels a devout Christian, Mrs. Swithin, is presented sympathetically.[7] Yet despite these intimations of interest in a traditional system of belief, nothing in *The Years* suggests a firm acceptance of faith. As in Woolf's earlier works, the moments of vision her characters are granted are intermittent. Woolf's own position at the end of *The Years* seems much the same as that expressed by Lily

[6]Woolf, *The Voyage Out*, 27.
[7]Hafley, 149.

Briscoe to *To the Lighthouse*: "The great revelation had never come. The great revelation perhaps never did come. Instead there were little daily miracles, illuminations, matches struck unexpectedly in the dark. . . ."[8]

For Eleanor, one such match was struck by Nicholas, who showed her that even in the midst of an air raid the events of their time could be placed in the long perspective of man's history on earth. Through Nicholas' exposition of his theory of the evolution of the soul another way of looking at daily life is presented. His view suggests that what can be experienced in one lifetime is insignificant, since the progress of civilization is so slow that it is barely perceptible to the individual, who sees only confusion. In the holograph, Elvira shares his long-range point of view; her remark about the way men of the future will look back on us with disgust (*TY*, 189) expresses her belief in man's progress—so that the way we live now will seem as brutish and bleak to the people of the future as the lives of cave men seem to us.

But Eleanor, whose personal search for order and meaning provides one of the threads of continuity in the novel, cannot long accept either an other-worldly religion or a utopian dream. She wants to believe in happiness here and now, with living people, and Woolf, who once thought of calling this novel *Here and Now*, seems to agree (*AWD*, 16 Jan. 1934, p. 215). In *The Years* one finds many moments of quiet celebration of ordinary things. Eleanor delights in technological advances: lights that go on in an instant and hot water that gushes from her taps. She has lived long enough to know the discomforts of the past, when rooms were dim and chilly, and servants struggled up steep stairs with buckets of hot water for their masters' baths. The modern world has freed her from the difficult master-servant relation; it has downed barriers so that subjects no one dared broach around the Victorian tea table are bandied back and forth between friends.[9]

Eleanor and Rose have seen women move out of the confines of the

---

[8]Woolf, *To the Lighthouse*, 240.

[9]In *Moments of Being*, Woolf describes the liberating effect of Lytton Strachey's use of the word "semen" in mixed company: "Can one really say it? I thought and we burst out laughing. With that one word all barriers of reticence and reserve went down. . . . Sex permeated our conversation." "Old Bloomsbury," in *Moments of Being*, 173–74.

drawing room into the professions; they have watched Maggie and Renny work out a marriage unlike any their parents could have known.

Even in the midst of the tumult of the final party, one finds these quiet moments when ordinary people, speaking in their natural voices, effect changes more meaningful than any that can be found in political programs blared from loudspeakers.[10] North, who went off to war because it was the "thing to do," has learned to despise ambition and empire-building—he wants to find a new way to live and turns to his cousins for advice. Peggy, fearing that marriage will trap him into conformity, tries to warn him. At first he misunderstands her, but their common childhood proves a bond that transcends their differences; they come together for a moment of affection and communion. And Eleanor, holding on to her knotted handkerchief, manages to remember to talk to Edward about a university education for the porter's son.

But in the context of the novel as a whole, these hopeful incidents fade in comparison to the powerful images of despair and disintegration that are reiterated throughout.[11] Though the Pargiter family is comfortably middle class, they live within the sights and smells of poverty, sickness, and decay. Unlike the Ramsay's seaside house or Mrs. Dalloway's drawing room, the stuffy house on Abercorn Terrace is no sanctuary of beauty and serenity. When the Pargiter children try to escape its confines, they find themselves forced to deal with the most unpleasant facts of city life: with grease-ringed bathtubs, conniving workmen, and undercooked, slimy food. And though the holograph and proofs are generally more grim than *The Years*, an ominous warning remains—the fat face of the dictator gesticulating on the front page of the newspaper.

Along with sickness and decay, death plays a prominent role in the lives of the Pargiters. The figure of death is always a presence in

[10]Comstock has used the contrast between the demagogues' loudspeaker and people talking in their natural voices as a basis for her interpretation of *The Years*. Comstock, 252–75.

[11]As Nancy Topping Bazin puts it, the "tone of horror coexists with but prevails over the tone of naive optimism." Bazin, *Virginia Woolf and the Androgynous Vision*, 180.

Virginia Woolf's novels, as it had figured so often in her life. But the form death takes is different in this work; it is a death that comes with a slow deterioration of body and mind, wholly unlike the romantic end that Clarissa Dalloway called a "defiance," an "embrace."[12] When people die in *The Years* they die slowly, in pain and loneliness; they do not leap from windows or perish in their youth of exotic tropical fevers.

This gloomy realism reflects the atmosphere in which Woolf lived as she was writing the novel, for this was a period which took its toll of those she loved most dearly. Leonard Woolf recalled, "The erosion of life by death began for Virginia and me in the early 1930's and gathered momentum as we went downhill to war and her own death. It began on 21 January 1932 when Lytton Strachey died of cancer. This was the beginning of the end of what we used to call Old Bloomsbury."[13]

Lytton's death and the suicide of his companion, Dora Carrington, soon after, left Virginia with a profound feeling of emptiness and despair. When she wrote her novels and essays, she was often stimulated by the thought of her friends' responses to her work, so that with the disappearance of her lifelong intimates her sense of communication was diminished.[14] Lytton Strachey, whom she had loved and admired for so long, seemed to have disappeared without a trace. In her diary that February she wrote: "I wake in the night with the sense of being in an empty hall. Lytton dead and those factories building. What is the point of it—life—when I'm not working— suddenly becomes thin, indifferent. Lytton is dead, and nothing definite to mark it. Also they write flimsy articles about him" (*AWD*, 8 Feb. 1932, p. 179).

The death of friends marked the growing turmoil in her world; ugly factories were springing up to block her beloved view of the Sussex hills, and the ominous rumblings of fascism abroad and

[12]Woolf, *Mrs. Dalloway*, 280–81.

[13]*DAW*, 250.

[14]When she learned of Stella Benson's death, Woolf wrote: "A curious feeling when a writer like S. B. dies, that one's response is diminished: *Here and Now* won't be lit up by her: its life lessened (*AWD*, 7 Dec. 1933, p. 214).

economic depression at home compounded her feeling that something had gone wrong.

In the face of these fears Woolf had begun to work on *The Years*, hoping that writing the novel would bring "order and speed" again into her world (*AWD*, 25 May 1932, p. 181). But given her experiences during these years, it is questionable whether Woolf could have created the kind of synthesis she had been struggling to achieve, whether in fact the novel's stubborn refusal to cohere came from a deep division within herself and within the society she was trying to come to terms with.

In Woolf's earlier works she had enclosed a portion of the world in a private vision, limiting her concern to a few people, a few events, a few memories. The first part of *To the Lighthouse*, which is, in my opinion, more complete than anything else she has written, was in fact an elegy, a recapitulation of the past. It represented the sunlit world of her childhood, a world no longer available to her by the time she wrote *The Years*. Leonard Woolf tells us that at the time she was struggling to complete *The Years* he took her to St. Ives, where she had summered as a child, hoping that a return to that familiar scene would soothe her jangled nerves.[15] But Talland House and Godrevy Lighthouse could no longer weave their spell—too much had happened in the intervening years.

What had happened was partly Woolf's own growth as a person and a writer, and her decision to break the mold of her earlier works, to include more of life in her novels. This greater openness is responsible for many of her problems with *The Years*, and she was not always able to solve them. Yet the very unevenness of the novel, its lack of resolution, reflects a willingness to take risks, a growing maturity. Later, looking back on her struggle with *The Years*, Woolf was able to see that whether or not it had succeeded as a novel, writing *The Years* has been a profound experience: "I also know that I have reached my point of view, as writer, as being" (*AWD*, 7 March 1937, p. 277). For her, the writing of *The Years* had been more than a creative process; it had been a means of self-discovery.

Despite the many difficulties it presents, *The Years* deserves a place

[15]*DAW*, 153–54.

as one of Virginia Woolf's great novels. Its dignity, its quiet, unadorned language, have a felicity all their own. *The Years* is a courageous novel: it eschews all easy victories. Its heroines are homely spinsters, its romances take place offstage, its scenes are set in the most ordinary of surroundings. Yet it manages to convey the excitement of life as it is lived by people who struggle to understand the meaning of what is happening to them, and to face the realities of war and poverty, ugliness and death. And throughout one hears a quiet voice that may be Virginia Woolf's own, telling us that happiness is possible; that life is interesting and worth living; that one must be open to the future; that against all odds, one must not despair.

APPENDIX

Galley Proofs of Episodes Excluded During Final Revisions of
The Years
The first unpublished episode is set in 1917, just before Maggie's
dinner party. As the scene opens, Crosby, the Pargiter's housekeeper,
who is retired now, is taking her landlady's grandchildren to the park.

WARTIME LONDON

STEP up, step up," Crosby grumbled at the two
gaping children who were gazing at the soldiers. A
company of young men in khaki were marching down
Richmond High Street. A drum beat a regular tick,
tick, tick, tick. They marched in time to it with their
collars undone and their faces red and shiny after the
march.

It was very warm. The sultry September sunshine
lay in broad stretches across the pavement. Crosby in
her respectable black was glad to reach the shade
thrown by an awning over a shop. She was taking Mrs
Burt's two grandchildren, Alf and Gladys, for a walk
in Kew Gardens after tea. She was always ready to
oblige Louisa—and in fact liked the task; it gave her a
sense of her own importance. "Step up," she repeated,
"step up," and the children trotted on. The soldiers
marched away. Now she reached out and caught Alf
in one hand and Gladys in the other, for there was a
road crossing in front of them. The street outside the
station was crowded. A train had come in, and people
were hurrying up the steps from the station and stream-
ing across the road with newspapers crumpled in their
hands. Newspaper boys, with fresh bales of newspapers
under their arms, were beginning to scatter through
the streets crying the latest news.

Crosby kept her hand on the children's shoulders
until it was safe to cross.

"Now—" she said, making the great decision; they
all scuttled over in a body. Now they were safe on the
long stretch of road that led without crossings to the
gate at Kew. Her legs pained her, so that her walk, as

she hobbled along, resembled the flutter of a steadfast
but uneasy hen. The children, however, could be
trusted to walk alone. Sometimes one or the other gave
a little caper, or lagged annoyingly, but for the most
part they walked obediently, hand in hand, with their
toys pressed close to their sides just ahead of her. At
their age, Crosby thought, Martin and Rose would
have been up to all sorts of tricks. She could see Martin
now, holding a bottle of milk above his head and
bringing it down with a smash on the pavement outside the Park. "Out of sheer devilry," she said to
herself. "And I had to laugh," she added, shaking her
old head, wrinkling her old cheeks at the memory. But
Alf and Gladys were sober, straight-haired children,
with no spirit in them, she thought, as they trudged on
along the dusty road just ahead of her.

When they reached the gardens Crosby hobbled off
to her usual seat under the tree near the gate, for her
legs pained her; she was too tired to walk further. She
sat down and looked about, resting her eyes vaguely
on the blazing beds of autumn flowers. Then she took
out her sewing and began stitching at the white calico
nightgown she was making. Her needle pricked along
the hem with a sound like a mouse nibbling. Every
now and then she looked up over her spectacles to see
that the children were not in mischief. No; they were
playing on the grass. Her eye rested once more vaguely,
like an insect sunning itself, on the red and yellow
flowers. Then she bent over her sewing again; she
made a little noise like tu-tut-tut as her needle pricked
through the stiff white stuff.

But though it was a fine evening, the breeze was

freshening; now and then a gold-spotted leaf came spiralling to the grass at her feet; her ankles felt chilly. Then the children began to worry her. They kept coming up and laying their toys on her knees, and asking what they were to play at next. They wanted to go to the lake, they said; Alf wanted to sail his boat. She stitched on imperviously until she had finished her hem. Then she rolled up her sewing.

"Come along, then," she said, putting her things in her bag. "And then we must go home," she added, checking her indulgence as if by instinct.

The little covey moved off in the direction of the lake. The gardens were rather full. Family parties were straying down the broad grass walks, middle-aged women for the most part, who sauntered, and chatted episodically, keeping one eye on the children. Some parties had brought their tea with them; there were rugs on the grass, spread with cups and bottles of milk. But it was getting late, and the mothers were putting the tea things away while the children played by the lake. The decorated water-birds, beautifully picked out with black and white, stepped statelily among them. Alf and Gladys went cautiously hand in hand down to the water's edge. Alf stooped and launched his boat. Crosby looked after her for a seat in the sun but out of the wind. She would give them a quarter of an hour before she took them home.

There was a seat, but it was already occupied by an old man eating something out of a paper bag; by a woman knitting; and by a young man who sat beside her making notes in a little book. But there was room for her if they sat closer. They edged together, and she took her place at the end of the seat. Nobody spoke. The young man went on jotting down notes, and the young woman went on knitting. Crosby disliked the old man who was eating out of a paper bag—now he was scattering crumbs to the birds and the sparrows came fluttering round, hopping and pecking. But she liked the young married couple—the little boy in a green jersey who was playing about was their first child, she guessed. Then there was a cry from the water; one of the geese had run at Alf and pecked him.

"Don't meddle with them birds, Alf!" Crosby cried. "They'll hurt you!"

Alf desisted. The goose waddled off.

"They're dangerous, those birds," she said, turning to the young married couple. But they paid her no attention. The woman called to her child; at the same moment the young man got up, put his book in his pocket and walked off. Crosby was put out. She had been mistaken. They were not a married couple. They did not even know each other. She was annoyed at having spoken, since nobody bothered to answer her.

The young man walked away from the lake down the broad grass sweep rather slowly, for he was totting up figures in his head. He was a traveller in men's underwear, and he was making a rough total of his day's sales. On the whole he hadn't done so badly; business was still fairly brisk, considering. He lit a cigarette and glanced casually at the trees and flowers. They were a fine show certainly. Many people had stopped to look at them. Some of the flowers were as big as a man's head; all curled. But he knew nothing about flowers, and he had a train to catch. His pace

quickened and he walked briskly through the gate, an down the street of villas that led to the station. He wa a trained traveller; he had an instinct which told him he walked fast, but not too fast, he would about catc his train.

He was right; the train came in as he arrived, an yet he had not hurried. He threw away his cigarett and swung himself on board. He found a seat too; bu he had to hold his bag on his knee for the train was fu of soldiers. They stood in a line down the middle of th carriage, hanging on to the straps, talking and jokin as if they had been out all day taking exercise togethe Their faces were red; the necks of their uniforms wer open. The civilian passengers kept looking up at them surreptitiously over the edges of their newspaper They looked at them admiringly; they smiled furtivel at their chaff. There was a good deal to be said for the job, Bert Parker thought—glancing at them, over h order-book; then he wetted his finger and turned th flimsy page—compared with his one. But he hadn done so badly, all things considered. He jotted down figure at the bottom of the page. Now they wer sliding into Hammersmith station. Most of the soldier got out there; they jostled and chaffed each other a they tramped down the carriage clumsily with the sacks on their shoulders, obviously conscious of th admiring glances that were cast on them. Newspaper were now lowered.

"What a nice-looking set of young fellows!" a elderly lady murmured, looking over her shoulder the soldiers who were now lining up on the platforn as the train started off. There was more room now Bert Parker put his bag on the seat beside him. Peop unfolded their newspapers, spreading the sheets wid so that "Three British Cruisers Sunk" was repeate again and again in large black letters on the front pag of one newspaper after another. The newspapers we turned over, as if the readers were searching for mor information. But they could find nothing more abou the disasters, only items. The wife of a postman Andover had been brought to bed of triplets; a baske of ripe strawberries had been picked at Sidmouth—that was all. They sat with their papers on their knee The train had left the open, and was rattling throug the tunnel. Now that the soldiers had gone there wa no laughter or chaffing; the passengers stared at eac other, or looked at their own reflections on the gla lined-tunnel.

The meagre white-haired old lady who had liked th look of the soldiers, had no paper and she screwed u her eyes and tried to read the headline on the man paper who sat beside her. But she was short-sighte He looked like a gentleman, however—he had a rin on his finger and he wore a grey suit—so that sh plucked up courage to say to him, rather nervously, the train ran into the station.

"If you've done with your paper, might I . . . "

He gave it her with a little jerk, and sat staring ahea of him. He had, she noticed, rather fierce blue eye Now that she had taken his paper he sat staring at th people in front of him. Since all movement or actio was impossible, they were all staring in front of them There was something in the passive and stolid appear ance of the other passengers that seemed to annoy hin He kept crossing and uncrossing his legs. He looke quickly up and down the row of faces. Nobody move

The Years—182

Nobody spoke. Since there were five more stations to be passed before he reached his station, and since each station took two minutes to reach, he must sit there for ten minutes longer. The train rattled and banged. Whenever he found himself shut up somewhere without anything to do, words seemed to come together in his head. His lips moved. What for, what for, what for, the train seemed to be growling as it rattled through South Kensington station. He looked at the respectable ladies in their drab hats and coats; he looked at a young man with a note-book puffing rings of smoke through his nose; he looked at a corpulent red-faced man with a heavy silver chain across his waistcoat. They were all of the respectable classes, save for a flower-woman with a basket at the door: Her naked arms were folded across her breast; a broad gold wedding ring was sunk into the fat of her fingers; and the feather in her bonnet jerked ridiculously as the train shook. Nobody moved or spoke. Everybody seemed to be gloating; to have fed on the garbage in the newspapers; and to be passively chewing the cud. He felt that if this went on he must get up and cry out. Suddenly he caught the reflection of his own face on the glass-lined wall opposite. He saw a red-faced man with a grey moustache staring back at him, quite indistinguishable from the others.

"Thanks so much," said the old lady, politely returning his newspaper. He grasped it in his fist as the train swept into the whiteness of the station. It was not his station, but he could sit there no longer looking at his own reflection in the glass. He got up and tried to push his way out between the slowly-moving bodies of his fellow passengers. But they moved with extreme slowness; he had to mark time behind them. People outside were pressing to get in. The conductor gave his automatic shout, "Passengers off first please!" as he warded off the new-comers. At last the man with the grey moustache forced his way out. Then the new passengers crowded in and took the places that had been left empty.

A girl in evening dress sat down on top of the newspaper that he had left in his seat. A young officer in uniform stood up in front of her holding on to the strap. The elderly lady who had borrowed the newspaper looked sidelong at them, smiling slightly; she strained her head on one side to catch what they said. "What a rush we had getting off!" the girl said, looking up at the officer. There was no need that she should say it; but she felt that people wanted to hear her speak. A vague sympathy, a dumb admiration, surrounded them wherever they went. She had to say something. They're having a last night together before he goes to the Front, the old lady thought, straining to hear what the fine young fellow in uniform was saying. But he hardly spoke. His hand went mechanically to his chin; little clipped words seemed to issue from his firm red lips. The old woman strained to catch what it was he said.

"Good," he said. "Good. Good," he repeated curtly, shortly. He seemed to be trained to stand stiffly and to speak shortly. She admired it very much. An officer, going to the Front, she thought.

The train ran into Piccadilly Circus. They rose and went out. Eyes glanced appreciatively after them, as the girl went first and the officer followed protectively behind her. The old lady looked over her shoulder

The Years—183

after them as they walked along the platform. They are going to the play, she told herself. Perhaps it's their last night together, she thought. Sad as the thought was, there was a sweetness in it which gave her a thrill of something like pleasure. But here the train stopped at Leicester Square, and she fluttered out onto the platform. It would have been a relief to her if somebody had asked her to help them; she looked along the platform in case any one wanted to be directed for instance to the Hampstead tube; but nobody wanted to be helped, and the liftman clanged the door in her face as she reached the gate.

Dear, dear, she said as she stood in the draught. How provoking! Now I shall keep her waiting. The draught swirled the skirts round her thin legs. But thousands of young men, she thought, are standing in the rain; thousands are lying wounded, she thought, clapping her hands to her skirts. Here the lift opened its door and she hurried in. I'm afraid I'm late, she thought, and perhaps she'll have gone in. Perhaps it had been foolish to tell her to get the tickets; it might have been better for each to have got her own ticket separately. Her sense of inefficiency, her usual little worries returned to her, as she hurried out into Leicester Square.

For a moment she was bewildered, for she had lost her sense of direction. The streets were glaring with light. Advertisements were popping in and out. The names of the theatres were framed in blue and red lines; there was a bottle of beer that poured and stopped, then poured again. The sky glared as if a red and yellow canopy hung down over it. Uncertain of her way, she trotted a few steps towards Trafalgar Square. Birds were making a high shrill squealing in the air. No, that was wrong. She stopped. It must be the other way. Of course . . . there was the Coliseum with its globe on top of it. Long queues stood in the street, moving slowly as if they were being gradually swallowed by a snake. The people were moving on step by step. Some of them were eating bananas; others were reading newspapers; men were turning somersaults and playing horns; but the queue moved slowly; then stopped; then moved on again, as if the snake had swallowed another mouthful. Taxis were arriving; people in evening dress were jumping out even before the kerb was reached; they were pushing through the swing doors into the brightly-lit hall. Miriam Parrish hurried along; peering anxiously this way and that, and at last caught sight of a woman standing just within the door whom she recognised.

"Oh, Eleanor, my dear!" she exclaimed, "I'm afraid I've kept you waiting!"

"Nothing to matter," said Eleanor; and they took their seats just as the curtain rose.

Now that the rush was over, the streets emptied themselves and became quiet. It seemed, in the theatre quarter, that everybody had gone indoors. The plays had begun; the feast of entertainment was spread; everybody had taken their places. An occasional taxi drifted along; the omnibuses scarcely waited and swooped along quickly with only a handful of passengers in them. The starlings which had been making a shrill discordant chatter on the eaves of St. Martins Church and round the walls of the National Gallery

The Years—184

ceased. Nelson's Column rose elongated, patched with yellow at the base; but as the night deepened the little figure and the coil of rope became dead black against the sky. Spangles, crescents of light, were reflected in the black water in the basins of Trafalgar Square. The moon was almost full, and within its radius the sky was clear and blue; but over the theatres it glared yellower and redder, and the signs, the advertisements, the bottles of beer that poured and stopped, the faces in the streets, became more and more clear-cut as the night deepened.

For an hour or two the neighbourhood had the air of a room that has been deserted; but just before eleven the rush of life began again. People poured out of the theatres; taxis wheeled circled and hooted; omnibuses drew up; were filled over and over again; and the streets were full of people in evening dress, or in their ordinary clothes, making their way to the tubes and the trains that were to take them home.

Eleanor and Miriam Parrish came out into the street together.

"I did enjoy that!" Miriam Parrish exclaimed. She gave Eleanor's arm a little squeeze as they stood for a moment in the crowd. "And I never guessed how it was going to end—did you?" she said.

"No," said Eleanor. "I never guessed. It took me quite by surprise." Until five minutes of the end, she had believed that the innocent man was the villain. She stood still for a moment; she was still under the influence of the play. She had to readjust all her ideas. She had been completely taken in.

"I suppose one ought to have guessed," she said, thinking of the plot. "But I didn't—no." They began to walk along the street. Miriam was going home by tube. They reached the station.

"How nice it's been, spending an evening together," she said, giving Eleanor's arm a little pinch. "Do let us meet again soon. Now where do you get your bus? . . ." She was beginning to fumble for her purse.

"Oh, just down there," said Eleanor. "I shall walk," she added. "Good night, Miriam." She turned away. Miriam disappeared down the lift.

It was a fine night and the air was refreshing after the hot theatre. She liked walking after the play. She would walk before she took her omnibus. She crossed into Trafalgar Square. It looked vast and empty, scattered here and there with small black figures. It was odd, she thought, how completely she had been taken in; not until five minutes before the end had she realised—she began to go over the plot again. But a voice said behind her, "Ah, but it's not a time for picking and choosing. . . ." At first she thought the words were spoken to her. She looked round. Two middle-aged men of the professional class were passing her. She stopped for a moment to let them go by. They were talking about the War; she had forgotten the War; she had been absorbed in the play. She had a momentary feeling of guilt. How childish, she thought, moving on, to have been absorbed in a story, when—when what? She looked up at the sky. The moon was almost full; it was so clear that the craters showed on it like engravings on a beautifully polished silver coin.

The Years—185

Not a cloud softened its sharp edges; the sky round it was dappled with yellow silver light. She looked at Cockspur Street lying in front of her.

There was nothing in particular to fix her eyes upon. Everything seemed much as usual. People were walking along, in couples, singly, rather quickly, as they did when it was late and they were anxious to get home. They were snapping up taxis; they were crowding into omnibuses. Yet somewhere—she glanced at the sky again—somewhere—she glanced at a great stone building—behind this, behind this—again she hesitated. Again she felt a feeling of guilt. There was something to see and she did not see it; something to feel and she did not feel it. She glanced back at the two men who had passed her. They were rapidly disappearing. They were feeling it, she thought, remembering their words—something about picking and choosing, while she had been absorbed in the play. But everything seemed much as usual. The air blew fresh on her face. She liked walking in London, at night especially, when the outlines of buildings showed; the detail that distracted one by day was lost; and it became larger and more dignified. She walked up the Haymarket, admiring the curve of the street. The dignity of the street, clear blue and spacious, made her remember, as she walked, how she had sat on a terrace, looking at hills. And the maid came out on the terrace, she thought, and said, Soldiers are guarding the line with fixed bayonets! There it was, sure enough; the familiar feeling. She sighed. And I said to myself, Not if I can help it, she thought, recalling the emotion with which, putting down her coffee-cup, she had looked at the hills fading into darkness, and had thought . . . some absurd thought about England: England in danger.

An omnibus stopped beside her. She had meant to walk; but she felt a sudden disinclination to walk by herself. It would be better to be with other people, she thought. Other people, she thought, getting into the omnibus, stop one from thinking. They're a help. . . . She sat down. She looked round the omnibus as she settled herself. It was almost full. All the other passengers looked sleepy, surly and rather tired after their night's outing. There was the usual City clerk and his young lady; the usual woman with a child on her knee; the usual nondescript elderly ladies who always puzzled her, since it was difficult to guess how they lived . . . but the conductor was collecting fares. He too looked surly. He was collecting coppers, taking them without a word. Now he had taken them, he stood in the door checking figures on a sheet. Nobody spoke; nobody moved. She glanced out of the window at the long line of shops on either side, the expensive shops in Piccadilly; that were all, at this hour of the night, shuttered, blank. There was very little traffic. At this hour of the night the omnibuses scarcely stopped; she saw a couple raise their hands; but the driver ignored them. The omnibus rushed on, swaying from side to side, as it took the long stretch of empty road at full speed.

"Papa's club," she said, looking up at the large building which she had passed so often.

The omnibus was so well-lit that she could have read, if she had anything to read. But she had nothing to read except the programme which she held in her hand. And the omnibus shook too much. They swept on. Here was Hyde Park Corner. She looked at the

yellow clock in the little house at the corner. At this
rate, she thought, I shall be home in no time. She
glanced at the faces again. The conductor was leaning
against the stairs, staring blankly in front of him. The
woman holding the child on her knee had put her
ticket in her mouth. Why take a child of that age out
at this time of night? Eleanor asked herself, and she
began to make up a little story to account for it—
perhaps she had been visiting her husband, who was
wounded, in one of the City hospitals—when the bus
stopped with a jerk; the woman got up and lurched,
carrying the child, down the gangway out onto the
pavement. She set the child on its feet; and the bus
swooped on. Perhaps she was a caretaker, Eleanor
thought, trying to go on with her story: but late at
night when people were too tired to talk, the little
stories that one made up in omnibuses were unsatis-
factory. Everyone seemed numbed and torpid. The
girl was dropping off to sleep with her head on her
young man's shoulder. She opened her eyes when it
swerved.

We're going much too fast, Eleanor thought, as
they cut round corners and swooped round lamp-posts
At this time of night the bus travelled at an enormous
speed. Here they stopped again. More people got out.
The conductor scarcely allowed them time to get off
before he touched the bell. Now she was the only
person left. The conductor leant with his back to the
stairs and half shut his eyes. The light seemed brighter
in this emptiness. She was rattled about like a pea in a
bladder, since there was nobody on either side of her.
She edged up so as to sit in the corner.

When it stops I shall get off, she said to herself. She
looked over her shoulder to see where they had got
to. I shall get off when we come to the public-house,
he decided. There were the lamps glaring, there were
the claret- and buff-painted walls of the public-house.
She got up and jumped off quickly. Almost before she
had found her feet the bus had started again.

"They don't give one much time," she said angrily,
looking after the disappearing omnibus. But it was a
relief to be on her own feet again; it was a relief to feel
the fresh air on her face, and out here in this suburb,
the night, without statues or advertisements, without
theatres, without the stare of faces under arc lamps, was
almost the natural night: the night itself. The streets
were deserted.

The long avenue curved before her with one sil-
houette. The houses were all small middle-class villas
with little front gardens, bow-windows jutting out,
and a flight of steps that ran up to the hall door. All
looked equally demure as she passed them; blind and
safely curtained for the night. People kept early hours
out here; the husbands had to go early to the City in
the morning. Now and then a tree broke the monotony
of the line; its shadows flickered on the pavement.
Leaves hung separate, for some had fallen; there was a
faint smell of the autumnal earth. Not a single figure
appeared in the whole length of the avenue. Only cats
were about, slinking silently close to the wall. The soft
green light in their eyes glowed at her for a second;
and then became suddenly extinct. She heard her own
footsteps tap on the pavement.

She had some way to walk before she saw the vast
block of flats in which she lived rising at the corner.
A company had pulled down half a street and built

them for "middle-class people of limited incomes,"
There was no lift; otherwise, as the advertisement put
it, they were "replete with every modern con-
venience"; and cheap, certainly. She rehearsed these
advantages often as she came in sight of her home. And
then there's the magnificent view, she always added; I
like being right on top. Here she looked up to the three
windows on the very top next the roof.

Everybody else was already in, she noticed as she
let herself in and looked at the board in the hall. In. In.
In. In. The Smiths, the Jenkinsons, the Beards, the
Ropers; the whole lot of them were in. They always
were at this time of night. She had to climb high up on
top of them to get to her own flat. She had six flights
of stone steps to climb before she reached her door.
But what a pleasure it still was, she thought, as she
toiled up and up, to come and go as one liked; to feel
that there was nobody—here she fitted her key in her
lock—sitting up for her. Her milk was standing outside; the newspaper was pushed through the letter-box;
and when she went in, letters were scattered in a fan
shape in the hall.

She still enjoyed the ease and rapidity of the "modern
conveniences." She touched a knob, and the sitting-
room was lit. She lit a match and the gas fire was
burning. There was her breakfast tray on the kitchen
table; and she had only to light the gas ring and the
kettle would be boiling in five minutes. Warmth, light,
comfort, sprang into being at a touch.

She still felt, when she came into her sitting-room, a
sense of being very high up. After living for so many
years on the ground floor at Abercorn Terrace, she felt
here high up, airy, exalted. The curtains had not been
drawn, and she looked for a moment at London lying
beneath her. She looked down upon innumerable
roofs, sloping, shining on one side, dark on the other.
Then there were the odd squares and divisions made
by walls; here and there a high building rose with a
streak of yellow light on it; and by day one could see
a blue line of hill in the distance which she always called
"the Surrey hills." That was now invisible. But tonight there was an extraordinary expanse of sky; the
moon was shining; there was a look of gaiety in the
sky, which was spread with that look of dappled
iridescence that comes sometimes when the moon is
full. Below was the yellow light that never ceased, the
glare of London.

She sat down to warm herself while the kettle
boiled. The little white skulls in the fire were already
dark red. The heat stole over her hands and face. She
sat for a moment spreading her hands in it. Then she
took the pack of letters from the table and began
shuffling through them. None looked interesting;
except Crosby's, for Crosby, she thought, opening the
cheap envelope, always writes as if she were talking;
without stops; capital letters at odd intervals; a volley
of sound, as if she were talking . . . but there was a
hissing in the kitchen. The kettle was boiling over. She
went into the kitchen; made her tea and came back
holding the cup in her hand.

The evening paper which she had thrown on the
table caught her eye. Three British cruisers sunk—she
had read that on all the posters already. She supposed
she must look and see if the list were out of what Mrs
Robins, her char, called "casualities." "Casualities,
casualities," she murmured as she spread the paper on

The Years—188

her knee. There were some names in the stop-press news; but none that meant anything to her until she came to the name Rankin.

That can't be the man I met at Morris's in the summer? she asked. She tried to remember. He had been a sailor. His Christian name—what was it? Lionel, she thought. This man was Lionel. She looked up. Captain Rankin; a nice ordinary man who had taught them how to make knots.

"Aren't sailors charming people?" Celia had said as he opened the door for them. "And they dance so beautifully." They had been going up to bed. She looked down at the paper again. It must be him, she supposed. For a second she felt a wish to put out her hand and stop him as he opened the drawing-room door. But how could I have stopped him? she asked herself. She had not stopped him. She saw the gently swaying waves lifting him up and down as he lay helpless in the moonlight. And they had gone upstairs. A sense of futility came over her. But how could I have stopped him? she said aloud. It was absurd. She ran her eyes hastily over the other names in the newspaper, but she knew none of them. And the paper went on with little separate items: ". . . the wife of a postman at Andover was brought to bed of twins," she read. And a basket of strawberries . . . she threw the paper away. She sat there staring at the gas-fire; then she looked round her bright clean room. There was her mother's picture over the writing-table; and the cabinet full of china. She felt as if she were perched up, dry, isolated, in a high, safe place, overlooking the sea. But what's the use of thinking? she said to herself angrily, and began to open her letters. One was a demand for rates; another to say that Edward would lunch with her on Tuesday; another that a committee would meet on Thursday at four instead of Friday at two. She had better write it down while she remembered it. She went to her writing-table and crossed out one engagement and added the other. All the little compartments were becoming full. Every day in the week had its

pencilled note. People were meeting. . . . And that was the day I meant to start for India, she thought, glancing at a certain Friday round which she had drawn a red ring. Then she stooped and turned out the gas; she waited till it made its little pop. The skulls began to fade. And the wife of the postman, she thought, glancing at the paper, has had triplets. It was odd—birth, destruction. She saw the three red faces under a flannel hood. The triplets seemed to throw a shaft of light into the future. She made a little calculation. If they were born yesterday, she thought, touching her fingers, in nineteen-twenty-four they'll be ten; in nineteen thirty-four, twenty; in nineteen-forty-four—when I shall be dead, she thought, getting up. No: possibly I shall still be alive, she thought. I hope so, she added. She wanted to go on living. It was odd.

She went into the bathroom. It gave her a thrill of pleasure. It was lined with gleaming white tiles; the taps shone silver; jars and brushes stood on a shining glass shelf. She lit the geyser; water instantly began to steam into the pure white bath. At Abercorn Terrace it always ran cold, she remembered. She began to undress. Yes, she thought as she slipped off her clothes and hung them on a silver hook, this is luxury, a hot bath. And to think, she thought, taking the pins out of her hair, that if I'd had a quarter of a millionth part of

The Years—189

that money—she saw Rigby Cottages again and the sunflower with a crack down the middle, I could have . . . But what's the use of thinking? she thought. The steam rose in a cloud; she turned on the cold tap. She waited for a moment for the water to be cool enough to get into. She was stark naked; the window had no blind. She stood looking at the dappled iridescence of the moon-lit sky, which seemed to make her bathroom whiter, cleaner, more dazzling in its purity than ever and then she stepped in.

The second unpublished episode would have appeared just before the final, or "Present Day" chapter. In the galleys it follows a passage that became the "1918" section of the novel, in which Crosby, older now and less fortunate, is crossing a busy street on aching legs and muttering to herself. (This passage ends with the second paragraph on galley 208: ". . . queue at the grocer's shop.") In the galley, three more paragraphs conclude the episode with Crosby catching sight of Kitty and Edward driving by in a limousine. After a break (on galley 109), the focus shifts to Kitty and Edward in the car. It is 1921 and they are meeting again for the first time in many years.

The Years—208

The broken words formed on her lips as she hobbled towards the ghostly line of trees. The roar of traffic sounded louder. She could see houses beyond the trees. She was approaching the High Street. Her pale-blue eyes peered forward through the mist as she made her way towards the railings. Her eyes alone seemed to express an unconquerable determination; she was not going to give in; she was bent on surviving. The soft mist was slowly lifting. Leaves lay damp on the asphalt path. The rooks croaked and shuffled on the tree-tops. Now a dark line of railings emerged from the mist. The roar of traffic in the High Street sounded louder and louder. Crosby stopped and rested her bag on the railing before she went on to do battle with the crowd of shoppers in the High Street. She would have to shove and push, and be jostled this way and that; and her feet pained her. They didn't mind if you bought or not, she thought; and often she was pushed out of her place by some bold-faced drab. She thought of the red-haired girl again, as she stood there, panting slightly, with her bag on the railing. Her legs pained her. The long-drawn note of a siren floated out its melancholy wail of sound; then there was a dull explosion.

"Them guns again," Crosby muttered, looking up at the pale-grey sky with peevish irritation. The rooks, scared by the gun-fire, rose and wheeled round the tree-tops. Then there was another dull boom. A man on a ladder who was painting the windows of one of the houses paused with his brush in his hand and looked round. A woman who was walking along carrying a loaf of bread that stuck half out of its paper wrapping stopped too. They both waited as if for something to happen. A topple of smoke drifted over and flopped down from the chimneys. The guns boomed again. The man on the ladder said something to the woman on the pavement. She nodded her head. Then he dipped his brush in the pot and went on painting. The woman walked on. Crosby pulled herself together and tottered across the road into the High Street. The guns went on booming and the sirens wailed. The war was over—so somebody told her as she took her place in the queue at the grocer's shop.

The sun was shining almost with summer heat, though it was still early in May, and the long line of cars that blocked Richmond High Street had been forced to come to a standstill. They kept up an intermittent, impatient hooting; but none of them could move. The sun struck on their glossy sides; it made bright spots on the silver-plated handles; on the glossy, varnished panels. The narrow street was completely blocked for the moment. Dazed with the hum and uproar, with the hooting, and throbbing of cars, Crosby stood on the pavement hypnotised into a trance. She looked like an old insect that has outlived the winter and suns itself upon a leaf.

Suddenly she straightened and stiffened. Her hands clutched her bag; her eyes became bluer, more prominent, and fixed themselves upon the face of a gentleman in the large car that was drawn up in front of her.

"Mr Edward!" she muttered. "There's Mr Edward!" He was only a hand-breadth from her; only the glass of the window between them. Her mouth hung open as she gazed. There was a lady beside him in black. She was talking; she turned her face towards Crosby as she said something.

"Miss Kitty!" Crosby murmured. And she was in

The Years—209

black because his lordship was dead; Crosby had seen his death in the newspapers. The cars hooted impatiently. People jostled behind her. But Crosby stood still, staring. She took in every detail; Lady Lasswade had a rug over her knees; she was greyer than she used to be, but still extremely handsome; and there was a great dog on the seat. If only somebody had been with her, to whom she could have pointed them out. . . . But here the car moved on; all the cars moved on. Crosby was left staring on the pavement. She kept her eyes on the car as if it were a vision, fading, slowly withdrawing from her sight. She could still see the back of Mr Edward's head; she could still see the great dog on the seat; but now an omnibus came between, and she could see the car no longer.

"It must have been higher up," said Kitty, as the car pulled out and swept smoothly up the hill. ". . . a little old house with a balcony."

She glanced at the houses on her right.

"We used to drive down and have tea," she said. "There was a lawn that sloped down to the river." Since her husband was dead, and this visit had been with him, there was a touch of sadness in her words; but she spoke cheerfully. There was nothing of the lugubrious draped widow about her, Edward thought. She looked extremely handsome in her black; and her complexion was still white and pink like a girl's; and that pleased him, for they were about the same age.

The car swept on up the hill. Then the houses stopped; and the view opened on the right.

"The view——" said Kitty, turning to look at it.

"The famous view——" said Edward. Down below opened a wide space with a far blue distance of fields, and immediately below on the flat, the river wound, silver, serpentine, set with little boats.

"Where does that come?" said Edward. "In what novel?"

"Dickens?" she said on the spur of the moment.

"No, no, no!" he expostulated, smiling.

Why no, no, no, she asked herself, feeling slightly piqued.

"Haven't an idea," she said. She slipped the rug from her knee and tapped on the glass.

"We'll get out here," she said, and the car stopped inside the Park gates. The great dog bounded out first, and then she got out and told the chauffeur to meet them at another gate. They were going to walk across the Park.

"And I shan't want this," she said, tossing her coat into the car. "It's too hot."

Indeed it was the first day of summer. The trees were sprigged with little green spears; but the leaves were still crinkled, half furled. Here and there a solitary tree rose, like a torrent, a torrent of black iron. But the air was so soft, so gummy, that it seemed as if buds and leaves must be forming even in the black tree under the iron bark. The hum of the traffic now muted, and the distance that lay so blue before them seemed to wrap the whole earth in the softness, the haze of fertility.

The great shaggy dog bounced through the bracken.

"He's enjoying himself," said Edward.

"Yes, he hates London," said Kitty.

The dog had been waiting in the car which had fetched them from the lunch party where they had met.

"He won't chase the deer?" Edward asked—there were deer feeding at a little distance in the bracken.

"Heel, Sultan," said Kitty sharply, and the dog slunk back to her side.

They walked on briskly in silence. The air carried with it little sounds—of branches creaking, of birds chirping—almost as if they were in the country.

"And you're leaving London?" said Edward, turning to her.

"Yes," she said, "—tearing things up. You can't think," she added, "what a lot there is to tear up after thirty years."

"Is it as long as that?" he asked.

"Well—" she paused, making a calculation, "I was married in eighteen-eighty-five, and it's now nineteen-twenty-one."

"That's thirty—that's thirty-six years!" he exclaimed. "Yes, it's a long time."

They were silent. The air and the movement had done away with constraint at first; but now they both felt a little shy. They had not met since her husband's death the year before. They were walking down a green drive, with a plantation on either side of them. The dog jumped over the palings into the wood. They could hear the dry twigs crackling under him as he leapt about snuffling among the dead leaves. Then horse's hoofs thudded behind them, and a couple on horseback came cantering past.

"D'you ever ride now?" said Kitty, watching the riders lurch up and down in their saddles.

"When I stay with Hugh at the Towers," Edward said.

"He was always a great man on horseback," she smiled. "How well I remember—Tony Ashton, Hugh Gibbs—the three of you!" she paused. "You used to ride together at Oxford," she said. She was silent, as if she were thinking back to their youth.

"Who's at the Lodge now?" she asked, keeping one eye on Sultan. There was a little herd of does in front of them, stepping daintily through the ferns.

"The Antonys still?" she enquired, rather absent-mindedly for she did not want Sultan to chase the deer.

"Heel," she said sharply. "Heel."

"The Antonys?" said Edward. He seemed a little surprised at her question. "No—he died, six months ago."

"Did he?" she said, keeping an eye on her dog. "And who's there now then?"

"Nobody," he said, "at the moment."

She detected some self-consciousness in his voice as she watched her dog snuffing about among the ferns.

"You, Edward?" she said lightly, "will they give it you?" He raised his hat and ran his fingers through his hair. She recognised the familiar gesture which made her feel at ease with him. And he was still very handsome; very distinguished-looking, she thought.

"Yes, of course," she said, as if she had suddenly realised something. He was silent. He did not deny it or confirm it. They always keep these things a mystery, she reflected with a little amusement.

"You'll live in the old house where we used to live," she said aloud. "How old!"

She saw the tree leaning on its prop; and the drawing-room; and her mother sitting there stitching at her embroidery.

"And is there electric——" But she stopped in the

middle of her question; for they had come out of the ride between the trees and stood on a little rise of ground looking down on a silver shield of water. A flight of birds came over in single file; they circled high then swooped low, trailed their legs in the water, and swam along.

"Wild duck!" she exclaimed.

"Yes. Wild duck," he said. "But you never liked it," he resumed, as they walked on down the hill, "Did you?"

"Oxford? No, not as a girl," she said.

She saw again the muslin blind blowing out across the dressing-table, and heard all the clocks striking, one after the other.

"One was so—cooped up there," she said; "I mean as a girl." She sighed. She wished now she had not quarrelled so often with her mother. But she stopped. A musical wooden clapper sounded in the wood behind her. She held her hand up.

"Listen!" she exclaimed. That's "a cuckoo!"

They listened. They heard the branches creaking; the wind sighing through the trees; but if there was a cuckoo it was silent; the sound did not come again. They moved on in the direction of the lake. It shone ruffled with gold scales as a breeze passed over it. Barred with slender trees, the lake lying beneath them reminded Edward of Italy for a moment. He pointed at it. But the dog began to bark violently. He had rambled off into the bracken and was barking at a couple who lay stretched out under a tree. The man raised himself on his elbow—he was lying with his arm round a woman—and threw something at him.

"Sultan!" Kitty shouted. "To heel, Sultan. To heel!"

They walked on past the lovers, lying stretched out on the grass. The girl's eyes were shut; she did not look up as they passed. But as they passed the man flung himself on the ground again, and Kitty, glancing back, saw that they were locked in each other's arms. It has all begun again, she felt; everyone was making love, everything was broken up, everything was moving on, she felt, as she heard the birds chirp and saw the branches tossing in the spring breeze.

"But you weren't quite fair, Kitty," Edward said, as they walked on side by side. He was a little hurt by something she had said—about Oxford, was it? He loved Oxford, of course, just as her father had loved it.

"But I never knew it," she said. "I left it so young. And it may be different now."

"No, I don't think it's changed," he said.

There was something in his voice, in the look in his eyes as he threw his head a little back, that touched her. After all, he had lived there all these years.

"You have those lovely rooms still?" she said.

"Where your mother brought you to tea," he said. "You wore a white dress," he paused, "with blue spots," he added, as if he remembered it.

"Did I?" she said. "I don't remember." There was some emotion in his voice. Perhaps it was merely the sentiment of the middle-aged about their youth. Or could it be—the thought flashed through her—making a steeple in the distance shine very white—that he was about to ask her to marry him again? A spasm of fear came over her, absurd though it was. No, no, no, she said to herself. No, no, no. And then, just as she used to do when she wished to brush aside something that was too emotional, she changed the conversation.

"There's my cuckoo!" she exclaimed. She stopped and pretended to listen. He stopped too. A bird was singing, but it was not a cuckoo.

"That's the wise thrush," he said, "that sings each song twice over." He spoke quite unconcernedly. She was relieved, but at the same time ashamed of her folly.

"Does a thrush sing its song twice over?" she asked.

"So the poet says," he observed. It was a quotation, and she had not recognised it. He always made her feel such a boor. That's why I didn't marry you, she said to herself, glancing sideways at his distinguished face—but his eyes were a little near together. Always saying what somebody else had said, she thought.

"I felt such a bull in a china shop," she said aloud; "I mean at Oxford," she added. "And then we married; and travelled, and the children came." She gave a little sigh. It was all over for her now, she was thinking.

"I'm so sorry, Kitty," he said. They had never spoken of her husband's death; but she felt his desire to express his sympathy, and she liked his shyness.

"I'm afraid you've been through a bad time lately," he said.

"So we all have!" she said.

"Yes, yes!" He threw back his head. Many of his pupils had been killed in the War; the young men he had been so proud of. And they had liked him too, she thought, remembering what her sons had told her. They laughed at him; there was some nickname they gave him—she could not remember what—but they respected him. And so did she. They have a standard, she thought as they walked on; people like Edward and Tony. And my father, yes, and old Chuffy. . . . But how different our lives have been! she thought, glancing at him as he walked beside her. She had travelled; she had married; she had borne children, while Edward had gone on year after year at Oxford.

"Tell me," he interrupted, "how's Dominick getting on?"

They talked about her eldest son, who had inherited the place.

"But I don't know if he'll be able to keep it up," she said. "The death duties are so heavy."

"It would be a great pity if he had to leave it," he said gravely.

Again she was irritated. Perhaps she was unjust; but he always brought back the feeling of that small, secure, self-complacent world that she had hated so as a girl.

"I hope it won't come to that," he said, "that he has to leave it."

"The place?" she said. She frowned. Other people were walking there already; seeing her woods, looking at her view. "They'll be forced to sell sooner or later," she said harshly, "like everybody else."

They had come to the edge of the lake. Her dog, excited by the quacking of the ducks, had plunged into the water and was swimming out among the little coveys of birds with great rough strokes.

"Oh that dog!" she exclaimed. "Sultan! Sultan!" she cried, striding to the water's edge and shaking her fist.

He wished she had not brought the dog. It made talk so difficult. But she always had a passion, he remembered, for big shaggy dogs. She's grown rather large, he thought, watching her. He had once thought her a nymph, a shepherdess—yes. He watched her

shouting to her dog. It was extremely difficult now to see what it had been in her that had so fascinated him. He half shut his eyes. He had been passionately in love with her. He could still remember the day. . . . But the dog had clambered out of the water and was shaking himself so that drops flew in a shower all over Kitty's skirt. She shook herself too. She beat him off with her bare hand. He was glad on the whole that he had not married her. She was too rough, too abrupt. But she was extremely vigorous for a woman of sixty. There was something about her vitality that charmed him still, he thought.

"Now you'll get into the car and make us all soaking wet," she said, speaking to the dog as she rejoined him.

And she talks too much to her dogs, he thought.

"I'm so sorry, Edward," she apologised, putting the dog on the chain. "I oughtn't to have brought him." They walked on.

"It wouldn't hurt Dominick to have to earn his living after all," she resumed, trying to return to what they had been saying.

"To earn his living . . ." he said. "But isn't it a good thing," he added, looking about him with his mild blue eyes, "that some people shouldn't?"

She felt that he was not giving the whole of his mind to what he was saying. He was looking about him; he was appraising, appreciating. He was swinging his stick and looking appreciatively at the view. He was getting old, she felt; he was content to take things quietly. How could she ever have thought, for a moment, that he meant to ask her to marry him? He was a scholar; he knew things of which she was ignorant. The soft air blew in their faces; he took his hat off and held it as if he enjoyed feeling the wind in his hair.

"How lovely it is!" he exclaimed, looking at the view.

"Yes," she said rather perfunctorily. "Lovely, isn't it?"

The view had the charm of a landscape in which there is space for different kinds of movement. There were the riders cantering; a troop of boys kicking a ball about; an old man riding on a grey cob, and in the distance a white house among some trees.

"But rather too crowded," she said, "—look at all those cars."

A line of cars moved down the road in the distance like a row of black beetles crawling. They were so distant that they seemed to move very slowly. They were so close that they seemed to make one long line of crawling blackness.

"There's Miles," she said, pointing to a large car drawn up by the grass at some distance. They walked on. She felt as they drew near the car that she had not made the most of her walk with a friend whom she had known so long, whom she saw so seldom. When she had seen him come into the room at luncheon she had said to herself with pleasure, "There's Edward!" but so much time was wasted getting into touch with people; so little was ever said. It was her fault largely.

"I'm so glad you'll be Master, Edward," she said impulsively. "Papa would have been so pleased. He cared so much for the college."

"Yes. What a wonderful book that was of his!" said Edward.

The Years—214

"The history, you mean?" she said. She saw again the ink slowly spreading over the fair page as she made a hasty movement.

"Dear Papa!" she exclaimed. She wished that she had been of more use to him; she wished that she had understood his work better.

"They were very good to me, your father and mother," he said simply, "when I was a young man."

"I think she cared as much for the college as he did," she said. She could see her mother now going up the stairs holding her candle in her hand, and saying, as she opened the door of the spare bedroom, "This is the room where Queen Elizabeth did *not* sleep!"

"Yes, I can see her," he said, "sitting in that low chair working at her embroidery."

They had reached the car. Miles held the door open for them.

"Sultan's been in the water," said Kitty, pointing to the wet dog. "You'll have to put a rug for him to lie on. And where shall we put you down, Edward?" she asked.

"If you could drop me at St. James's Street," he said, as they got in.

Movement and the look of things passing lulled them both; and the comfort of the car after walking. Soon they were crossing Hammersmith Bridge; it was all blue and silver, spring-like, ruffled into little waves as they passed over it; and the eights were out like water-beetles skimming beneath. But they were over it in a flash. At Hammersmith, however, the car was held up. The pavement bobbed with heads that jerked and dodged but remained fixed as if something clogged their feet. However much they bobbed and hooted, both the people on the pavement and the cars in the street remained fixed. The sun beat down on them; there was a slight smell of petrol.

"Soon it'll be quicker to walk than to drive," said Kitty impatiently. Then the car shot ahead. There was a clear run to Kensington High Street, and then again the crowd of women shopping thickened; the traffic coagulated; and they crept at foot's-pace behind an omnibus.

"I always wonder," said Edward, glancing at the great festooned windows, with their gleaming silks and their banners of bright ribbon, "what is the fascination of that particular activity?"

"Shopping?" said Kitty, glancing at a dress in a window. That was the manner, she thought, ironical, polite but slightly condescending, that always irritated her when she was a girl.

"You don't enjoy it?" she said aloud. She looked at the women with their faces pressed against the great plate-glass windows like fish in an aquarium. She had meant to shop too, to buy covers for the chairs in her new house, in Paddington, if he had not asked her to put him down at St. James's Street.

"When I was rich," she said as they passed on, "I hardly ever went into a shop. Now I'm poor, I shop too. . . . I rather enjoy it," she added.

"But my dear Kitty," he began, "I hope . . ." He paused. She knew what he was thinking, and she liked him for his shyness.

"I hope you're speaking," he continued, "in the comparative sense merely?" They had turned into

The Years—215

Kensington Gardens. They were rolling luxuriously past the Albert Memorial.

"Look! The poor Prince is all black," she said, pointing to the bowed figure under the canopy.

Edward raised his glasses and looked at the statue. "And Morris and Eleanor used to swear they'd seen him being gilt!" he said. They left the Prince behind.

"Oh, I'm not poor," Kitty went on. "But I don't want——" she hesitated. "Dominick has a great many calls on him," she said.

·Edward bent his head.

"Yes," he said. "It's going to be a question of cutting down everywhere for us all."

Probably he was very generous; he gave away a lot of money to young men, she expected. They were silent. They were driving past the Barracks. A sublime figure in red and silver was striding up and down with a red tuft on his helmet. Little companies of children on ponies were cantering along the Row. Dashing young men with their billycock hats pulled down over their ears went past at a gallop. At the end of the Row, the riders pulled up their horses and turned round. Since it was a fine afternoon cars were drawn up; the green chairs were full of people basking in the sunshine. The swelling flower-beds were thickly planted with blocks of bright-red and yellow flowers. Clouds grained with gold went toppling over the roofs of Park Lane houses, and the windows were spotted with blue and gold reflections.

The season was beginning, and they were held up at the gates of Apsley House to let the cars come in from Hyde Park Corner. Then they too passed out of the gate and swept down the long slope of Piccadilly. And we shall soon part, Kitty was thinking; and how little we've said, she thought. What was he doing? she wondered. Editing something as usual? She glanced at him. He was looking about him, as he had looked at the view in Richmond Park—with approval, with appreciation.

"I was dining with Bankes the other night," he said, turning to her. "You know him, don't you?"

"The Bankes who used to be at the Embassy?" said Kitty.

"Yes. Ralph Bankes. He's over now with his wife."

"The lady with large arms?" said Kitty.

"And a pretty daughter," said Edward. "And when I asked him what impressed him most"—he spoke slowly because he was looking round him, at the clubs, at the Park—"after the War—this was his first visit to London——"

"Wasn't he at the Hague?" Kitty threw in.

"Yes. At the Hague," Edward confirmed her. "He told me that the thing that had impressed him most, when he came back after five years, was——"

The car slowed down. They had reached St. James's Street.

"Oh, here we are," he said. "I'll get out here."

He got out and stood on the pavement with his hat in his hand. He had not finished his sentence.

"You won't come back with me?" she asked. "I've got Eleanor coming?" she suddenly remembered.

"No. I've got to meet somebody. . . . It's been very nice seeing you, Kitty," he said. They shook hands and looked into each other's faces with real affection.

"You'll come and stay with me, won't you?" she

The Years—216

said, "when I'm settled in?" And he bowed.

How handsome she still is, he thought as he turned away. The years had given her another kind of beauty; and she was wonderfully vigorous for a woman of her age. Had she really cared for her husband? he wondered as he crossed the street. Lasswade had always seemed to him an excellent fellow, but rather on the dull side.

The car moved on. The dog jumped across and sat in the seat that Edward had left. The dog felt a pang of disappointment as she looked round and saw Edward with his head tilted rather on one side walking down St. James's Street. He didn't even finish his sentence, she thought. What had he been going to say? Something about Piccadilly? Things going on, she supposed. She saw him again, standing in the Park with his hat in his hand looking at the view. She smiled. But I made a fool of myself over that quotation, she thought. The wise thrush . . . what was it the wise thrush did? She shook her head. She had forgotten. And then I thought he was going to ask me to marry him. Well, that's one thing I needn't regret anyhow, she thought as the car turned in to Grosvenor Square. One thing, she said as the car drew up at the door.

The leaves of the door sprang open as if at the touch of a spring, and displayed the black-and-white squares in the hall that always made her feel as if she were stepping across a chess-board.

"Miss Pargiter's waiting in the drawing-room, m'lady," said the footman, taking her things.

"Waiting is she?" said Kitty. She looked at the clock with compunction. She was ten, no, she was fifteen minutes late, and she had kept Eleanor waiting. She hurried upstairs.

"I'm so sorry, Eleanor," she said as she opened the door. She looked round, for she did not see her at once in the large room. Where had they put her? she wondered. Then she saw her, over there by the fireplace in the large chair reading a newspaper.

"I'm so sorry," she repeated as she came across the room. "I've been walking in Richmond Park with your brother."

She kissed her, and then sat down by the tea-table on which a great silver kettle rode, like a ship swinging between two silver stays. Kitty was stiff with her usual shyness for a moment; and noticed the very white gloves that Eleanor held on her knee. But she was wearing her usual clothes; her usual ring; she was the same, now oldish, woman with whom she had broken the swing at Oxford years ago when they were young.

"How nice to see you!" she began. "And then I'm late. But it was Edward's fault. We had to go round by Piccadilly."

"Oh, don't mind that," said Eleanor. "I've been sitting here, in the lap of luxury." She put down the paper she had been reading, and took off her glasses.

"I met him at lunch," Kitty explained, as she fidgeted with the tea things. "And then we went for a walk; I'd not seen him for so long. He told me," she added, "that he's going to be the new Master."

"He told you?" said Eleanor. "I thought it was a secret."

The Years—217

"So it is," Kitty laughed. "A profound secret—but I guessed."

"But Nigs told me——" Eleanor began.

"Nigs!" Kitty interrupted her. "That was the name! I couldn't remember. Nigs . . . Nigs," she said.

She carved herself a slice of cake and ate like a schoolboy, breaking off great mouthfuls. The dog came up to the table and sat there waiting for his share.

"Nigs didn't like you, did he, Sultan?" said Kitty, tossing him a curl of bread and butter.

"But," said Eleanor, hesitating a little, "I thought nothing had been settled yet." She too felt a little shy; her feeling of dowdiness returned to her. Kitty herself had changed slightly; she was all in black; she was not perhaps so highly groomed as she used to be. They had not met since her husband's death.

"Dear old Nigs. . . . No. It's not settled. But it will be," said Kitty. "How charming he is!" she added. "D'you know what came over me in the Park?" she said suddenly. She looked at Eleanor opposite her. "I thought he was going to ask me to marry him again!" She felt quite at her ease, as if they were girls again. "Wasn't it absurd?" she added.

Eleanor paused.

"I sometimes wish you had," she said.

"No. It wouldn't have done," said Kitty. "And he's done very well without me," she added.

"You made him very unhappy," said Eleanor, looking at Kitty and thinking of her as a girl.

"Did I?" said Kitty.

"Yes," said Eleanor. She remembered how Edward had cried, sitting on the edge of her bed, one night. Kitty stopped eating for a moment. She was surprised, but flattered. She could scarcely believe it; he had always made her feel such a boor.

"What a brute one is!" she said aloud. "How little one knows what other people are feeling!" She was silent for a moment. Then she drank up her tea and lit a cigarette.

"But I like him . . ." she said. "He's such a—what's the word I want?" She waved her hand. "Not 'gentleman'—it's what I feel with you, Nell; and with Martin, when he dined here, when we had a party here, and he said to me, 'What damned dull people you know, what damned bad pictures you have!' " She laughed and waved her cigarette at the portrait of herself over the fireplace. "I like it," she added. They have a standard, she was thinking, feeling largely flattered.

"Trust Martin to say what he thinks," said Eleanor; "especially if it's something disagreeable." She looked up at the picture. She had been looking at it while she waited.

"Who painted that?" she said.

"Oh, I forget," said Kitty, puffing her smoke out. "Thank heaven I shan't have to sit under it any longer."

"You're leaving?" said Eleanor, smoothing out her white gloves on the arm of her chair.

"Yes," said Kitty, "I'm only here tearing things up. There's a lot of things to tear up after thirty-six years. . . . I'm going to live in the country. I've bought a little house in the North . . ." She had a photograph of the house. She wanted to show it to Eleanor. It was a charming house; a little manor house, that had been used as a farm-house. She was going to alter it. But perhaps Eleanor would not be interested.

"It'll be a nice little house when I've altered it," she

The Years—218

said. "Quite small; quite humble. None of this. . . ." She waved her hand at the room, with its innumerable tables, chairs and ornaments.

Eleanor looked round; her eyes rested on an elaborate basket of flowers by the door in which each flower stood separate, as if a wire had been run through it.

"Always made me feel as if I were living in an hotel," said Kitty. "I always wanted to take a knife and scrape it all off. But what was the use? If I altered anything Charles used to come in and say 'Where's Uncle Bill on the old cob?' and back it had to go again," she laughed. It was the first time she had mentioned her husband. Why had she married him, Eleanor wondered, and not Edward? She thought of the good-natured man with the heavy face and the fine drooping eyes who used to march in when she was visiting Kitty and shake hands very cordially, and say "Lest we forget! Lest we forget!" reminding Kitty of some engagement; and then go out again rubbing his hands.

"I expect it looked very nice in the evening," she said, looking round her, "when there were lots of people about." The room had impressed her, as she sat waiting. She liked high rooms. There was an opulence about it. All her senses had seemed to expand as she sat there; with the footmen bringing in silver dishes, and all the papers laid head to head on a round table.

"Yes," Kitty agreed absentmindedly. "It did look nice sometimes, in the evening." In some ways she would mind leaving it, she thought. "But why a fire on a day like this?" she said.

There was a fire burning; and the room with its hothouse flowers was rather warm and sweet-scented. She got up and flung open the window. The noise of the street came in; they heard the rushing of wheels and the hooting of cars at the corner.

"I like big rooms," said Eleanor. She was comparing it with her own rather meagre flat. "I like the sense of space they give one."

"But you'd never come here," said Kitty. She was standing in front of the fire with her arms behind her back like a country gentleman.

"You always made some excuse, Nell, for not coming," she added, smiling at her.

"Did I? Yes. Perhaps I couldn't afford the clothes," said Eleanor, smiling back at her. She stooped and picked up one of the white gloves that had fallen on the floor.

"That's so silly," said Kitty, looking at the white glove.

"Not when you're young," said Eleanor. "When you're young you mind—not looking like other people." She looked at Kitty. She was very well dressed.

Kitty sat down again by the tea-table and took another cigarette.

"How nice it is not to be young," she said. "How nice not to mind what people think. . . . Now one can live as one likes," she added, lighting another cigarette. "Now that one's sixty."

They sat silent for a time, smoking their cigarettes and listening to the hooting of the cars under the window.

"Pity one can't live again," said Kitty suddenly. She held out her hands with the cigarette in them. They were strong hands with short, square-tipped fingers.

"Look at those hands," she said. "I ought to have

The Years—219

been a farmer. . . ."

She got up and strode about the room: she was always restless. She never seemed to altogether to fit in, Eleanor thought. She might be going to say something about her marriage. Perhaps she would, perhaps she would not. She was a queer mixture of candour and reserve. She was still very handsome; she moved vigorously. The dog got up and walked with her. When she reached the door she stopped, as if he expected her to go out. She ought to be walking on a moor with her dogs, Eleanor thought, looking at her. But she came back to the fireplace and stood with her hands behind her back.

"Human relationships aren't very satisfactory, are they?" she said. "It's so difficult to say what one feels." She was thinking of Edward; of their little random scraps of talk; of the sentence he had left unfinished as he stood on the pavement; and how Eleanor said she had made him unhappy.

"Just what we were saying last night," said Eleanor, wondering what she was thinking about, "at dinner."

Kitty looked at her. The words pricked her curiosity.

"Who were you dining with?" she asked.

"Oh, nobody you'd know," said Eleanor. "A foreigner." Kitty felt slightly nettled. She did not mean to tell her, she thought. What sort of people did Eleanor know, she wondered; whom did she dine with? Other people's lives always seem more interesting than one's own, she thought.

"And what did you say?" she asked.

What had they said? Eleanor could not remember. She saw again the smoky restaurant; a parrot in a cage; a girl with a feather in her hat; and Nicholas leaning across the little table, talking.

"Oh, just that . . ." she said. "How difficult it is to know people—how afraid we all are of each other." She stopped. She saw Nicholas touching the fingers of his hand with his familiar gesture.

"Afraid of each other?" said Kitty blankly. It was a new idea to her, it seemed. She considered it for a moment.

"That's true," she said, after a pause. "That's true of me anyhow." I was afraid of Edward this afternoon, she thought, afraid he was thinking me a fool. That was why she had made herself appear more brusque than she was; why she had talked to her dog. "Heel, Sultan! heel, Sultan!" she had said in order to cover up her shyness.

"But is it true of everybody?" she asked. It's not true of Eleanor, she was thinking.

"That's what we were saying," said Eleanor. It was one of the things that they had been saying; but they had said so many other things as well.

"You and your foreigner," said Kitty. She visualised a black man with a beard; the sort of man who wore a red tie. She felt a little envious; it sounded to her as if their evening had been so much more interesting than her evening. She had dined alone with her son and daughter-in-law. They had talked about racing.

"We were saying——" said Eleanor as Kitty waited, looking at her. She could not remember how the argument went. It was very difficult to repeat a conversation; she muddled things up. How had they reached that point about being afraid?

"Dressing up," she said suddenly. "Trying to make

The Years—220

out one is what one isn't," she paused. She was muddling it up. She flicked the white glove on her knee. "Isn't that because we are afraid?" she said. I bought these gloves in order to come here, she was thinking; but they ought to have been yellower.

"And power," she said suddenly, as if she had got her cue. That was what they had been arguing about, she remembered; that was what had started the conversation.

"Power?" said Kitty.

"Yes. People wanting power," said Eleanor; she could remember how it went now. But would Nicholas have been able to say all that here? she asked herself. Her eye rested on the gilt basket of flowers by the door, She smiled. No, she could not possibly tell Kitty what they had been talking about. Power, patriotism, love, sex and all the rest of it.

"But power's what people want," said Kitty. "They'll do any thing to get power."

She saw again the men filing into the drawing-room after dinner, and the women rising like a flock of gulls to receive them. Dear Eleanor, she thought, looking at her. She's very innocent. She hasn't seen as much of the world as I've seen. The thought pleased her rather.

"It's what they live for," she said, throwing away her cigarette. "And after all, it's human nature," she added, brushing away some of the ashes that had fallen on her lap.

"And we can't change . . ." Eleanor began.

"Human nature?" Kitty smiled. "I don't know," she said. "I find it quite hard to give up the little bit of power I had myself," she sighed. It was true. She still felt a lingering desire for the old life that she had disliked so much when she had it.

"No more people being nice to one; no more people making up to one, now that I'm pensioned off like an old servant," she said rather bitterly. Eleanor noticed the little wrinkles, the little hardnesses and hollows in her face that made her look her age as she spoke in spite of her vigour.

"But that's not what I mind," Kitty went on vehemently. "It's losing the place. It's the thought that I shall never walk in those woods again——" The tears started to her eyes; she pulled out her handkerchief, and dabbed them roughly like a schoolboy.

"Isn't it absurd," she said, "to cry for a wood when there's so much else to cry for? But walking with Edward, hearing the pigeons this afternoon——" She blew her nose. That is what she minds, Eleanor thought; not his death.

"That's what I mind," said Kitty. "Anybody can have this——" she waved her hand round the room ". . . all the people who used to come here; the women such fools, and the men only caring for their sport, their politics . . ." She broke off. That's what she minds Eleanor thought, leaving a place.

They sat listening to the dull sound of traffic that came through the open window. Somebody was playing a cornet in the street below; the dismal strain wailed through the air as if a dog had lifted up its head and was baying for the moon. The horns hooted; the cornet wailed; it was disturbing; unrestful. Like a piece of jangled music, Eleanor thought as she sat there listening.

"And what a mess they made of it!" Kitty added, throwing away her cigarette. "What a horrible mess!"

The Years—221

The little clock on the mantelpiece chimed the hour with quick, petulant strokes. Eleanor began to draw on her gloves, pulling the fingers down, for they were new and fitted tightly.

"Well," she said rising, "perhaps the younger generation——"

"No, no," said Kitty. She picked up one of the illustrated papers and glanced at a shiny brown photograph of a race meeting.

"They're just the same—Ann, my daughter-in-law," she said. She pointed to a woman in tailor-made clothes with field-glasses slung round her shoulders at a race meeting. "Just the same," she said. She threw the paper away. She got up.

"But you must come and stay with me in the country," she said, "when I've got my house ready." She wanted to fetch the photograph, but perhaps Eleanor would be bored.

"It'll be quite a nice little house when I've cut down the trees and dug up the beds. It's a little Tudor manor-house. . . ."

Eleanor had put on both her gloves now and was standing by the window.

"I'll come if you ask me," she said. Kitty stood beside her looking out over the square. "Next spring then—that's a promise," she said. "Spring's so lovely up there," she added. She looked down on the usual stream of business people who were hurrying along after their day's work. It was the crowded hour. The pavement under the trees was dappled with floating shadow; the little figures, foreshortened from this height, looked oddly insubstantial as they went in and out of the floating lights, and the shadows. And all round them were the great ring of houses, red gold in the evening haze.

"How I hate London!" Kitty exclaimed.

"How I love it!" said Eleanor. They both laughed.

"People are so interesting," said Eleanor. "I couldn't, live in the country." She was looking at the man who had been playing the cornet. He had stopped playing and was holding out his cap to each passer-by. Two, three, four people went by without stopping. But the fifth, one of those shabby-looking old women who are always to be seen in London squares, stopped, fumbled in her purse and dropped in a copper. Eleanor smiled.

"I knew we would!" she said, turning round.

"Well, we shan't convert each other," said Kitty, turning away. "And where are you off to now?" she asked, as she walked with her towards the door. "Some Committee?"

"No," said Eleanor rather awkwardly; "nowhere in particular." She won't tell me, Kitty thought. She is hiding her life as we all do. A queer feeling of blankness, of frustration, came over her as she stopped at the door. She broke off one of the hothouse flowers and gave it to Eleanor.

"A flower for your buttonhole, Nell," she said, giving it her.

"But that's a shame . . ." said Eleanor, looking at the velvety streaked petals.

"It'll only die in this hot room," said Kitty. "No, Sultan," she said, pulling the dog back. "You've got to stay with me." She shut the door.

Eleanor made her way down the great staircase. A

large picture with pale-green water and lemon-coloured buildings hung on the wall. Venice? she said to herself. She would have liked to stop and look at it, but there were flunkeys lurking somewhere, she supposed; and holding herself rather more ·erect than usual, she passed on down the stairs. Bright sunshine made an angle across the black-and-white squares. There was some commotion in the hall; a lady was coming in; the footman was holding the door open for a young woman in black. They passed each other in the hall. She was tall and fair and dressed very simply in black. She bent her head with a veiled smile of discreet courtesy as she passed Eleanor, for they did not know each other.

"Ann—the daughter-in-law," Eleanor thought. She recognised her from the picture in the illustrated paper. "The woman at the races," she thought. "But black suits her better," she thought. She was very lovely.

The footman asked her if she had a car. No, and she did not want him to call a taxi; she would walk. She wanted to walk; she felt the need to walk off some little quickening of feeling, caused by,—what? The big room; the staircase; the footman; the lady in black. Her lips moved as she walked.

. . . dressed in black, just as I came out, very lovely, Kitty's daughter-in-law, she said as she walked on without thinking where she was going. "I went to tea with Kitty," she went on, arranging the story to tell somebody. Yes, I went to tea with her, she said. She went—she'd been walking in the Park with Edward. We talked of Edward. . . . Have I forgotten my bag? she asked herself suddenly. No, she had it under her arm, but she was holding the flower so tight in her abstraction that she did not know that she was also holding her bag. Her lips began to move again as she stood on the pavement to let the traffic go by. We talked about Edward, she said, going on with her story. I don't think that she's very happy. . . . She's restless. . . . She's going to live by herself in the country. . . . A little house in the North.

She crossed the road. There was something that she wanted to tell somebody about Kitty; something that had struck her at the time; something that had seemed to her interesting; but she could not get hold of it in this crowd. Here she came to a shop window in which she saw her own reflection against a mound of some black stuff. So that's what I looked like, she said to herself, putting her hand to her hat. My hat's on one side. Was it like that all the time? she asked herself. She hoped not. There were dresses in the window; evening dresses and muslin summer frocks with ribbons floating, semi-transparent. For the young, she said to herself, thinking how charming they were. Then her gaze rested on a gold-spotted dress with a long skirt. That's the sort of dress I might wear, she thought. I still feel it, she mused. That was the feeling, she thought, looking at the dress; she remembered the feeling of bare arms, and skirts twining round her ankles. That was the feeling, she thought, remembering the old sensation as she came into a room of glitter, of festivity; and she turned to a young woman who was standing beside her, gazing at the clothes. There was something avid, feasting, like the rapture of a butterfly on a flower in the eyes of the young woman, edging closer to the window, sizing up the clothes quickly, and then fastening her gaze on the thin flounced muslin. Yes, that was the feeling, said Eleanor, as if the

girl's feeling had transmitted itself and supplemented her own.

I went to tea with a cousin who lives in Grosvenor Square, she began again. But now she was telling the story to Nicholas, because he was always interested in hearing about other people's lives. A Rigby, she married a man called Lasswade. It's a very big house . . . a great high room full of furniture. . . . But I doubt if you'd have found it easy, she continued, to say exactly what you thought. She smiled, as she remembered her own attempt to repeat the argument. My brother Edward was in love with her, she broke off. Very much in love . . . very much, she went on. He sat on the edge of my bed; he cried. It was in the paper, I think, or I had had a letter . . .

The crowd bothered her. She turned down a back street. There were always dingy streets just behind the shopping streets; streets that were rather empty; streets that were full of warehouses; houses that had been turned into workshops. She glanced automatically into the basements as she walked.

I remember, I read it out, she continued, "Kitty's engaged. . . ." And he said nothing; we were all there. . . . She stopped. There was a man in an apron down in the basement working at a case of type. She watched him. His bare arms were veined and his fingers were knotted, but they were incredibly dexterous. She watched him, fascinated by the way he flicked type into a great box with many compartments; there, there, there; rapidly, expertly; until, becoming conscious of her gaze, he looked up over his spectacles and smiled at her. She smiled back. Then he went on, making his quick half-conscious movements.

She had forgotten what she was saying. She walked on. This is the part of London I like, she thought, looking along the narrow eighteenth-century street where all the houses were let out in work-rooms, in apartments, and yet kept some tinge of ancient dignity. I like this part of London, she repeated. Her tension, her grip she had kept on her flower, on her bag, had relaxed. A fig tree grew out of the basement here; its leaves were beginning to unfurl; its branches spread a wide pattern over the wall. Within she could see women, ironing pink and blue stuff on long trestle tables. She stood and watched them; the irons ran over the crumpled stuff, leaving it pressed out and smooth. The sensation transmitted itself to her own body.

How quickly, she said, as she walked on, one loses the—what do you call it? She meant the tingling, the tension, that she had felt when she came out of the big house, and saw the woman coming across the angle of light in her exquisite clothes. It had become a picture now; she could look at it impersonally. The face was hard, she thought; the eyes glassy, perhaps. . . . What did Kitty say about her when she threw down the paper? She could not remember. But she could see Kitty walking up and down the room with the dog following her. And I thought to myself, she continued, Now she's going to confide in me—But she didn't. . . . The tears came into her eyes though. Yes, that was interesting; her feeling about the woods, the place— "That's what I mind," she said. That's what she minded, she said, turning to Nicholas again; not his death, but leaving the place, down in the country. . . . You may say it's ridiculous, she continued, but then, people are like that. It's human nature, Nicholas! And

The Years—224

if you'd been there, she asked him, could you have spoken perfectly freely? I wonder.

She looked along the street. It was somewhere here that she had dined the night before. It was the foreign quarter. The shops had French and Italian names over them; they sold maccaroni; they sold red rubber tubes. It was a dubious neighbourhood. There were people standing at a bar gesticulating. The chairs and little tables in front of doors reminded her of Italy or of France. Children seemed to pullulate. They were playing in the road. They were squatting on doorsteps. A woman came towards her with the swaying movement of a woman about to have a child. She had the suffering, drugged look of a person whose whole energies are absorbed in some physical process. And my mother . . . Eleanor thought, looking at her as she passed. My mother . . . She seldom thought of her mother, but now the brass bed, the sallow picture of the man in uniform, with a high light on his nose, hanging above it, and her mother lying there, came before her, She had ten, she thought. Ten, counting the three who died. And Papa, she thought . . . He had hidden the letters in the long drawer of the bureau, the letters from the lady with yellow hair. What had their relationship been, she wondered—her father's and her mother's? Had they been "in love?" Perhaps. But it was too long ago; too far away; she could not remember her mother, for all the children she had borne! she was a shadow lying there.

That was where we dined last night, she said as she passed a restaurant with bay trees in tubs. There was the grey parrot on the counter; and that was where we sat, she thought, looking at an empty table in the corner. They had sat on and on and on, talking. But I won't dine with you again, she said to herself, seeing him put his hand in his pocket, unless you let me pay my share. It's all very well, she added, to say you're making enough to live on now . . . but I won't dine with you unless you let me pay my share. It was I who ordered the wine. He's so easy in some ways, she thought; so conventional in others. About being nobly born, she smiled. Oh that family, the Poles, the noble Poles, from whom he was descended—how they bored her! But when he talks about what he's doing, about his work in the hospital, she added, then I love him: then we can talk all night. Then she felt, remembering the argument again, the complicated argument, it's like being two minds looking at the same thing from different angles, so that I can tell you any silly little story like this, about going to tea. . . .

A child was running along the gutter; and she guarded it half consciously with her eyes, holding herself ready to dart forward if it ran out into the street; for she heard a car coming. But the car passed; and the child ran on. She roused herself. She looked round to see where she was.

Everything seemed to stand out in sharper relief than usual. It was a fine spring evening. The street hummed with the swarm of people who were walking down the middle of the road. There was the usual barrel organ. The shops were still open; the shabby miscellaneous shops of this foreign quarter; but there was a sense of relief from work; of people standing at their doors, lounging about talking. She felt as if she were abroad—in France, or Italy; in some Southern country where the heat seemed to generate a feeling of

The Years—225

well-being. Even the beggars, she remembered, seem to enjoy life in Italy. It was late though; she was a long way from home.

"Why should I go back though?" she said aloud, looking at her watch. There was still a whole section— she took its measure at a glance—to do what she liked with. Her freedom from ties still sometimes came on her with a clap of surprise. Nobody was expecting her. So I can do what I like, she said, hesitating. How can I make the most of this?—she saw the section; it was roughly four hours. She felt in a mood to enjoy herself. Her mind was full; her being brimmed populous with sights, with sounds, with half realised ideas. She had been talking to Kitty; to Nicholas; then to herself. She had been bringing things together; building up new combinations as she walked; adding fresh ideas to old ones. Every sight, every sound, the man in the basement, the women ironing, the clothes, the people in the streets—all seemed to her to add themselves up easily and naturally. She walked on.

It's not being with people as much as being with them, friendship, she thought, looking at the long French rolls with their crisp crust in a baker's shop, as she passed. Why, then, regret death, the death of the body, or age, if that's true? she said, looking at the loaves; life may be more real when one's not living it? who knows? Except of course, she added, that "I" have to be—the thought slipped her.

"Latest winners," she read on a placard. A great deal of betting went on here. San Toy. Gemini. Star of the East—those are the names of racehorses, she thought. A great deal of betting went on here. These men in shirt sleeves, for example. Who's the Derby favourite this year, she wondered? For it would soon be Derby Day She had a mind to go there this year with Renny, who had a passion for racing. She found herself in Oxford Street. But I must dine somewhere. Who could I dine with? she asked herself. She had had enough of solitary musing; she wanted to hand her thoughts on to somebody else; so that they could be changed and broken up and given a body to. "Who could I dine with?" she said aloud. She ran over a list of names. Delia was in Ireland; Martin—he would be dining out; Morris had his family; and then and then and then—— She rejected them all for one reason or another. She had left it too late. She stood still in the crowd that pressed down Oxford Street. The sun was setting and the windows were lit. People came by with rosy faces. Some came quickly, as if they had engagements; others strolled lounging and looking about them as if they were merely taking the air; enjoying themselves. The weight of the day was off them! they too, she guessed, felt what she was feeling—garrulous, sociable, inclined for conversation. But how could she stop them and talk to them? It was absurd to let all this stir, potency, fecundity, run to waste, it was pouring past unused. Here was a man with a chip out of his cheek who looked as if he had knocked about the world; he passed! and another, trim, shaven, hollow-cheeked, who reminded her of her brother Morris; a nice man; in some office, she guessed; he passed; and another and another and another, all those nondescript elderly women whose existence puzzled her; and then a woman with bright little eyes, and a great flop of white hair, wearing a sprigged muslin dress under an old fur coat.

Eleanor laughed aloud. Why walk down Oxford Street wearing white tennis-shoes? she asked herself. She looked at the jaunty, disreputable, amusing old woman, pecking her way along the street, rather sidelong, capriciously, like a bird on a perch. But she checked her merriment. She wished she had somebody to laugh with. Sally? she thought suddenly. She loved laughing: she was a born mimic. But it was too late, she thought; and she walked on, smiling. And why not laugh, she asked herself. For she had half blamed Sally for laughing. Why do we always blame the laughers? she asked herself. Why stick seriousness as a label on top of—hats? she added inconsequently; she was passing a hat shop with a flight of hats on rods. Why not laughter? No, I'm not like that, she said, seeing her own reflection in the glass; her respectable elderly woman's reflection. Kitty had ticked her off to her irritation as a woman who sat on Committees, she thought. Where are you off to? Some Committee? she had said. I've done with all that nonsense long ago, she said to herself. But I must dine somewhere. I shall dine by myself; I shall have a good dinner and a bottle of wine, she said, looking about her for a restaurant. But there were only dress shops.

A feeling of expansion, of freedom from surface-marks of identification, possessed her. [That's the advantage of growing old, she thought; as Kitty said; one needn't care what other people think; for they always think wrong—always, always. . . .] It's a good state, age; she thought; as Kitty was saying: one needn't care what other people think: no need to pose; no need to cut a figure any more; one can be oneself. Don't you agree, Nicholas, she asked him, that it's best —she held her hand out, holding her flower, that it's best,—she tried to remember one of his pompous phrases, for he had never got the hang of English; he still used phrases like "exposing the greatest possible surface of the soul"—don't you think it's best, she repeated. Without disguises? She saw him again; touching the outspread fingers of his hands. But he bored her sometimes with his theories: with his ancestors. That she had thought before.

She looked up. When one began to repeat a thought, it was a sign one should change the subject—ask somebody to dine. But who can I ask . . . she began; and then lost the end of the sentence, because the sky above the roofs of the big shops reminded her, with its look of a blue-tinted ceiling, with one plume of fiery cloud, with its aloof alien look, that was so incongruous above the fretted outline of chimneys, of another scene; of the country. She was in the country; walking down a Welsh valley alone. And a little black solitary figure came down the hillside opposite; came nearer and nearer; till they both stopped beside a thorn-tree at the same moment; and said Good day, and stood there talking. He was a builder from Cardiff, she remembered; going to visit his mother who was ill in a farm; and he had written his name on a page of his pocket-book in case she ever came there, and she gave him her name, not liking to feel, as they parted, that they would never meet again.

Which was natural, she said. Human beings like each other surely, by nature—she turned to Renny; don't they Renny? By nature, surely they do? she repeated; turning to Renny, whom she loved, because he always said, "Eleanor, don't be a fool." He always

said what he thought. Perhaps I could dine with them? she thought. Shall I ring them up? No, she thought, shaking her head as she passed a post-office, when people are so happy they are glad to be alone together in the evening. "Damn that telephone," he would say; and Maggie, letting fall her socks . . . But she must dine. she was hungry. Here, she said; and stopped short; as if all the time she had been meaning to dine at this very place.

It was a large restaurant; cheerful, opulent-looking. She pushed through the revolving doors. There was an instant buzz and chatter as she came in, which she liked. It at once dissipated all her thoughts. The roar of the street seemed to have found a human voice. Not a word could be distinguished, but there was a general babble of sound. They were all eating, talking, companioned. It seemed as she stood there for a moment, as if she had come in upon a festival already in full swing. But there was no empty seat; all the tables were already taken.

She was about to go up the marble stairs to see if there were a place in the upper room, when, just as she moved, a man at a table in the corner rose and left. She went and took his seat. A waitress leant over the table, swept it clean of crumbs and glasses, and placed a coffee-splashed card in front of her. Then she dashed off somewhere else. What shall I have, Eleanor asked herself, looking at the menu. The three-and-sixpenny dinner? Yes, it saved the trouble of thinking; and she would order half a bottle of wine.

She laid her bag, her gloves and her flower on the table-cloth and waited. She liked the look of the place. Everyone looked festive. On each table an electric lamp burnt red through a tight shade fringed with glass beads. All the faces therefore were tinged with pink light. And everybody was in their best clothes.

There was the usual music; somewhere behind a column they were playing the usual waltz. But it was distant—a pulse of sound merely that surged up and down beneath the clatter. She sat there listening and looking about her, amused, distracted by the many voices, by the many movements all round her. They were very busy; people were coming in and going out. She waited. Gradually she became aware of a thudding sound in the background. She identified it. From where she sat, rather at the back, rather at one side, she could see a swing door opening and shutting. A file of waitresses went in; came out; they went in with dirty plates; they came out with the clean ones. She caught a glimpse of them snatching their dishes from a counter in the kitchens beyond. The machine at this hour of the evening was working smoothly but at full pressure. All the time new diners kept arriving; passing between the tables; coming in; going out. She waited.

She looked about her. At the next table was a couple dining together; a young man and a girl. They had finished one course; and they were waiting too. The girl had opened her bag and was carefully and deliberately powdering her face; then she took out a little stick and reddened her lips. The young man hitched up his trousers and nonchalantly, as if half consciously, ran his hand through his hair as he caught sight of himself in the glass. He might be a salesman in a motor-car business, she thought, and she a girl in a manicure

The Years—228

establishment, for they were both rather lustrous and shiny. And they were both on their best behaviour. "Preening," Eleanor said to herself with a smile. That is, she added, showing off; acting a part, naturally, she thought, after their day's work in a shop.

Then the *hors-d'œuvre* was dabbed down in front of her—little pink strips of fish and a potato salad. There was not much to it, she thought as she tasted the skimpy food, but it was a change from what one had at home after all. She poured out her wine; she never drank wine when she was alone either. And what, she wondered, as she glanced covertly at the couple at the next table, are they pretending to be? Something gay, smart, up to date and shiny—like the people in the illustrated papers? she wondered. They were neither of them quite at their ease; they were on their best behaviour, curious of people looking at them. She swallowed her *hors-d'œuvre*; it was salty and slippery and not very agreeable. . . . Still. . . . She waited.

How long are they going to keep me waiting? she asked, glancing at the menu. It was a long one. Five courses; *hors-d'œuvre*; fish; meat; pudding; dessert. It might have been better to order one dish and have done with it, she thought. She watched the waitresses hurrying round, half turning as they hurried, to pacify customers who were getting impatient. The swing doors seemed to thud more and more quickly. At last her own waitress, whom she had marked because of her queer pale face and a twist in her mouth, approached, dealing plates as she passed. To Eleanor she dealt a plate of white fish with pink blobs on it. She looked jaded and harrassed.

"Very busy tonight?" said Eleanor. She wanted to make her smile naturally.

"Yes'm," murmured the waitress as she turned, with a little twitch of her lip as if it hurt her to depart from the pursed-up expression which was somehow connected, Eleanor felt, with the weight of the tray she was carrying. It must be heavy—all those dishes, carried in front of one like that.

The music burst out again.

They oughtn't to make her carry all that, Eleanor thought, prompted, perhaps by the burst of music, sentimental as it was, to a sudden rush of pity. They could easily afford, she thought, looking round at the crowded room, more waitresses. They must make huge profits. She began to eat her fish. It was an insipid fish, watery and full of bones. She looked at the menu. We don't want all this, she said, looking at the long list of courses that still remained to be eaten. Why not have one dish; and that a good one? That's what we want; then why don't we have it? she asked, laying her knife and fork down. She pushed away the little pile of skin and bones. Why do they force us to have all this? Why can't we say . . . She yawned slightly. Her mind flagged. She wished that there was somebody to talk to; or failing that, something that she could read. But she had forgotten to buy a paper. She sat there listening to the thudding of the doors; to the violins scrambling over the notes so that they missed the tune. She listened. There was no tune; it was only a scramble of bungled notes.

It was getting hot too. People had begun smoking: the smoke hung down. A weight, made of the heat, and the clatter, and the thud and the music, seemed to be laid on top of her head. She felt as if a headache

The Years—229

were beginning. She put her knife and fork together. She had finished her fish. She had nothing to do but sit and look at her own smeared plate. Her exultation was ebbing.

Though the music continued, the glow, the dazzle and the gaiety were going. The clothes that had seemed at first sight so festive, now seemed, as she looked round her, drab; browns and blacks; almost all the same. At each table there was a respectable middle-aged couple, passively eating, passively waiting. And what was the next course? She looked. Poulet Marengo—some kind of titivated chicken she supposed. Whatever it was, they took their time about it. She opened her bag in case she had something there to read. But she had read both the card and the letter. The card was from Miriam, in Italy. It was the usual picture postcard; great white oxen standing in an olive garden with flaps hanging down beneath their chins; an arch behind them; cypresses, and something scribbled on the top about being back on Saturday and sitting in the sun. She put it down. The letter was from her nephew North, in Africa; but she had read it before. It was a non-committal nephew's letter about sheep; and the drought, and how some man she had never heard of had gone away so that he was alone on the farm. She used to like North, but he had been abroad so long she scarcely knew him now, she thought, as she pushed the letter back into its envelope. She looked blankly at the table before her. There was the silver vase with its one carnation; the pink lamp with its fringe of beads; and the orchid that Kitty had given her, lying among the metal knives and forks on the coarse table-cloth. Dazed by the noise and the ineffective efforts of the orchestra to impose some sort of tune upon the jumbled mass of tunes, her eye rested upon the table impassively. Things seemed to lose their meanings. That's an odd assembly of objects, she thought, dully observing the shapes and positions of the things on the table; though they were knife, fork and flower, they had for a moment lost their identity. Black marks on a white ground they seemed to be for a moment; a pattern; something fixed. If there were a pattern, she mused, what would it be? If accidentally scattered objects, were yet in order? If to a mind outside her mind they meant something? as to a painter they meant something? If there were a world beyond this world . . . but the thought slipped.

She raised her hand and beckoned to the waitress; but her waitress had vanished through the swing doors. How would it be, she began again, if this fork, this knife, this flower and my hand—she laid it on the table—were thought together by another mind, so that what seemed accidental—vegetable, animal, metal—were in fact all one? She looked at her hand. There it lay. Then she roused herself. What nonsense I'm thinking, she said, and took up the flower Kitty had given her, and looked at it. It was an orchid, streaked and pouched, with the exotic beauty of those strange flowers. It had a row of yellow dots on its pale-yellow pouch.

She drummed on the table. She wished she could attract somebody's attention. She wanted somebody—anybody—that man reading the paper for example—to take her thoughts and carry them out of this broken darkness into some hard certainty. She tried to hear what they were saying at the next table. But they were

The Years—230

completely silent. There they sat, staring, as if they had
ceased to exist, as if they had come to a blank wall, and
stood staring at it. Nothing is more depressing, she
thought, than the look of people sitting silent over
their food. Say something, she felt inclined to cry
aloud. Speak!

The orchestra which had faded into silence, now
burst into its tune again. They always started with a
rush, all together; and the first notes, striking into a
rhythm, even though it always petered out, threw her
mind on again. Listening to music, even to cheap
music, always until it became boring, ran things together. For a moment as she looked at the table; it
seemed to her that the connection she had half grasped
now ran between the different things; as if she could
live from the fork to the flower, from the flower—she
put out her hand and touched it—to the spoon. Adventurously, boldly, as you would say, Nicholas, she
thought. Adventurously, boldly, she thought, half
shutting her eyes; yes boldly, adventurously, since we
know so little, about anything is: from the fork to the
flower; she smiled. And so, she continued, speaking to
herself, and raising her hand to her head conscious as
she was of pressure on the top of her head, break up
this weight, this unreality, the dumb passivity—she
looked at the couple again; they were still staring ahead
of them. Break it up? Break it up! she said, tapping
lightly on the table. They haven't said a thing to each
other for the last five minutes, she thought. Not a
thing; and yet here they are having a night out together
and they haven't said a thing.

She turned abruptly. Would they never bring her
chicken marengo? There was no sign of her waitress.
Why was I such a fool as to come here? she asked
herself, when I might have cooked my own dinner,
at home?

She tapped urgently on the table. It's the only way,
she thought; nobody is going to attend to me unless I
make a fuss. She tapped again. The man who was
reading a paper propped on the cruet near her looked
up. She tapped again. And now the waitress came and
slapped her chicken down on the table in front of her.
She took up her knife and fork hastily and began to
eat. But it was not appetising. There was only a rag of
flesh on the skinny little bird; and it was luke-warm. It
must have been waiting on the counter, forgotten. She
had soon finished it. Now she would have to wait again
The next course was what? She looked at the couple
next her. They were always a course ahead of her, and
now they were eating something whitish out of a
metal cup.

"Péche Melba," she concluded, looking at the menu;
that's what it is. But why do they make us have all
these courses? Why do they do it? She looked at the
menu. The restaurant was owned by a large company;
it had branches all over London; there was a list of
them. But who are the people who do it? she wondered
who is it who makes us eat through a dinner like this?
Some rich man? Some company with a rich man on
top? A rich man who began very humbly, and then—
she had finished her chicken and pushed the smeared
plate away from her—like that man whom Celia's
always grumbling about—what's his name? The one
who built a house; the one who spoilt the view—"but
one has to be nice to them because they're so rich"—
she could not remember his name. But she could see

The Years—231

him. He walks about like an advertisement of riding
breeches, she thought. And they all laughed at him,
because he rode to hounds without knowing "the stem
of a hound from the stern"—was that the expression?
Anyhow they laughed at him. . . . What apes and cats
we are, she thought, lifting her glass but the wine was
poor; taking his money and laughing at him . . . what
apes and cats we are, she thought, for whatever aspect
of life presented itself to her seemed at the moment
equally sordid; and connected with the smeared plate
and the skinny bird. But here her Péche Melba was
delivered. It was a greyish-white mound that slipped
about, already half melted, at the bottom of a metal
cup.

The couple at the next table had eaten theirs; they
had finished; they were going. The young man was
paying the bill; the girl was setting her hat straight at
her little hand mirror. They were still acting; the young
man, as he surveyed his silver nonchalantly was acting
some rich man; the girl, arranging her hat coquettishly
sideways, was acting some rich girl—some Lady-this-
or-that in the illustrated papers. Why must they do it.
Eleanor asked herself, lifting her spoon to her lips,
when they're not like that? She watched them. As they
got up they turned and smiled at each other. When
they're so nice underneath, she added. They disappeared through the swing doors.

She swallowed a spoonful of the sweet stuff; but it
had a distinct taste of salt in it. She put down the spoon
again; it was impossible to eat it. She would get her
bill and go. But her waitress had disappeared again.
She sat looking about her. In front of her were pillars
cased in imitation marble; then there were arches with
horse-shoes of fretted woodwork that reminded her of
the Alhambra. It seemed to be a combination, what
with the plush and the arches of Buckingham Palace
and the Alhambra, she thought. There was not a square
foot free from ornament of some kind. At one side, in
order to cut off the kitchens, there was a glass screen;
but even the screen had leaves painted on it. Vine
leaves, she said to herself, looking at them. And last
year she had been in Italy, and had sat in the courtyard
of a little inn under a vine. And the man said to me, she
thought, remembering a scene, "Take it," when I
admired the jar with olives in it. "It belonged to my
wife," he said. And here we have glass beads on pink
lamp-shades, she thought, pushing away her metal cup
still half full of the whitish-grey liquid. She would pay
her bill and go.

She saw her waitress attending to the next table.
Two men in bowler hats had taken the seats of the
couple who had just left. The waitress had brushed off
the crumbs; tidied the table; and was placing the menu
before them. Eleanor beckoned to her. Now they're
going to eat through the whole of that dinner again,
she thought. It irritated her unreasonably that they
should be going to eat through the whole of that
dinner again. She beckoned. But the waitress was
attending to the City men; she saw one of them wink
at her as he gave his order. She beckoned. At last the
waitress came and totted up her bill. Then she paused;
she held her pencil suspended as if to make sure that
nothing had been forgotten.

"No, I didn't have coffee," Eleanor said, to help her.
"Half a bottle of wine, but no coffee," she said. She
watched her adding up the sum. She looked harrassed.

She still wished, even now at the last moment, to make her smile. The only way would be to give her a larger tip than she expected. She did it; she slipped back a coin, a larger coin than the girl expected. And the girl smiled. She looked at her for a moment as if the heavy weight that had been caused by the trays were momentarily lifted.

She liked me, Eleanor thought, for a moment. Then she added, no, it was my tip. Still, she thought as she made her way out deviously between the many little tables, it was a nice smile, considering she's been on her feet, how many hours?

She pushed her way out through the revolving doors and found herself on the pavement of Oxford Street. It was darker now, and the long avenue with its dipping line of lights looked empty. Only an hour or so ago it had seemed to her teeming with life; sociable, garrulous, hospitable. Now, as she walked, a little wind blew a dirty scrap of paper scraping along the pavement in front of her. And she was alone; the weight of her own being came back to her. There she was, walking along Oxford Street, an elderly woman in no way remarkable, going home, carrying a pair of white gloves. She held the gloves in front of her. It seemed to her ages since she had drawn on those gloves She had stood at a window, she remembered, looking down, and there was a man playing the cornet; a man with a hat in his hand. And she had turned to Kitty and said, "I like people—they're so interesting." And that was a lie, she said: the kind of lie she hated most; the becoming pose—she who had said that she did not pose. The lie that makes one out a lover of one's kind, she thought. She walked on. And I don't love them, she thought. No, she thought, thinking of the men who had winked at the waitress, I hate them. There they still were, eating. There they all were, staring passively at their food. I despise them, she thought. She stopped. The pavement was stained red with ruby light from a picture palace. There were revolving doors and page-boys with rows of gilt but on their jackets. People were shopping; they were going in. She had half a mind to finish her evening at a picture palace. But she hesitated. Outside hung two over-life-size photographs of film stars kissing. And they, she said to herself, looking at the pouting faces, the curled moustaches, the red thick lips, put Nicholas in prison. She walked on.

She half meant to walk home through the Park. She would go to the Marble Arch, she thought, and walk part of the way back under the trees. But suddenly as she glanced down a back street, fear came over her. She saw the men in the bowler hats winking at the waitress. She was afraid—even now, even I, she thought . . . afraid. Afraid to walk through the Park alone, she thought; she despised herself. It was the bodies fear, not the minds, but it settled the matter. She would keep to the main streets, where there were lights and policemen.

The shops were still lit; they still kept their hats, their clothes on view though the doors were locked, so as to tempt people to buy. People still looked and sauntered; people came tapping past on the pavement. The pavement was barred with stripes of light and darkness. The faces were now lit up, now obscured. The faces, she said to herself—here a group of young men lurched past, bawling out a coarse, defiant song,

their arms linked together, so that she stepped off the pavement to avoid them—the faces of beasts, she thought, in a jungle.

She walked on. One of the big shops was being pulled down, a line of scaffolding zigzagged across the sky. There was something violent and crazy in the crooked lines. It seemed to her, as she looked up, that there was something violent and crazy in the whole world tonight. It was tumbling and falling, pitching forward to disaster. The crazy lines of the scaffolding, the jagged outline of the broken wall, the bestial shouts of the young men, made her feel that there was no order, no purpose in the world, but all was tumbling to ruin beneath a perfectly indifferent polished moon. For there it hung, the new moon, the lovely slip, cut sharply in the sky. There it hung high up over Oxford Street, as she disappeared down into the tube.

SELECTED BIBLIOGRAPHY

Unpublished Documents

In the Henry W. and Albert A. Berg Collection of English and American Literature of The New York Public Library, Astor, Lenox, and Tilden Foundations:

Brace, Donald. Letters to Leonard Woolf. Harcourt, Brace, 383 Madison Ave., New York, 27 April 1936, 29 June, 1936, 31 July 1936. Listed in Berg as: (Woolf) Harcourt Brace and Co. 55 T.L.S., telegrams to the Hogarth Press or Leonard Woolf. Folder 15.

Woolf, Leonard. Letter to Donald Brace. The Hogarth Press, 52 Tavistock Square, London, W. C. 7 July 1936. Listed in Berg as: (Woolf) Harcourt Brace and Co. 55 T.L.S., telegrams to the Hogarth Press or Leonard Woolf. Folder 15.

Woolf, Virginia. Diary, unpublished, 30 June to 1 Oct. 1903. Listed in Berg as: (Diary) 7 holograph notebooks, unsigned, each dated. No. 2: "Hyde Park Gate," pp. 1–8.

————. Diary, unpublished, 1 Jan. 1915 to 24 March 1941. Listed in Berg as: (A Writer's Diary) holograph, unsigned.

————. Letters to Ethel Mary Smyth. Monks House, 24 Jan. 1931. Listed in Berg as: 363 A.L.S., 32 A.L., 13 T.L.S., 34 miscellaneous pieces to Ethel Mary Smyth, 30 Jan. 1903, 10 March 1941. Folder 13.

————. "Professions for Women." Holograph. Listed in Berg as: (The death of the moth. Professions for women) Speech 21st Jan. 1931. Holograph fragment of drafts, unsigned. In her: (Articles, essays, fiction and reviews) vol. 4, 1 June 1930, pp. 117–33.

————. *The Years*. Galley proofs. Listed in Berg as: The Years (London: By L. and V. Woolf at the Hogarth press, 1936) Galley proofs, incomplete. 17 March (13 April) 1936 and 14–(15) April 1936.

————. Holograph fragment. Listed in Berg as: (The years) Holograph draft (incomplete) unsigned and undated, 17 pages.

————. Holograph notebooks. Listed in Berg as: (The years) The Pargiters; a

181

novel-essay based upon a paper read to the London, National Society for Women's Service. Holograph, unsigned, 11 Oct. 1932–15 Nov. 1934. 8 volumes.

————. *The Years*. Page proofs. Listed in Berg as: page proofs of section "1917" pages 1–23, 15 Dec. 1936. With galley proofs.

————. *The Years*. Typescript. Listed in Berg as: Typescript (incomplete) with the author's ms corrections, unsigned and undated. 11 pages.

————. *Three Guineas*. Early holograph draft. Listed in Berg as (Three Guineas?) Draft for Professions, in articles, essays, fiction and reviews, 6, 125-145. Holograph fragment, unsigned, 14 April 1935. 11 pages.

————. *Three Guineas*. Holograph and typescript. Listed in Berg as: (Three Guineas) Holograph and Typescript, with the author's ms. corrections, both fragments, unsigned, 21 Sept. 90 pages; 49 pages.

————. *Three Guineas*. Holograph reading notes. Listed in Berg as: (Three Guineas) Holograph reading notes, unsigned and undated. 39 pages. Identification based on several passages similar to passages in published version.

————. *Three Guineas*. Later typescript. Listed in Berg as: The second guinea. Later typescript, unsigned, 28 June 1937.

In other repositories:

Bell, Quentin. Letter to Grace Radin. Cobbe Place, Beddingham, Lewes, Sussex, England, 5 May 1975.

Woolf, Virginia. *The Years*. Typescript fragment, undated and unsigned. In Sussex University Library, Falmer, Brighton, Sussex, England, pp. 361–64, 366–67, 380–81.

VIRGINIA WOOLF'S PUBLISHED WORKS

The Captain's Death Bed and Other Essays. London: Hogarth Press, 1950.

Collected Essays. 4 vols. New York: Harcourt, Brace, 1966. Vols. 1, 2.

The Common Reader: Second Series. London: Hogarth Press, 1932.

The Death of the Moth and Other Essays. London: Hogarth Press, 1942.

The Diary of Virginia Woolf; Volume One: 1915–1919, Volume Two: 1920–1924, ed. Anne Olivier Bell. New York: Harcourt, Brace, 1977–78.

Flush: A Biography. London: Hogarth Press, 1933.

Granite and Rainbow. London: Hogarth Press, 1958.

A Letter To a Young Poet. The Hogarth Letters, No. 8. London: Hogarth Press, 1932.

The Letters of Virginia Woolf; Volume One: 1888–1912, Volume Two: 1912–1922, Volume Three: 1923-1928, Volume IV: 1929–1931, Volume V: 1932–1935, ed. Nigel Nicolson and Joanne Trautman. New York: Harcourt, Brace, 1975–79.

Moments of Being: Unpublished Autobiographical Writings, ed. Jeanne Schulkind. New York: Harcourt Brace Jovanovich, 1976.

Mrs. Dalloway. New York: Harcourt, Brace, 1925.

The Pargiters: The Essay-Novel Portion of The Years, ed. Mitchell Leaska. New York: Readex Books, 1977.

A Room of One's Own. London: Hogarth Press, 1929; rpt. New York: Harcourt, Brace, 1932.

Three Guineas. New York: Harcourt, Brace, 1955.

To the Lighthouse. 1927; rtp. New York: Harcourt, Brace, 1955.

The Voyage Out. 1915; rpt. New York: Harcourt, Brace, 1948.

The Waves. 1931; rpt. in *Jacob's Room and The Waves*. New York: Harcourt, Brace, 1959.

A Writer's Diary, ed. Leonard Woolf. London: Hogarth Press, 1953.

The Years. 1937; rpt. New York: Harcourt, Brace, 1965.

CRITICISM AND BACKGROUND READINGS

Annan, Noel. *Leslie Stephen: His Thought and Character in Relation To His Time*. Cambridge, Mass.: Harvard Univ. Press, 1952.

Austen, Jane. *Emma*. London: J. M. Dent. New York: Dutton, 1952.

Bazin, Nancy Topping. *Virginia Woolf and the Androgynous Vision*. New Brunswick: Rutgers Univ. Press, 1973.

Bell, Quentin. *Virginia Woolf: A Biography*. 2 vols. in 1. New York: Harcourt, Brace, 1972.

Comstock, Margaret. "The Loudspeaker and the Human Voice: Politics and the Form of The Years." *Bulletin of The New York Public Library* 80 (Winter 1977), 252–75.

Critics On Virginia Woolf, ed. Jacqueline E. Latham. London: Allen and Unwin, 1970.

Delattre, Floris. Review of *The Years*, by Virginia Woolf. *Études Anglaises* (July 1937), 289–96.

De Salvo, Louise. "A Note On the Beginning of *The Years*." *Bulletin of The New York Public Library* 80 (Winter 1977), 139–40.

de Selincourt, Basil. Review of *The Years* by Virginia Woolf. *The Observer*, 14 March 1937, p. 5.

Fawcett, Millicent Garnett. *Women's Suffrage: A Short History of a Great Movement*. London: T. C. and E. C. Jack, n.d.

Fleischman, Avrom. *Virginia Woolf: A Critical Reading*. Baltimore: Johns Hopkins Univ. Press, 1975.

Forster, E. M. *Aspects of the Novel*. London: Edward Arnold, 1927.

———. *Virginia Woolf*. The Rede Lecture, 1941. London: Cambridge Univ. Press, 1942.

Frye, Northrop. *Anatomy of Criticism: Four Essays*. Princeton: Princeton Univ. Press, 1957.

Garnett, David. Review of *The Years* by Virginia Woolf. *The New Statesman and Nation*, 20 March 1937, p. 481.

Guiget, Jean. *Virginia Woolf and Her Works*. 1962; trans. Jean Stewart. New York: Harcourt, Brace and World, 1965.

Hafley, James. *The Glass Roof*. 1954; rpt. New York: Russell and Russell, 1963.

Hicks, Granville. Review of *The Years* by Virginia Woolf. *New Republic*, 28 April 1937, p. 363.

Hoffman, Charles C. "Fact and Fantasy in *Orlando*: Virginia Woolf's MS Revisions." *Texas Studies in Literature and Language* 10 (Fall 1968), 435–44.

———. "From Short Story to Novel: The MS Revisions of Virginia Woolf's *Mrs. Dalloway*." *Modern Fiction Studies* 10 (Summer 1968), 171–86.

————. "Virginia Woolf's Manuscript Revisions of *The Years*." *PMLA* 84, No. 1 (Jan. 1969), 79–89.

Hulcoop, John. Review of *Mrs. Dalloway's Party* by Virginia Woolf, ed. Stella McNichol. In *Virginia Woolf Miscellany* (Spring 1975), 4.

Jack, P. M. Review of *The Years* by Virginia Woolf. *New York Herald Tribune Book Review*, 11 April 1937, pp. 1 and 27.

Kelly, Alice Van Buren. *The Novels of Virginia Woolf: Fact and Vision*. Chicago: Chicago Univ. Press, 1973.

Kirkpatrick, B. J. *A Bibliography of Virginia Woolf*. 2nd ed. London: Oxford Univ. Press, 1968.

Lawrence, D. H. *The Quest for Rananim: D. H. Lawrence's Letters to S.S. Koteliansky, 1914–1930*, ed. G. J. Zytanuk. Montreal: McGill-Queens Univ. Press, 1970.

Leaska, Mitchell. "Virginia Woolf, the Parjeter: A Reading of The Years." *Bulletin of The New York Public Library* 80 (Winter 1977), 172–210.

Leavis, F. R. *"After To the Lighthouse." Scrutiny* 10 (Jan. 1942), 295–98.

Lehmann, John. "Working with Virginia Woolf." *The Listener*, 15 Jan. 1955, pp. 60–62.

Lewis, Wyndham. *Men Without Art*. London: Cassell, 1934.

Lipking, Joanna. "Looking at the Monuments: Woolf's Satiric Eye." *Bulletin of The New York Public Library* 80 (Winter 1977), 141–45.

MacAfee, Helen. Review of *The Years*, by Virginia Woolf. *Yale Review* 26 (Summer 1937), x.

McLaurin, Allen. *Virginia Woolf: The Echoes Enchained*. Cambridge, England: Cambridge Univ. Press, 1973.

Marcus, Jane. *"The Years* as Greek Drama, Domestic Novel, and *Götterdammerung." Bulletin of The New York Public Library* 80 (Winter 1977), 276–301.

Marder, Herbert. *Feminism and Art: A Study of Virginia Woolf*. Chicago: Univ. of Chicago Press, 1968.

Mellers, W. H. Review of *The Years* by Virginia Woolf. *Scrutiny* (June 1937). Rpt. in *The Importance of Scrutiny*, ed. Eric Bentley. New York: New York Univ. Press, 1964, pp. 378–82.

Middleton, Victoria. *"The Years:* A Deliberate Failure." *Bulletin of The New York Public Library* 80 (Winter 1977), 158–71.

Muir, Edwin. Review of *The Years* by Virginia Woolf. *The Listener*, 31 March 1937, p. 622.

Novak, Jane. *The Razor Edge of Balance: A Study of Virginia Woolf*. Coral Gables, Fla.,: Univ. of Miami Press, 1975.

O'Brien, Josephine Schaefer. *The Threefold Nature of Reality in the Novels of Virginia Woolf*. The Hague: Mouton, 1965.

Owens, Olga. Review of *The Years*. Boston Evening Transcript, 10 April 1937, p. 2.

Patmore, Coventry. *The Angel in the House*. In *The Poems of Coventry Patmore*, ed. Frederick Page. London: Oxford Univ. Press, 1949, pp. 61–205.

Pritchett, V. S. Review of *The Years* by Virginia Woolf. *Christian Science Monitor*, weekly magazine section, 31 March 1937, p. 10.

Quennell, Peter. *A Letter to Mrs. Woolf: A Reply to A Letter to a Young Poet*. London: Hogarth Press, 1932.

Radin, Grace. "'I Am Not a Hero': Virginia Woolf and the First Version of *The Years*." *Massachusetts Review* 16, No. 1 (Winter 1975), 195–208.

————. "'Two enormous chunks': Episodes Excluded during the Final Revisions of *The Years.*" *Bulletin of The New York Public Library* 80 (Winter 1977), 221–51.

Recollections of Virginia Woolf by Her Contemporaries, ed. Joan Russell Noble. London: Peter Owen, 1972.

Renan, Ernest. *Vie de Jésus*, trans. Charles Edwin Wilbour. New York: Carleton, 1864.

Richter, Harvena. *Virginia Woolf: The Inward Voyage*. Princeton: Princeton Univ. Press, 1970.

Showalter, Elaine. "Killing the Angel in the House: The Autonomy of Women Writers." *Antioch Review* 32, No. 3, pp. 339–53.

Smyth, Ethel. *Female Pipings in Eden*. London: P. Davies, 1933.

————, *et al*. *Little Innocents*. London: Cobden Sanderson, 1932.

Spalding, Morris. Review of *The Years* by Virginia Woolf. *Life and Letters Today* (Summer 1937), 156.

Sparrow, John. Review of *The Years* by Virginia Woolf. *Spectator*, 19 March 1937, p. 526.

Spilka, Mark. "New Life in the Works: Some Recent Woolf Studies." *Novel* (Winter 1979), 169–84.

Stevens, George. Review of *The Years* by Virginia Woolf. *Saturday Review of Literature*, 10 April 1937, p. 15.

Strachey, Rachel. *The Cause: A Short History of the Women's Movement in Great Britain*. London: G. Bell and Sons, 1928.

————. *Our Freedom and Its Results*. London: Hogarth Press, 1936.

————. *Women's Suffrage and Women's Service*. London: London and National Society for Women's Service, 1927.

"The Things that Pass." Review of *The Years* by Virginia Woolf. *Times Literary Supplement*, 13 March 1937, p. 185.

Troy, William. Review of *The Years* by Virginia Woolf. *Nation*, 24 April 1937, p. 363.

————. "Virginia Woolf, The Novel of Sensibility." *Symposium* (Jan.-March 1933), 53–63.

Virginia Woolf: The Critical Heritage, ed. Robin Majumdar and Allen McLaurin. Boston: Routledge and Kegan Paul, 1975.

Ward, Mary Augusta Arnold. *A Writer's Recollections*. London: W. Collins, 1918.

Weiser, Barbara. "Criticism of Virginia Woolf from 1956 to the Present: A Selected Checklist, with an Index to Studies of Selected Works." *Modern Fiction Studies* 18 (Autumn 1972), 477–87.

Woolf, Leonard. *Beginning Again: An Autobiography of the Years 1911 to 1918*. New York: Harcourt Brace Jovanovich, 1964.

————. *Downhill All the Way: An Autobiography of the Years 1919–1939*. New York: Harcourt Brace Jovanovich, 1967.

————. "Kot." *The New Statesman and Nation* 49 (5 Feb. 1955), 170–72.

Wright, Elizabeth Mary. *The Life of Joseph Wright*. 2 vols. London: Oxford Univ. Press, 1932.

Wright, Joseph, ed. *English Dialect Dictionary*. London: Froude, 1903.

INDEX